Introduction to Blender 3.0

Learn Organic and Architectural Modeling, Lighting, Materials, Painting, Rendering, and Compositing with Blender

Gianpiero Moioli

Apress®

Introduction to Blender 3.0: Learn Organic and Architectural Modeling, Lighting, Materials, Painting, Rendering, and Compositing with Blender

Gianpiero Moioli
Milano, Italy

ISBN-13 (pbk): 978-1-4842-7953-3
https://doi.org/10.1007/978-1-4842-7954-0

ISBN-13 (electronic): 978-1-4842-7954-0

Managing Director, Apress Media LLC: Welmoed Spahr
Acquisitions Editor: Spandana Chatterjee
Development Editor: Laura Berendson
Coordinating Editor: Divya Modi
Copy Editor: Kim Wimpsett

Cover designed by eStudioCalamar

Cover image designed by Freepik (www.freepik.com)

Distributed to the book trade worldwide by Springer Science+Business Media New York, 1 New York Plaza, New York, NY 10004. Phone 1-800-SPRINGER, fax (201) 348-4505, e-mail orders-ny@springer-sbm.com, or visit www.springeronline.com. Apress Media, LLC is a California LLC and the sole member (owner) is Springer Science + Business Media Finance Inc (SSBM Finance Inc). SSBM Finance Inc is a **Delaware** corporation.

For information on translations, please e-mail booktranslations@springernature.com; for reprint, paperback, or audio rights, please e-mail bookpermissions@springernature.com.

Apress titles may be purchased in bulk for academic, corporate, or promotional use. eBook versions and licenses are also available for most titles. For more information, reference our Print and eBook Bulk Sales web page at http://www.apress.com/bulk-sales.

Any source code or other supplementary material referenced by the author in this book is available to readers on GitHub. This is the codes repo link https://github.com/Apress/Introduction-to-Blender-3.0. For more detailed information, please visit http://www.apress.com/source-code.

Printed on acid-free paper

For Giancarlo Marchese, my professor of sculpture at the
Brera Academy of Fine Arts.

Table of Contents

About the Author

Gianpiero Moioli is a sculptor, architect, and professor of sculpture and virtual architecture at the Brera Academy of Fine Arts in Milan. He has been a certified instructor (BFCT) with the Blender Foundation since 2008.

Gianpiero graduated with an MA in sculpture from the Brera Academy of Fine Arts in Milan and received his MA in architecture from the Polytechnic University of Milan.

In 2008, together with Stefania Albertini, he created the Brera Academy Virtual Lab, a virtual sculpture and architecture laboratory at the Academy of Fine Arts of Brera. He started using Blender in 2004 and presented his first results with this open source software in three Blender conferences in 2008, 2010, and 2011.

About the Technical Reviewer

 **Ajit Deolikar** is a mechanical engineer from Pune, India, and has experience in new product design and development. Since his childhood he has been passionate about art and started making artistic videos for marketing industrial products using open source graphics software like Blender, GIMP, etc. He is also involved in Blender training, customization, and automation using Python scripting and is constantly re-learning Blender because of regular enhancements by developers.

He is currently creating various short animation projects in the education field using Blender. His mission is to extend his collective experience with animation tools and create training modules on various topics.

In his spare time, he likes to play chess and analyze game strategies played by great grandmasters. He would someday love to write at least one book on those approaches. He can be reached at ajitb502@gmail.com.

Acknowledgments

I want to thank Ton Roosendaal and the Blender Foundation's and Blender Institute's team for maintaining this fantastic creative tool.

I would also like to thank the staff of Apress who helped me create this book, in particular, Laura Berendson, Spandana Chatterjee, and Divya Modi.

A special thanks go to Ajit Deolikar for his invaluable review of this book.

Introduction

When you try Blender for the first time, you'll immediately notice its two main features: the open source license and the possibility to use it as a tool for expanded artistic and design expression. The first feature gives you the freedom to use and modify the software in every way including for commercial purposes. The second feature allows you to work with a myriad set of tools for many uses, from 3D modeling to simulation, from video editing to motion tracking, etc.

I teach sculpture and virtual architecture at the Brera Academy of Fine Arts in Milan, and Blender is essential to my academic activity. We use it for art, architecture, design, 3D printing, and exporting 3D objects and environments to online virtual worlds. It is a flexible software that adapts continuously to new design and communication needs and new technologies.

Due to its ability to adapt to the times and the rapid network changes, Blender follows real-time art and design modifications, even at the cost of essential changes in the interface and structure.

The improvements that Blender Foundation brings from time to time make it a software that is always in line with the current needs of people doing art, design, architecture, game development, physics, and many other disciplines.

This is why I decided to write this book.

This book is suitable for those who know the basics of Blender and want to switch to version 3.0 quickly, but it is also for those who have never used Blender and want to take advantage of the new features. I also introduce the theoretical foundation that underlies digital painting, sculpture, and architecture when necessary. These fundamentals, such as color theory, digital spaces principles, nodes, and material nodes theory, are essential to understanding what you are doing when you create in 3D spaces.

In this book, I have tried to demonstrate the wide range of realization and creative possibilities in Blender, limited only by the artist's imagination. I hope I have succeeded.

CHAPTER 1

Introducing Blender 3.0

This chapter will explore the main changes introduced in the latest versions of Blender that are included in the 3.0 release. First, we will look at the differences between Blender 3.0 and the previous version. After that, we will learn how to install Blender.

Setting up Blender is quick and easy, and it takes up extraordinarily little space on our computer's drive. Next, we will cover installing the stable and experimental versions, the so-called daily builds, with the newest features.

Also, we will get familiar with the new interface, navigation techniques, menus, workspaces, editors, and views.

Finally, we will get to know some of the most important innovations of the 3.0 version of Blender: the Eevee and Cycles X rendering engines.

In this chapter, we are going to cover the following main topics:

- Main changes in the new 3.0 version

- How to install Blender 3.0 and older versions

- The new user interface and user experience

- How to use new keyboard shortcuts

- Eevee, the new real-time renderer

- Cycles X, the new, improved version of the physical-based path tracer renderer

This chapter will present all the necessary knowledge to get familiar with the Blender 3.0 interface. It is both for new users and for users accustomed to previous versions.

© Gianpiero Moioli 2022
G. Moioli, *Introduction to Blender 3.0*, https://doi.org/10.1007/978-1-4842-7954-0_1

Exploring the Main Changes in Blender 3.0

Starting with version 2.83, the Blender Foundation has decided to produce two different series of Blender.

- Long-Term Support (LTS) is the stable Blender version that can be used for long-term projects and will remain stable for two years. This version is currently 2.93 LTS.

- Semantic Versioning Specification (SemVer) is the conventional release numbering divided into major, minor versions, and patches. Thus, the first version of this series is 3.0. Later versions will be 3.1, 3.2, etc. After two years, version 3.0 will become 4.0.

This change highlights the growing importance of Blender for business use, and it also seems to mark the end of an era when Blender was considered unconventional software unlike any other.

Figure 1-1 shows the development scheme of the two Blender series proposed by the Blender Foundation.

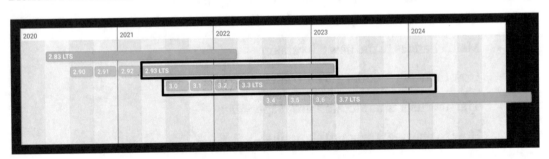

Figure 1-1. *The Blender release schedule from the Blender Foundation*

Figure 1-1 shows we have two versions: the orange is the leading version, currently 3.0. The blue one shows the LTS, dedicated to companies that need a more stable interface over time for their long-term projects.

Blender 2.8 included a makeover of the user interface, becoming much more user-friendly and intuitive. In Blender 3.0, compared to the earlier versions, many things have been changed to simplify and speed up using the software. The settings now are much more consistent, and Blender developers have reorganized the menus to be more orderly.

The next section will quickly present the most critical changes in the latest versions leading up to 3.0.

Left Button Selection (LBS)

Before version 2.8, by default, object selection was done with the right mouse button.

Considering other benchmark software such as Photoshop, 3D Studio Max, etc., Blender developers changed the default selection method to the left mouse button. However, the user can alter the selection method to the right mouse button if that is its preference.

Asset Browser and Pose Library

A modification introduced recently is the Asset Browser. This local user library makes assets available from one Blender file to another and lets us drag and drop them directly into the 3D Viewport editor.

Figure 1-2 shows the Asset Browser interface.

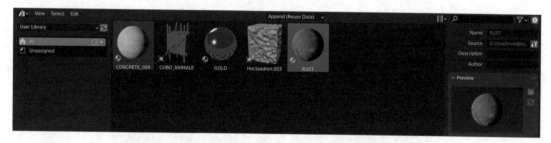

Figure 1-2. *Asset Browser*

There are different types of assets within Blender: materials, objects, textures, etc. With this new type of editor, we can import them directly.

Workspaces

Workspaces are another substantial modification that replace the old layouts. They are in the Topbar, next to the main menus, as shown in Figure 1-3.

Figure 1-3. *Workspaces in Blender 3.0*

The primary workspaces are Layout, Modeling, Sculpting, UV Editing, Texture Paint, Shading, Animation, Rendering, Compositing, and Scripting. We can use each of them for a specific function.

We can also customize these default workspaces and create our own based on our needs; to do this, we click the + sign on the right of the menu.

For example, by switching from Layout to the Modeling workspace, we enter directly into the subobject modification mode called Edit mode, speeding up the work. The Sculpting workspace takes us straight to Sculpt mode, and shows only the tools needed for that mode; in addition, the Timeline disappears, and the 3D view expands.

The Blender 3.0 Toolbar (T)

A significant feature, especially for those using Blender for the first time, is the Toolbar, which we can find on the left of the Blender interface, as shown in Figure 1-4.

Figure 1-4. *The Blender 3.0 Toolbar in Object mode*

In Blender 3.0, in Object mode, the Toolbar is divided into four parts, from top to bottom:

- In the first part, we find the following:

  a. Some selection tools

  b. The button to change the cursor position in the 3D Viewport

- The second part has the main transformations: Move, Rotate, Scale, and Transform.

- Then we find some tools for annotating and measuring: Annotate and Measure.

- Finally, we have a button to add some primitives interactively in the 3D Viewport.

With the toolbar, we can immediately move our objects in the 3D space, scale, and rotate them easily with gizmos.

Tip   There are two main ways to model in Blender: Object mode and Edit mode. In Object mode, we work with the main transformations at the object level, while in Edit mode, we work more specifically on subobjects such as vertices, edges, and faces.

The Tab key is the keyboard shortcut that allows us to switch from Object to Edit mode quickly.

In the toolbar in Edit mode, we can find the transformations and the most critical tools for subobject modeling. Again, these tools help Blender users because they don't need to learn the keyboard shortcuts for these operations immediately.

With this tool, we can perform the essential modeling operations by simply clicking the icon of the desired device and performing the procedure in the 3D window. Only a left-click and drag action is required.

Most of these tools also have customized manipulator widgets, making the devices more accessible and more intuitive to use. This change is significant for beginners, but we still recommend learning the keyboard shortcuts that allow a faster workflow.

Tip   If the toolbar is not present in 3D view, click the T button to make it appear on the left side of the viewport and press it again to hide it. The N key opens and closes the sidebar on the viewport's right. We can also open and close the toolbar in the 3D viewport at the cursor position by pressing Shift+spacebar. To open the toolbar's hidden tools, we need to click and hold the left mouse button on the icon's arrow in the lower-right corner and choose the desired device.

Eevee

Another phenomenal change included in the Blender 2.8 version is Eevee, the new real-time rendering engine. In version 3.0, this renderer has been improved and made a lot faster, as you will see later in this chapter and in Chapter 6.

With the introduction of Eevee, Blender's 3D Viewport became interactive and allowed us to work in real time in rendered shading, just like the best game engines.

The Cycles render engine is the previous renderer of Blender. It's a path tracer, and it is currently irreplaceable for the realism that a path-tracing engine produces.

Eevee is a lot faster than Cycles.

For some materials or effects, we have the same results in Cycles and Eevee; however, in other cases, Eevee does not have the same realistic and high-performance rendering results as Cycles.

For example, rendering transparent objects with real-time engines like Eevee does not give the same photorealistic rendering quality as Cycles. Eevee also needs more interface settings to be fixed before starting work.

Cycles X

Cycles X is a facelift of Cycles and has a redesigned architecture. The source code of Cycles X is different, so it is much faster than Cycles. Since the interface has not been altered, how we set up our work does not change.

We will discuss Cycles X in more detail in Chapter 6.

Workbench

Another renderer that comes to our aid to model in the viewport is Workbench.

It is for quick preview rendering, dedicated to precisely rendering and defining the model. With well-defined shadows, different colors, and cavity shading, the details of the objects we model are more apparent, and we can work with greater ease and precision.

Scene Collections

Another fundamental change that allows us to work in a much more orderly way is the introduction of Scene Collections instead of layers. Before version 2.8, Blender allowed us to use up to 20 layers; now, we can add as many collections as we need, give them a name, and organize them as we prefer.

We will discuss scene collections in detail later in this chapter when we speak of the Outline Editor.

Grease Pencil

The Grease Pencil was already present in previous versions of Blender, but it was a simple tool, usable only for writing and making notes in the viewport. However, since version 2.8, it has emerged as an exciting painting and animation tool.

We can continue to use the Grease Pencil for annotations. Still, now we can also do much more: we can use Draw, Object, and Edit modes for Grease Pencil brushes, and we can add dedicated modifiers and new materials.

In version 3.0 of Blender, the Grease Pencil provides many tools such as points, lines, and strokes, as well as a new workspace, modifiers, visual effects, materials, and many more features capable of producing entire 2D animated films.

In addition, with this tool, we can draw strokes and turn them into meshes or three-dimensional objects.

Geometry Nodes

Another exciting feature in Blender 3.0 is the Geometry Nodes modifier, which is helpful in editing objects' geometry by procedural modeling.

These nodes join and partly replace the modifiers and exponentially increase the possibilities of building objects having much more complex geometry.

With this tool we can create rich scenes from simple assets and then modify them and make them more complex through the modification of parameters.

In 2019, the Blender Foundation started working on Everything Nodes' critical project. It aims to extend the control of nodal systems to geometry, particles, simulations, collections, textures, materials, animations, etc. We can say that geometry nodes are part of this.

We will learn about the principles of this new modeling system in Chapter 3.

USD Importer

Universal Scene Description (USD) is an open source standard developed by Pixar for its animated films and used to create complex scenes collaboratively in a 3D world.

Pixar released USD as an open source file format.

Nvidia, starting from this file format, has built Omniverse. This application allows the real-time collaboration of many creatives on three-dimensional scenes and renders it with real-time path tracing.

Therefore, this format is significant and could be the future of 3D modeling production.

Blender already exports in the USD format, and the Blender Foundation and Nvidia have the ability to import USD files in version 3.0.

In this first section, we briefly explored the main innovations introduced in the new interface of Blender 3.0. These features make the software more robust and improve the user interface. In addition, the workflow is optimized.

The approach of this book is practical; to explore all the topics more technically, we can refer to the online Blender 3.0 Reference Manual here: `https://docs.blender.org/manual/en/dev/index.html`.

For any questions about using the software, we can also refer to Blender Stack Exchange at `https://blender.stackexchange.com/`; this is a great site where users quickly respond to questions.

Now let's learn how to install the software on our computer.

Installing Blender 3.0

In this section, we will see how to download the latest versions of Blender 3.0 from the official website:

- We can download the ***stable version*** from `https://www.blender.org/download/`.

- We can download the ***experimental versions***, some of which are still unstable but contain the latest features and cool bug fixes, from `https://builder.blender.org/download/`. Several experimental versions are accessible in the menu of the same page, divided into various builds: Daily, Branch, Patch, Library, Buildbot, Builders, and Latest Changes.

We will see how to proceed with installation in the following sections.

The Blender Foundation Website

The first thing to do when we start using Blender is to connect to the site `https://www.blender.org/` where we can download all the installation files and a lot of materials to use and extend Blender.

The site also contains a series of information and updates essential for those who want to use the software from beginner to expert levels.

In the menu at the top of the page, we can find the sections Features, Download, Support, Get Involved, About, and Store.

Let's not forget Donate, where we can make a small donation to support software development.

Let's quickly see what the sections contain:

- On the Features page, we immediately get an idea of what we can do with Blender.

- On the Download link, we find the latest stable version of the software for the various operating systems.

- The Support section is where we find a lot of documentation, different tutorials, and many free and paid courses to learn how to use Blender.

Figure 1-5 shows the page of the support section.

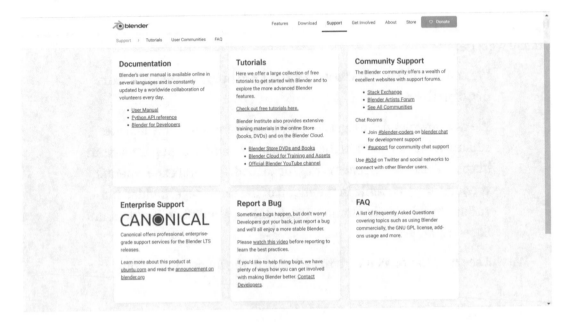

Figure 1-5. *Blender site, Support section*

As Figure 1-5 shows, we can quickly access this page's documentation, tutorials, and community support.

This page allows access to several international communities worldwide, ideally according to this motto: "It's all about people. Anywhere you are, there's a community for you."[1]

Installing Different Versions of Blender 3.0

Now let's install Blender.

We will start with the official version, the stable one. It is straightforward, and the software takes up very little space on our computer's hard disk: the current zipped folder is about 200 MB.

Figure 1-6 shows the download page for the many official versions for different operating systems and the source code.

---

[1] This is the motto on the Blender Foundation's Community Support page at `https://www.blender.org/community/`.

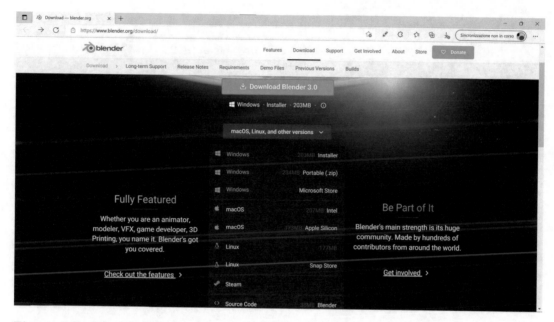

Figure 1-6. *The Blender 3.0 download page of the official versions*

As you can see in Figure 1-6, we can install two versions for each operating system: the executable one, which installs the software on our computer's hard disk, and the portable, or zipped, which we can also use from a memory stick. On this page select Looking for Blender LTS? to find the link to install Blender LTS.

We can install the official versions with a few clicks:

1. Navigate to the download page at `https://www.blender.org/download/`.

2. Click the button "macOS, Linux, and other versions" and open the drop-down menu.

3. Choose the appropriate operating system for you (Windows, macOS, or Linux) and start downloading the zipped folder files by clicking the relevant button.

4. Follow the instructions on the screen.

This installs the recommended, stable version.

Instead, if we want to install a more recent but not yet stable version, we go to the bottom of the download page and click the Download Blender Experimental button. This operation will redirect us to another page that shows several experimental software versions, as shown in Figure 1-7.

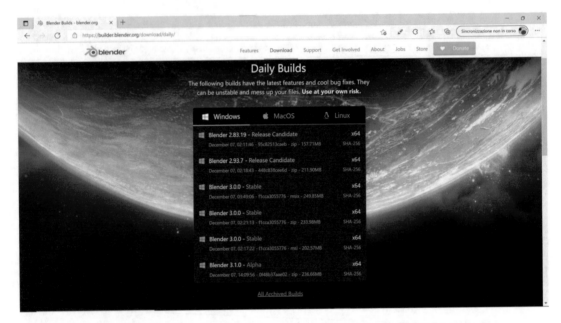

Figure 1-7. *The Blender 3.0 download page for the experimental versions*

From here, we can download both the official beta and alpha versions, called the *daily builds*. In addition, we can download the release candidate. These are specific versions to test the subsequent releases of the software.

Not all of these versions are stable. In fact, the page says, "The following builds have the latest features and cool bug fixes. However, they can be unstable and mess up your files. Use it at your own risk."[2]

There is also a dedicated page to download previous versions of Blender, including the 2.7 series and every earlier version of Blender; see `https://www.blender.org/donload/previous-versions/`.

Now we can open our software by clicking the Blender icon on the screen if we have installed one of the stable versions with the installer package. We do not have to install the experimental versions on the computer. Instead, we start them by clicking the Blender icon inside the main folder; the Blender application is the only one with the Blender icon visible.

So, we can have two or more different Blender versions on the same PC.

---

[2] This is the warning that we will find on all the download pages of the experimental versions of Blender. But, according to my personal experience, I must say that in many years of using the experimental versions of Blender I have had few problems.

This section taught us how to install the stable release of Blender and the experimental versions. Now let's start getting to the heart of the chapter by analyzing the user interface.

Using the Default Interface of Blender 3.0

After installing Blender 3.0, let's look at the interface to orient ourselves in the 3D Viewport and start using it.

When we open it for the first time, the interface looks like Figure 1-8.

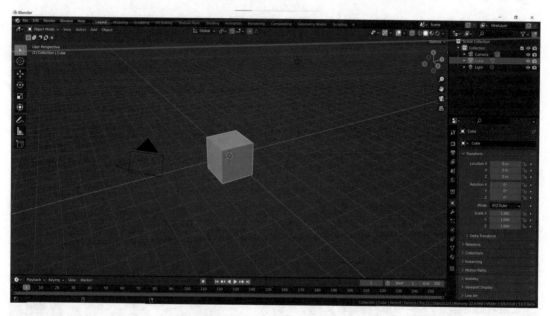

Figure 1-8. *Default user interface of Blender 3.0*

As we can immediately notice, the most crucial window is the 3D Viewport, the central workspace in which most of our activities will occur. It is a three-dimensional space in which three objects are already present: a Cube, a Camera, and a Light.

We can begin creating objects in Blender and start working immediately with these three elements.

But let's take it one step at a time; later in the book, we'll look at the elements we mentioned here. Right now we will take a closer look at the interface.

Main Areas

The Blender interface was developed in OpenGL and has several excellent possibilities for personalization so that everyone can organize their own working space to operate most efficiently and quickly for them.

The new Blender 3.0 interface is orderly and user-friendly.

First, we'll look at the areas, editors, menus, and workspaces in Blender to understand the software more effectively.

Let's start by looking at the main elements of Blender's interface, as shown in Figure 1-9.

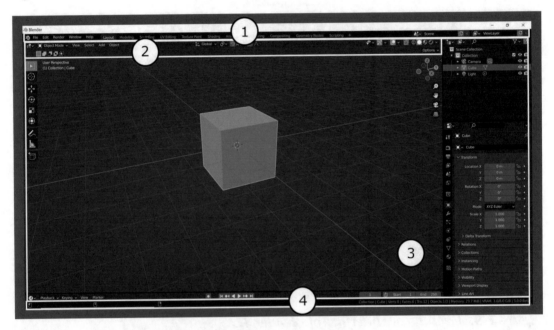

Figure 1-9. *The four main areas of the user interface*

Here are the four main sections:

1. The Topbar is at the top of the Blender interface and contains the main menu, workspaces, scenes, and layers.

2. The header is directly below the topbar. It contains the head of each window or editor with menus, tool settings, and essential tools that interactively change with the editor type.

There are two sections: the Toolbar Information Header above and the Tool Settings below. By right-clicking in the 3D view header, we open a window with which we can control the visualization of the two bars. If the header is not displayed, we can click the arrow in the upper-right corner of the viewport to recover it.

3. The editor area is the central screen space for the editor type.

4. The status bar provides information about keyboard shortcuts, the selected object, and the software version in use.

After a quick look at the general structure of the interface, we will now see how the main toolbars and windows are structured, and we will study in more detail the editors and views.

Topbar, Header, Toolbar, and Status Bar

The Topbar, header, toolbar, editor area, and status bar are the elements that make up the Blender 3.0 interface when we launch the platform.

When we open Blender, there are four editor types. In the center, we find the 3D Viewport editor, on the right are the Outline and Properties Editor. Instead, the Timeline is at bottom of the interface.

Across all platforms, Blender's user interface is consistent.

The Topbar

Let's start with the Topbar, the first line at the top of the interface containing the main menu, default workspaces, scenes, and layers.

On the left of this bar, the main menu contains File, Edit, Render, Window, and Help, as shown in Figure 1-10.

Figure 1-10. *Blender main menu*

File collects the most important File operations. Edit contains the editing operations and the Preferences window, which allows us to customize the interface, which we will learn about later. Render includes the processes related to making a rendering. Window collects the actions on the windows. Finally, Help connects us with Blender sites, including the manual, the tutorials, and a lot of informative material.

Another vital part of the Topbar is the one containing different workspaces, as shown in Figure 1-11.

Figure 1-11. *Blender 3.0 workspaces, scenes, and layers*

Multiple workspaces and their default settings help speed up workflow. In the next section, we will see how.

With the Scenes section, we can organize our work much better.

From the New Scene button in the Topbar, we can create multiple scenes with different objects within the same Blender file, as shown in Figure 1-12.

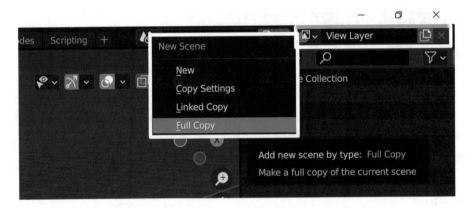

Figure 1-12. *The options for a new scene and the Render Layer button*

As we can see in Figure 1-12, we can build a new scene differently from the default scene or replicate a scene already present in Blender and then modify it. In addition, working with other scenes allows us to create different versions of the same environment within the same file. Then we can change those scenes independently.

Next to the scenes, we find the render layers on the right, dividing the rendered image into several levels to edit them separately and subsequently merge them into a final image. We will see render layers and passes in Chapter 6.

Now let's learn about the tools of the editor type's header.

The Header of the Editor Type

On the second and third lines from the top, we find the header of the editor type composed of two bars, as shown in Figure 1-13.

Figure 1-13. *The upper part of the 3D view interface: the 3D View Header*

At the top, we find the Toolbar Information Header, and below we can see the Tool Settings. Both these bars contain essential tools for working in Blender.

On the left of the header, the Editor Type Selector is the button to switch between the different editors, as shown in Figure 1-14.

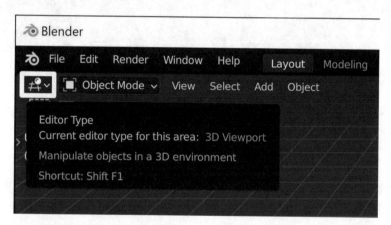

Figure 1-14. *The Editor Type Selector*

We can switch between the various editors that we will learn about one by one in the "Introducing Editors and Views" section of this chapter.

Next, we find the Object Mode selector and the Header menu, as shown in the figure.

Object Interaction Mode Button

In the Object Interaction Mode button, we can choose our working mode.

Next, the 3D View Header menu changes according to the editor type. For example, in Object mode, we find View, Select, Add, and Object; instead, in Edit mode, we have View, Select, Add, Mesh, Vertex, Edge, Face, UV, etc. We will learn about these menus in this chapter's "Menus and Workspaces" section.

Let's learn about the different object modes now; each has specific functions to perform certain tasks with 3D objects, images, videos, etc.

In Figure 1-15, we see a complete list of all the object modes summarized in brief.

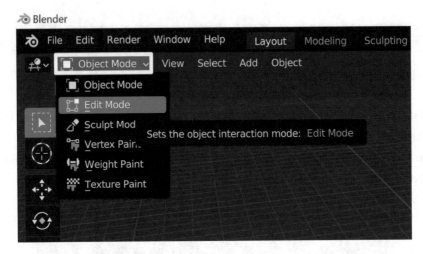

Figure 1-15. *Object modes*

Figure 1-15 shows only the modes related to the mesh objects. But there are others associated, for example, with the Armature objects, etc.

Let's look at each mode individually:

- Object mode is the default modality available for every type of object. In this mode, we work on the thing as a whole, and we modify the entity's position, rotation, and dimension, the so-called object data-block editing, while the topology does not change.

- Instead, we use Edit mode for subobject editing. In this modality, we work on the individual elements of the object; for example, vertices, edges, and faces for meshes and control points for curves, surfaces, etc. Thanks to the main transformations and other modification tools, we can modify the object's geometry by acting on its subobjects.

- Sculpt mode is a mesh-only mode for creating organic shapes in real time and realistic sculptural modeling with virtual clay. In this mode, the tools are brushes/chisels like Draw, Clay, Flatten, etc., and work on the Blender's meshes by changing the mesh's topology.

- Vertex Paint Mode is a mesh-only mode, where the tools become brushes that allow us to change the color of the mesh's vertices. This operation gives vertices color without affecting the surface, geometry, texture, or material. We will use this color to apply different changes, as we will see in Chapter 5.

- Weight Paint mode is a mesh-only mode that assigns a weight to each vertex defined with a scale of values ranging from blue to red, from 0 to 1, and from the absence of influence to the maximum weight value. We use it for rigging and animation, for particle systems, and for each modification in which we need a change in the value of the amendment itself.

- Texture Paint Mode is a mesh-only mode; it allows us to paint meshes or create textures in various ways with multiple tools.

Let's see some other editing tools of the header now.

Transformation Orientation, Transform Pivot Point, Snap and Proportional Editing

We can find other essential tools even further to the right, as shown in Figure 1-16.

Figure 1-16. *Transformation Orientation, Transform Pivot Point, Snap, and Proportional Editing*

Figure 1-16 shows the buttons for multiple features, from left to right, including Transformation Orientation to modify the alignment of the transformation axes, and the Transform Pivot Point and Pivot Center tools for rotating and scaling, which precisely establish the center of modification of the transformations.

Next, we find the Snap system and the Proportional Editing panel, which we can activate with the shortcut O.

Here we have different snaps available when performing the main transformations, as shown in Figure 1-17. In addition, snaps help move the selection to any defined point.

Figure 1-17. *The snap options*

The defined points are Increment, Vertex, Edge, Face, Volume, Edge Center, and Edge Perpendicular. Each gives us a different snap function that we will explore throughout the book.

By contrast, the Proportional Editing panel makes a balanced selection of objects in Object mode and subobjects in Edit mode, as shown in Figure 1-18.

Figure 1-18. *The Proportional Editing options*

The selection takes place according to the selected object and the falloff type. Then, by rotating the mouse wheel, we proportionally increase or decrease the size of the sphere of influence of the selection.

On the right of the interface, we can see a few more visualization tools: View Object Types, Show Gizmo, Show Overlays, Toggle X-Ray (Alt+Z), and Viewport Shading.

Visualization Tools

In this section we'll learn about the Visualization buttons of the header.

There are five elements related to visualization on the right side of the 3D view's header, as shown in Figure 1-19.

Figure 1-19. *The visualization buttons to the right of the 3D view's header*

Let's look at each of these in more detail:

- The View Object Types list controls the visibility and selectability of each type of object. Visibility is indicated by the eye shape image button, while the arrowhead image button indicates the selection. By clicking this button, we can turn on or off the visibility or restrict the selection for each object such as Mesh, Curve, Grease Pencil, Armature, Light, etc., as per our requirements.

- The Show Gizmo list shows gizmos of all types, including Viewport, Object, Empty, Light, and Camera gizmos. From here, we can show or hide all the gizmos.

- The Show Overlays list displays overlines as gizmos and outlines. Thus, we can check the visibility of the grid, the axis, the 3D cursor, etc.

- The Toggle X-Ray button, which we can also access with Alt+Z, allows us to hide or show the back of our objects in 3D view in both Object and Edit modes. With the button active, the objects are displayed as transparent. The tool is handy in Edit mode because it also acts on the selection, and it also allows us to select the hidden subobjects.

21

- Viewport Shading controls the display of 3D view and allows us to change the type. We have different types of shading:

  - The Wireframe shading is the so-called "wireframe" display that shows only the outlines and edges of objects.

  - In Solid shading, we display the thing as a solid; it is the best shading mode for modeling and editing the elements.

  - Material Preview represents the objects with the materials applied, displaying the textures, transparency, reflection, etc.

  - The Rendered shading presents the 3D View workspace with the same characteristics as the final render, with materials, reflections, lights, and shadows reproduced in the selected render engine.

Then, we can control some visualization characteristics in the Properties Editor, which will be explained later in the chapter.

In the Viewport Display window of the Object Properties panel of the Properties Editor, we can control different characteristics of our objects; for example, we can show the name in the 3D view. Furthermore, in the Viewport Display window of the Material Properties of the Properties Editor, we can change the object's color in 3D view to Solid viewport shading regardless of the material' color applied.

But now, in the second bar, let's look at the Tool Settings on the left.

Tool Settings

The second line of the header contains the Tool Settings, shown in the white rectangle in Figure 1-20.

Figure 1-20. *The selection Tool Settings*

In Object and Edit modes, as shown in the figure, we can see the Select functions, whereby we can directly perform different types of selection.

In the Tool Settings, we can decide what kind of selection to make: extend, subtract, invert, or intersect the current selection.

We find the tools to create and edit brushes and chisels in the same bar in Sculpt, Vertex Paint, Weight Paint, Texture Paint, and Draw modes.

Depending on the visibility requirement of the 3D Viewport editor, we can change the position of the tool settings. We can do this by right-clicking the Tool Settings and then selecting Header; this will pop up a toolbar. Next, we can choose Flip to Bottom. With this done, the Tool Settings will move to the bottom-left side of the 3D Viewport editor such that we can have a clean 3D Viewport on the top side. We can also revert this change.

Let's look at the toolbar now.

The Toolbar

The toolbar is an essential instrument of the new Blender interface that is especially useful to those who are just starting to use Blender. The toolbar contains several tools.

This window has other instruments according to the various object modes. So, it will always have several characteristics in Sculpt, Vertex Paint, Weight Paint, and Texture Paint modes.

We can show the various devices, functions, and keyboard shortcuts by hovering the mouse over the icons, as shown in Figure 1-21.

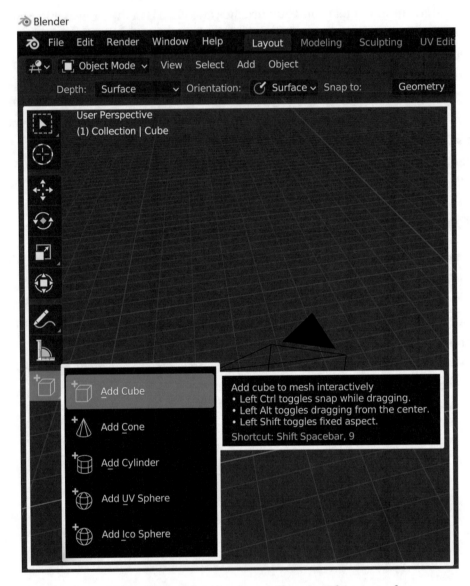

Figure 1-21. *The Add Mesh function in the toolbar in Object mode*

Figure 1-21 shows the Add Mesh function with its different tools: Add Cube, Cone, Cylinder, etc.

In Object mode, the toolbar has the following tools in order:

- Selection to select objects.

- Cursor to switch from selection to cursor mode and move it; we can also access this tool with the Shift+spacebar shortcut.

- The main transformations are Move, Rotate, Scale, and Transform, and we can also access these tools, respectively, with G, R, S, and T.

- We can perform all three basic transformations simultaneously with a complete interactive gizmo.

- We use Ctrl to make precision changes in increments of 1 grid unit or press Shift+Ctrl to allow 0.1 grid units. We can modify the increments by opening the Viewport Overlays panel from the Overlays button in the 3D view header and changing the Scale. For example, if we set the Scale value from 1 to 0.1, the Ctrl increments will be 0.1 grid units instead of 1 grid unit. If we set Scale to 5 increments will be 5 grid units.

- The Add Mesh tools, as shown in Figure 1-21.

In Object mode, we also have the following:

- The Annotate key to make annotations directly in 3D view

- The Measure key to inspect the distances and angles of the created objects

In Edit mode, there are several tools for modifying and modeling the mesh such as Extrude Region, Inset Faces, Bevel, Loop Cut, Knife, Poly Build, Spin Smooth, Edge Slide, Shrink/Fatten, Shear, and Rip Region.

In Sculp mode, we have all the chisels or brushes.

Finally, in Vertex Paint, Weight Paint, Texture Paint Mode, we have brushes for editing vertices and textures.

In the Tool Settings of the 3D Viewport header, we have the controls for the toolbar tools we have just seen.

The Status Bar

At the bottom of the interface, we find the status bar. It changes depending on what editor our mouse cursor is in. It shows suggestions for keyboard shortcuts on the left. On the right it shows information relating to the objects.

This bar can be helpful if we don't know or remember some keyboard shortcuts. For example, when we move an object, the left part of the status bar in Object mode looks like Figure 1-22.

Figure 1-22. *The Status bar in 3D Viewport editor, in Object mode*

Figure 1-22 shows the shortcuts to perform operations on objects.

On the right side of the status bar, we have all the information relating to the objects, as shown in Figure 1-23.

Collection | Cube | Verts:8 | Faces:6 | Tris:12 | Objects:0/3 | Memory: 22.9 MiB | VRAM: 4.6/8.0 GiB | 3.0.0

Figure 1-23. *The Status bar*

Figure 1-23 shows the name of the collection of the selected object, the object itself, the number of vertices and faces, the number of tris (triangular faces), the weight of the scene in the computer memory, the RAM usage, and the installed version of Blender.

We can access this information by right-clicking the status bar and activating what we are interested in the window that appear, for example, the Scene Statistics box.

This section has studied the essential tools to work effectively with the Blender 3.0 interface. Since version 2.8, the developers have modified the interface to work more practically and effectively.

In the next section, we start to see two fundamental Blender tools in more detail: editors and views.

Introducing Editors and Views

We already had a general overview of the editors used in Blender. Now, let's look at a more specific and in-depth analysis of the tools of the Blender 3.0 interface with the study of the editor area.

As we have already seen, the Editor Type Selector allows us to switch from one editor to another.

Editors are the most disparate. Let's look at them one by one, starting with understanding what they are and what they're for.

Editor Types

The editors are the heart of Blender. Each of them is a window with tools for different purposes. These instruments give the software great flexibility and perform many disparate functions with similar interfaces.

In most cases, we can use the same keyboard shortcuts for similar tools in different editors. For example, if we need to move an object in the three-dimensional space of the viewport, we use the G key; we also use the same key to move an armature in Pose mode or move a strip in the Video Sequencer.

There are four groups of editors: General, Animation, Scripting, and Data.

We can see all the types of editors available in Blender 3.0 in Figure 1-24.

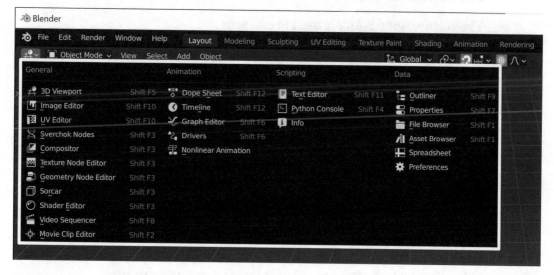

Figure 1-24. *The editor types*

We also see the keyboard shortcut to open each editor type in Figure 1-24. Analyzing them one by one, this is what is in the General section:

- The 3D Viewport is the most used Blender editor. It is the three-dimensional space in which we work on our objects.

- We use the Image Editor to see and edit two-dimensional images, such as the textures for the materials. New textures can be created by clicking the New button in the Texture Node editor or by clicking the New control in the Texture panel.

- The UV Editor is one of the crucial editors mainly used to apply images and textures to three-dimensional objects and to edit UVs.

- Here we make mappings to apply textures on a three-dimensional model. We do this operation in the UV Editing workspace, and Blender has several built-in algorithms that automatically unwrap

3D shapes. In Chapter 4, we will learn about the various methods to perform this operation.

- The Compositor allows us to edit images and videos directly inside Blender by importing photos or videos through the Image or Movie Clip nodes and using the other nodes to modify them. We can consider Compositor as part of the post-process.

- The Texture Node Editor is used to edit textures.

- When Blender launched the 2.92 version, it was with a Geometry Node editor. The idea is to create geometry procedurally.

- In version 3.0, we can create complex geometry with excellent control such as base assets, modular pieces, particle instances, etc.

- With the Shader Editor, we can create and edit node materials.

- Both Cycles X and Eevee use node materials, as we will see at the end of this chapter and, more thoroughly, in Chapter 6.

- The Video Sequencer is a complete video editing system that allows us to edit videos and add effects. We can import different images and video clips and edit them together, adding transitions and effects of various types; we can also add and edit audio files to complete our movies.

- We can use the Movie Clip Editor for tracking or masking movies.

In the Animation Editor Type section, we find the following:

- Blender's Dope Sheet is an editor inspired by the traditional animation-making method. It gives the animator a total view of the entire animation process; it presents all the keyframes and animation movements in a general scheme.

- The Timeline is the strip at the bottom of the interface just above the status bar. This editor displays the frames for the animations and provides simple tools to move between them. We use it to reproduce animations and physical simulations. The blue vertical line that we can move by clicking and dragging the cursor is the playhead, and it shows the current frame number at the top.

- The Graph Editor allows us to edit animation curves, F-Curves, for everything that can be animated.

- Drivers shows the settings for a driver. Drivers are a way to control property values using a function or mathematical expression.

- With Nonlinear Animation, we can manipulate and reuse animations more quickly than editing keyframes. We use it to make significant changes in the animation of an object in a relatively simple way. The NLA can also reuse an already animated sequence.

In the Scripting section, we find the following:

- We use the Text Editor to write Python scripts and develop custom add-ons for Blender.

- The Python Console is a tool to execute commands quickly; it is also a way to explore the possibilities of Python for Blender.

- The Info Editor records our software's accomplished operators, alerts, and error messages. We can also select documented reports by clicking them.

In the Data section, we have the following:

- The Outliner is an essential window because it contains all the scene collections and objects of the current Blender file.

- The current version of Blender contains a critical modification: the Scene Collection.

- This layer system can include the different types of objects and can be shown or hidden in the 3D Viewport or the rendering.

- The collections replaced the old layer system were limited to 20 levels and did not have a proper name. This innovation brings order and improves the work performance in Blender because it allows direct control of groups of objects. Now, we can have unlimited collections.

- The Properties Editor contains all the most basic Blender commands such as as render properties, output properties, modifiers, physics properties, etc., so we will discuss it separately.

- We use the File Browser Editor in operations related to files, including, for example, opening, saving, and choosing new locations for existing files as images, materials, videos, etc.

- The Asset Browser works as a local user library. It allows us to save all Blender assets to make them available from one Blender file to another by dragging and dropping them directly into the 3D Viewport, as already happens with Unity.

- The Spreadsheet Editor is directly connected to the Geometry Node Editor and is used to control the geometry attributes employed by the geometry nodes themselves.

- Preferences is the editor we use to customize Blender and change the Blender's default configuration; we will present this editor in Chapter 2.

After a brief overview of the different editor types, let's look at a fundamental one in more detail: the Properties Editor.

Properties Editor

The Properties Editor allows us to edit the active object's properties and scenes and related data blocks. Many Blender functions are gathered in this editor.

Arranged vertically, on the right of Blender's interface, this editor enables us to access different tabs that contain almost all the main functions of Blender.

This provision replaces the previous version with a more straightforward and rational distribution of the commands shown in Figure 1-25.

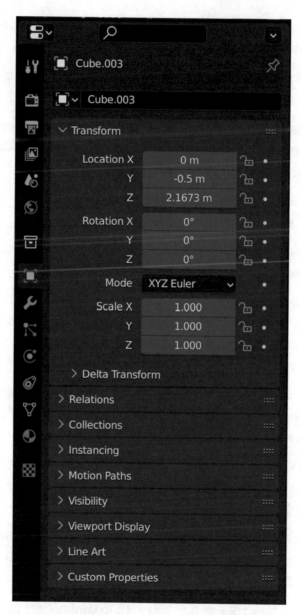

Figure 1-25. *The Properties Editor*

Each of these tabs has a specific function different from the others; let's look at each in more detail:

- The Active Tool and Workspace Settings tab presents the tool selected in 3D view and the current workspace. For example, it contains Sculpt mode features and brush controls for sculpting.

- Render Properties contains all the settings to control the image and video rendering.

  The Scene window allows us to select the active render engine: Eevee, Cycles, or Workbench.

  With the Sampling window, we can control the quality of our image or video, increasing render samples with the Render and Viewport boxes with a reduction of aliasing.

  Ambient occlusion simulates softer lights and shadows by generating smooth shading even without direct lighting.

  We can use the Depth of Field window to control the lens aperture and the camera focus to simulate typical camera blurs.

  Subsurface Scattering simulates semitranslucent materials on which light partly bounces, partly penetrates, and then disperses inside and bounces back later, like human skin, fruit, gelatin, honey, wax, tomatoes, etc.

  Screen Space Reflections is an option for rendering glass objects in Eevee. Eevee will not correctly give transparent surfaces if we don't select this and also select Refraction.

  The Shadows window controls the characteristics of the shadows. In addition to the Shadow window of the active light's Object Data properties in the Properties Editor.

  If we want technical rendering, an exciting window is Freestyle, which we must select if we're going to get a rendering with a drawing effect.

- The Output Properties section allows us to control the output characteristics of the file, its information, and save settings.

  The Dimensions window gives us control over the resolution of the rendered files.

  In the Output window, we can define the destination folder and the file format. We can choose different professional formats for images (BMP, PNG, JPEG, etc.) and videos (AVI JPEG, AVIRaw, and FFmpeg).

We can also choose images or videos in black and white, RGB, or RGB with an Alpha channel for transparency.

- View Layer Properties controls the visibility of the collections, allowing us to select them and set their options. Finally, this editor will enable us to render each layer separately to compose them in post-production and apply them to compositing effects independently.

- In the Scene Properties window, we can set the scene features.

  We can set the unit system as None, Metric, or Imperial in the Units window. Blender then automatically switches from the metric system to the Anglo-Saxon system.

  Then we have the Gravity window, where we can modify the force of gravity. The default gravity value is set to $-9,8m/s^2$ in the z-axis parameter value.

- World Properties shows the environment settings. The Surface window contains the general settings for the background and its lighting.

- Collection Properties contains some boxes to adjust some features of the collections used to organize the scene logically.

- We work with scene objects in the Object Properties Editor. First, we use them to modify the characteristics and properties of the selected object. For example, we can change an object's visibility and name here. Then we find the Transform window to identify and modify the object's location, rotation, and scale.

- We use Modifier Properties to add the various modifiers to the selected object. Each of them modifies the object in a different way. They allow us to work flexibly by altering the element indirectly. Moreover, we can apply or delete them at any time.

  Blender provides four categories of modifiers: Modify, Generate, Deform, and Physics. We will gradually see the most stimulating of them one by one throughout the book.

- We can use the Particle Properties Editor to create particle systems.

To add a particle system, after selecting an object, we click the + button on the right of the panel. There are two types: Emitter and Hair. We can choose either. Then we need to provide the necessary data in the respective fields to get the particle system working.

- Physics Properties is the editor from which we add the physical simulations. We have several options: Force Field, Collision, Cloth, Dynamic Paint, Soft Body, Fluid, Rigid Body, and Rigid Body Constraint.

- In Object Constraints Properties, we assign an object's relationships with other elements to create interactions, such as the path of a camera on a curve for an architecture walk-through. We can establish four different types of links: Motion Tracking, Transform, Tracking, and Relationship.

- Object Data Properties contains several functions related to the selected object. Vertex Group's window is helpful in control groups of vertices to assign different effects, animations, and custom particle systems.

  Shape keys help add keys to the mesh and then animate facial expressions and more. We can also generate vertex colors to affect mesh movements and animations.

- We use the Material Properties window to assign the material to the object and change its characteristics.

  From here, we can modify all the properties of the substance. As we will see later, we can also perform the same functions with nodal materials directly inside the Shader Editor.

- Texture Properties is the panel where we can assign the textures to the substance by clicking the New button (+).

  Blender sets a bitmap texture, which is an image.

  Then we can assign the image, in the Settings window, from the New or Open button.

We have to create an image from scratch with Blender's Texture Paint tools with New. Instead, with Open, we can import an existing image.

If we want a procedural texture, we can choose the type by clicking the Image or Movie button and selecting one of Blender's procedural textures, as Clouds, for example. We will discuss the topic in more detail in the Textures section of Chapter 4.

Here we have introduced the Properties Editor summarizing its main features without listing all the functions; refer to the Blender 3.0 Manual for a complete list.

Let's now learn about menus and workspaces.

Menus and Workspaces

Now let's take a closer look at four other essential elements of Blender's interface:

- The main menu on the top left of the Topbar

- The 3D View Header menu alongside the object modes

- The Pie menus

- The workspaces

Let's look at these four elements in more detail.

The Topbar Menu

The main menu in the Topbar contains the items File, Edit, Render, Window, and Help. The names already give us an idea of their functions, but let's look at them one by one carefully.

File

In the File window, we have the New item (Ctrl+N) to create a new file and the Open item (Ctrl+O) to open an existing file. The Open Recent item opens a recently opened file.

Then we have the Recover Last Session and Autosave menu items; the files are automatically saved by Blender every few minutes in a temporary file that we can access if necessary.

Tip   In the File menu, we can recover lost files using File ➤ Recover ➤ Last Session or File ➤ Recover ➤ Auto Save. With the first function, we retrieve the last session, while with the second one, we open a window from which we can open different files saved automatically by Blender.

Next, we can use Save, Save As, and Save Copy to save the current file in different ways.

We use Link and Append to import objects, materials, etc., from other Blender files.

With Append, we can import an independent copy of the asset. In contrast, we can import a linked duplicate that we cannot directly modify with Link. With this, we can reuse already created stuff as per our requirements.

In Blender 3.0, we will use the Asset Browser, an agile content management tool that we will learn more about in Chapter 3.

Then we have the Import and Export items, which we use to import and export files from other software into Blender.

The most important file formats are already available in the menu that we open by typing Import or Export, as shown in Figure 1-26 for Import.

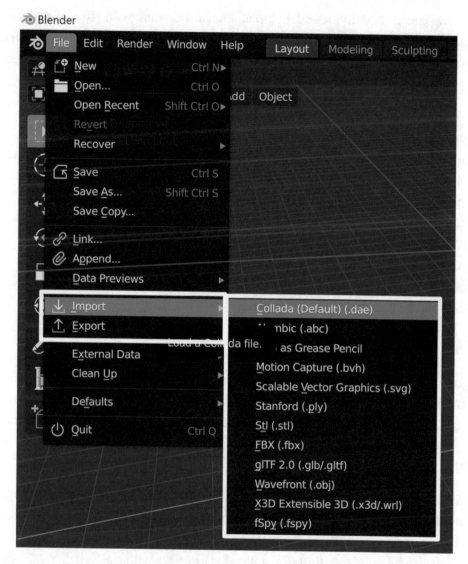

Figure 1-26. *The default import file formats*

We can activate other file formats in the User Preferences from the add-ons window (in the Topbar menu, select Edit ➤ Preferences ➤ Add-ons ➤ Import Export ➤ search and enable the file format you need).

Another critical item in the File menu is External Data to pack external data into the Blender file in use.

Also, we can embed different data types, such as textures, inside the `.blend` file by clicking Pack Resources. This command is crucial if we have to move the file, put it on a thumb drive, or upload it to the cloud so we don't lose the external data such as textures.

Edit

Let's move on to the Edit item.

The Edit item opens a window with essential entries such as Undo (Ctrl+Z) and Redo (Shift+Ctrl+Z), which, as in other software, are used to cancel or repeat the last operation performed.

Undo History opens a window with the procedures performed and allows us to recover them.

Finally, we will find the Preferences button at the bottom of this menu item. This fundamental button opens the User Preferences, from which we can customize practically all the functions of this software.

Render

Let's go to the Render window with its two menu items: Render Image (F12) and Render Animation (Ctrl+F12). These render the video or the image. We can also use View Render (F11) and View Render Animation (Ctrl+F11) to see the rendered clip or picture.

Window

In the Window menu, we can open a new window through the command New Window.

We can show or hide the status bar at the bottom of the screen by checking Show Status Bar.

We can also take a screenshot of the Blender interface with the Save Screenshot item.

Help

The Help item contains links to open the Blender 3.0 Reference Manual, the Support website, the User Communities, the Developer Community, and the Python API Reference. In addition, we can open the Blender 3.0 Python API Documentation to help familiarize ourselves with the Python Blender language.

Now let's look at the 3D View Header menu.

The 3D View Header Menu

We can find this menu in the 3D view header next to the object modes for which it is interactive.

The items in this menu automatically adapt to the active mode. So, we will have certain tools in Object mode, others in Edit, others in Sculpt, etc.

The menus are as follows in Object mode: View, Select, Add, and Object. In Edit mode, we have View, Select, Add, Mesh, Vertex, Edge, Face, and UV.

We will look at these menus rather rapidly because we do not use them often. After all, we apply almost all the same functions more quickly with the keyboard shortcuts, the bars, or other tools in the interface.

Let's see the items one by one in both Object and Edit modes. First, here are the items in Object mode:

- We use the View window to show or hide some bars, for example, the toolbar, sidebar, Tool Settings, etc.

  We can also edit the work areas using the Area button at the bottom of the list.

  This menu is also helpful for different operations connected with cameras and navigation.

- We use the Select item for different types of selection that we will see in detail in the next section dedicated to selection methods.

- We add all objects into a scene with Add.

  We can add Modeling and Grease Pencil objects, cameras, lights, speakers, force fields, and so on. We can also use the shortcut Shift+A to add the same objects.

- The last item in Object mode is Object, which allows us to do all the operations on objects: from Transform to Set Origin to Snap. Furthermore, it will enable us to duplicate things and change the element's display from Shade Smooth to Shade Flat.

  It will help us apply Quick Effects (i.e., Fur, Explode, Smoke, and Liquid) automatically and immediately and convert one type of object to another and also delete it.

In Edit mode, we will find View, Select, and Add, which are similar to those in Object mode. We also will find the following menus:

- Mesh concerns operations such as objects but performed on a mesh such as Transform, Mirror, and Snap. Others like Extrude, Split, and Convex Hull are more specific to subobjects.

- Vertex, Edge, and Face allow us to act on individual subobject types with more specific 3D modeling operations: Extrude (E) and Bevel (Ctrl+Shift+B). To name just the most useful, we have the following:

  - In the Vertex window: New Edge/Face from Vertices (F), Rip Vertices (V) and Rip Vertices, and Fill (Alt+V) and Merge Vertices (Alt+M)

  - In the Edge window: Bridge Edge Loops, Subdivide

  - In the Face window: Extrude Faces, Triangulate Faces (Ctrl+T), Tris to Quads (Alt+J), Wireframe

- UV instead reports all the various ways to unwrap our three-dimensional object that we will see in detail in the following chapters.

In Sculpt, Vertex Paint, Weight Paint, and Texture Paint, we have the specific tools for these modes: View, Sculpt, and Mask in Sculpt mode; View and Paint in Vertex Paint; View and Weights in Weights Paint; and View only in Texture Paint.

We will carefully see all the most essential tools from time to time throughout the book.

Pie Menus

The pie menus are interactive functions that open directly in the interface.

They are a fundamental innovation since Blender 2.8 because they introduce a new, quick way of working with menus and keyboard shortcuts.

It's a slightly different system of working that requires a little mnemonic effort, but it's worth it to speed up the work.

The shortcuts are similar to that of standard actions, but they open entire menus.

For example, usually shortcut A allows us to select all the objects present in the scene. If we enable the pie menus, shortcut A opens a menu for all types of selection, as shown in Figure 1-27.

Figure 1-27. *Pie selection menu*

Before obtaining the window shown in Figure 1-27, we must activate the pie menus. So, we open the Blender User Preferences and select Add-on 3D Viewport Pie Menus (in the Topbar menu, select Edit ➤ Preferences ➤ Add-ons ➤ Import Export ➤ Interface: 3D Viewport Pie Menus), as shown in Figure 1-28.

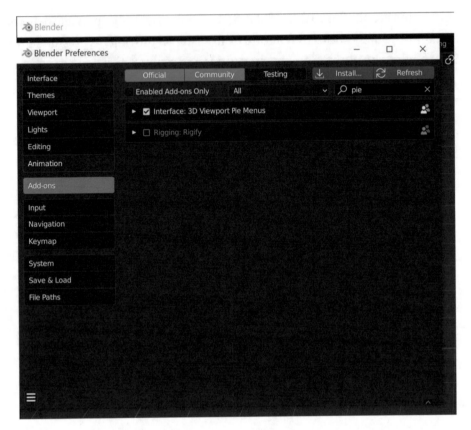

Figure 1-28. *Activate 3D Viewport Pie Menus add-on*

Next we need to learn the keyboard shortcuts to open these menus directly in the 3D Viewport.

In the current version, we have 15 pie menus. First, let's see a brief description of each menu.

- The Animation menu (Shift+spacebar) allows us to control the Timeline, insert keyframes, and activate the auto keyframe.

- The Apply Transform menu (Ctrl+A) enables us to apply the selected object's location, rotation, and scale transformations or clear them.

- The Edit Align menu (Alt+X) works in Edit mode (Tab) and aligns vertices/edges/faces on the axis.

- The Edit Delete menu (X), in Edit mode, allows us to delete or dissolve subobjects. It also contains the commands Merge by Distance, Delete Edge Loops, and Edge Collapse.

- We can use the Editor Switch menu (Ctrl+Alt+S) to change the editor type quickly.

- The Interface menu (Ctrl+U) allows us to save/open files.

- The Manipulator menu (Alt+spacebar) shows and hides manipulators.

- The Mode Switch menu (Ctrl+Tab) changes between different object type modes.

- The Origin menu (Ctrl+Alt+X) allows us to change the origin of the selected object, which usually is in the geometric center of the thing itself.

- The Save/Open menu (Ctrl+S) opens, saves, and imports files into Blender.

- The Proportional Edit menu (Shift+O) applies proportional selection to an object or subobject.

- The Sculpt menu (W) quickly opens brushes in Sculpt mode.

- The Select menu (A) selects and deselects each object type.

- The Shading menu (Z) changes the display in the 3D view.

- The View menu (Alt+Q) edits views in the viewport.

All these menus are exciting and allow a faster workflow inside Blender.

Now let's see another important innovation of the last Blender version: workspaces.

Workspaces

Every workspace is suitable for a different function; the default one is Layout.

Other default workspaces are Modeling, Sculpting, UV Editing, Texture Paint, Shading, Animation, Rendering, Compositing, Scripting, etc. Each one is suitable for a different function.

We can create, customize, name, and save our workspaces for later use, so they are a way to tailor our interface.

Each Blender feature has a dedicated workspace, and we identify it with its name. So, for example, the Layout workspace is the primary space in which we start working at the object level. Then if we want to start working at a subobject level, we can either change from Object mode to Edit mode or go directly to the Modeling workspace, where we already have the object in Edit mode ready to be edited.

Let's look at the primary workspaces:

- The Layout workspace allows us to work directly at the object level.

- The Modeling workspace instead is already set up for subobject level modeling.

- The Sculpting workspace is ready to sculpt. We work directly in Sculpt mode with the toolbar and the Properties Editor open on Active Tool and Workspace settings, ready to sculpt our object.

- We have a UV Editor on the left in the UV Editing workspace and then a 3D Viewport set in Edit mode. On the right, we find the Outliner and the Properties Editor's Object Data Properties panel commands to unwrap the selected object in the 3D Viewport.

- In this environment, we can quickly develop the surface of our three-dimensional objects on a two-dimensional plane to apply bitmap textures in the best possible way.

- In the Texture Paint workspace, we paint textures on the Image Editor on the left or directly on the object in 3D Viewport on the right.

  To start painting, we have to create a new texture or import an existing bitmap texture with the New or Open button.

- The Shading workspace is ready for the visualization and modification of the materials; at the top center, we have a 3D Viewport editor in material preview Viewport Shading Mode. Thus, we already have an immediate display of the material characteristics.

Below we have a Shader Editor to modify the nodes of the material. We have a File Browser at the top and an Image Editor at the bottom to create or modify the image textures on the left.

Finally, on the right, we have the Outliner at the top and the Properties Editor set to World Properties at the bottom.

- The Animation workspace's interface is set with the Dope Sheet at the bottom to create and edit animations.

Below that there are several other types of workspaces.

Even further to the right, we have a plus sign (+) that allows us, by clicking it, to open other types of workspaces or create our own.

For example, if we want to create a second Layout workspace, we can click the plus sign (+) and then click Duplicate Current to create a new workspace; we rename it by double-clicking the name in the Topbar, and then we modify it as we want.

Now, let's continue with the user preferences to customize our interface deeply.

Blender Customization

The User Preferences window allows us to modify the default configuration of our software.

We can access it from the Edit item of the main menu in the Topbar (Topbar ➤ Edit ➤ Preferences).

We can see the different functions on the vertical menu on the left through the tabs Interface, Themes, Viewport, Lights, Editing, Animation, Add-ons, Input, Navigation, Keymap, System, Save and Load, and File Paths, as shown in Figure 1-29.

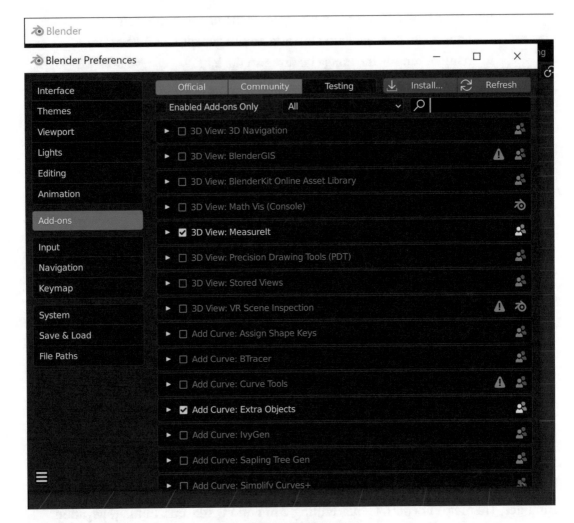

Figure 1-29. The Add-ons panel of User Preferences

Let's see what these sections are for:

- Interface controls some customizable aspects of the UI and allows us to modify its elements and their display.

- The Translation window enables us to change the interface's language and tooltips.

- In Themes, we can customize the theme of the Blender interface, which includes the appearance, colors, etc.

- Viewport allows us to control the 3D view aspects such as Show Object info, view name, gizmo size, etc.

- The Lights panel allows us to install custom studio lights, MatCaps, and HDRIs.

- Editing contains the menu to align the newly created objects to World, View, or 3D Cursor.

- Animation allows us to modify some ways of displaying the interface in animations.

- The Add-ons section extends Blender's functionality with internal and external plugins. We will learn about it in detail during the book when we need to add new objects or new tools to our software. We can see part of this panel in Figure 1-29. Figure 1-29 shows how we can activate several pre-installed add-ons directly by checking their boxes in the window. In addition, we can install other add-ons by downloading their zipped installation files from the Internet.

- The Input panel contains the option Emulate Numpad that allows those who use a laptop without a number pad to use the keyboard's numeric keys to change the 3D view. We can also select Emulate 3 Button Mouse. The panel also includes the buttons needed to use a tablet, such as pressure sensitivity adjustments.

- Navigation allows us to settle the navigation parameters and helps us to move around the 3D interface, for example, with the Orbit Around Selection button, which, if selected, rotates the view while navigating around the selected object. Or we can zoom to the mouse position.

- Keymap controls the Blender's tools shortcuts and allows us to customize them.

- The System panel controls graphics card options, memory limits, and sound settings.

- Finally, we have the Save and Load and File Paths panels to modify files and file path functions.

Slowly we're covering all the essential elements of the user interface by following Blender's graphical layout. First, we saw the main areas, such as the Topbar, Tool Settings, toolbar, status bar, and primary tools. Then we saw the heart of Blender: the editors where we do all the creation and editing work.

The following section will explain the navigation techniques, selection tools, and new features of version 3.0 of our software.

Selecting, Navigating, and Transforming

As we have already said, one of the most critical changes in the latest versions of Blender is the switch from left-clicking to right-clicking selection.

For many years, Blender and the Blender Foundation developers resisted, maintaining the selection of the objects with the right button.

But, with the transition to version 2.8 and subsequent versions, this "epochal" change has happened.

In Blender 3.0, we select with the left mouse button.

This modification makes Blender more similar to other software and more suitable for the graphics tablet. This change also frees up the right button for other functions, such as the new Object Context Menu that we will see shortly.

Let's start by learning how to navigate the 3D interface, select objects, and move them around in 3D view.

Navigation Techniques

Knowing how to navigate in 3D view is essential and allows us to work quickly and easily. The best thing is to get used to employing the mouse together with the keyboard shortcuts so we can work with one hand on the mouse and the other on the keyboard.

By clicking the Ctrl+spacebar key combination, we can maximize or minimize 3D view. With the shortcuts T and N, we can open or close the bars on the right or left —the toolbar and the sidebar— and work with the 3D Viewport that occupies the whole screen using the full-screen definition.

Blender 3.0 makes editing the user interface easier, and we can change the layout of the window's interface more quickly.

When the mouse cursor is on a window's dividing black line, a double arrow appears, and we can press and drag the left mouse button to adjust the dimension of the window.

When we right-click the line when the double arrow appears, we open the Area Options menu. So, we can create other windows by clicking the Vertical Split and Horizontal Split buttons: a line appears that we can move with the mouse. When satisfied with the window's dimensions, we click the left button to split the existing window into two parts at the chosen point.

We can join two areas by right-clicking the Join Areas button in the same window and clicking again with the left key.

Finally, using the Swap Areas button, we can invert the contents of the two windows.

This system inside the 3.0 version is faster and more intuitive than the previous one and makes the UI more user-friendly.

We can easily navigate the 3D Viewport using only the middle mouse button:

- We rotate the middle mouse button to zoom in and out on the 3D Viewport.

- By clicking this button and moving it, we rotate the 3D view.

- Also, by clicking the middle mouse button while holding down the Shift key, we change the position in 3D view in Pan mode.

We can use almost identical keys and the same movements to navigate the panels or the other windows: by rotating the middle mouse wheel, we zoom; by clicking and moving it while holding down Shift, we pan.

In the 3D Viewport, using the Numpad keys, we can modify the various views: by clicking 5, we change from Perspective view to Orthogonal and vice versa; with 7, we enter Top view; with 1, we enter Front and with 3, we enter Right view.

With identical keys, but keeping Ctrl pressed, we have opposite views to those mentioned: Ctrl 7 Bottom; Ctrl 1 Back; Ctrl 3 Left.

If our laptop does not have a Numpad, we can use, as shown previously, the option Emulate Numpad in the Input panel of User Preferences.

We can also navigate the 3D Viewport using the tools on the right side of the interface, with the Navigate gizmos, as shown in Figure 1-30.

Figure 1-30. *The Navigate gizmos*

As Figure 1-30 shows, we rotate the object's view by clicking the LMB and dragging the mouse on the gizmo's sphere. We can move in the respective Orthogonal view by clicking the corresponding letter: X, Y, Z or -X, -Y, -Z.

Below this gizmo, there are the buttons to zoom in/out, pan the view, toggle from camera/orthographic view and, the last button, to toggle from orthographic projection to perspective.

Now let's begin to explore the selection methods.

Selection Methods

In Blender, many selection methods work in Object and Edit modes simultaneously.

As we have seen, we can also select the objects with the Select menu in the header of the 3D Viewport, but it is faster with keyboard shortcuts.

We can also choose the different selection modes from the window that opens by clicking the A shortcut if we activate the pie menus as we have seen before (in the Topbar, select Edit Preferences ➤ Add-ons ➤ Interface: 3D Viewport Pie Menus).

But let's see what the main keyboard shortcuts for selection are.

Object Selection in Object Mode

We select one single object with the left mouse button selection.

To add or remove elements from the selection, we must hold Shift and click the left mouse button on the item. So, we can add or remove it from the selection.

With the A key (Select All), we pick out all the 3D view elements, while with Alt+A, we can deselect all the items (Deselect All). We also deselect everything by clicking with the mouse in the interface to a point where there are no objects.

Ctrl+I (Invert Select) reverses the current selection.

With the button B (Box Select) selected, we open a rectangular selection window defined by clicking and dragging the left mouse button. We can deselect by clicking B and then clicking with the central wheel.

With button C (Circle Select) selected, we define a circular selection area of which we can control the width by rotating the central wheel of the mouse or using the + and - keys of the numeric keypad.

We can select items randomly by clicking Select Random from the 3D View Header Menu ➤ Select ➤ Select Random.

We also have several advanced selection methods; with Shift+G, the Select Grouped key appears as a menu that allows us to select the Group objects differently.

Another menu opens with Shift+L (Select Linked), allowing us to select objects linked in Object and Edit modes differently. Pressing the L key and passing over one item will also select all other entities related to the first one.

Subobject Selection in Edit Mode

In Edit mode, we work at a subobject level.

We select vertices, edges, or faces by left-clicking the selectors in 3D view's header or pressing 1 for vertices, 2 for edges, and 3 for faces.

We select one single subobject with the left mouse button selection.

We add other subobjects to the selection by holding down the Shift key in Object mode and by left-clicking subobjects. To add elements to the selection, we must press Ctrl and Numpad + until all the items of interest are selected. Then, by pressing Ctrl and Numpad, we subtract from the selection.

We use all the selection methods used in Object mode. Then we have some more specific ways for Edit mode.

In vertex or edge select mode, we can select edge loops either from the menu (Select ➤ Select Loops ➤ Edge Loops) or with Alt+LMB. At the same time, we can press Shift+Alt+LMB for modifying, removing, or adding existing selections.

In Edge or Face select modes, we can select face loops with keyboard shortcuts Ctrl+Alt+LMB in Edge mode or Alt+LMB in Face mode for selecting.

We can also modify the current selection with Shift+Ctrl+Alt+LMB in Edge mode and Shift+Alt+LMB in Face mode.

With the Toggle X-Ray button, we can modify the 3D View shading, making objects and subobjects transparent; this transparency also influences the selection. By enabling this tool with Box Selection, pressing B, and dragging, we select all the elements that fall in the selection window, even hidden ones.

Now that we have seen the essential selection methods, we can apply the transformations to the objects to modify them.

Basic Transformations

In the 3D Viewport, we can apply three fundamental transformations: Translation, Rotation, and Scale.

These changes allow us to move, rotate, and scale our objects in Object mode. In Edit mode, we can do the same operations and transform subobjects, as we will see in Chapter 2.

We can do the basic transformations in both Object and Edit modes in three ways:

- *Using the gizmo of the function Transform*: We can activate it from the toolbar by left-clicking (LMB) on the respective icon, then clicking and dragging the different manipulators, and releasing the mouse when satisfied with the transformation.

- We perform snapped transformations by holding down the keys Ctrl and Ctrl+Shift while clicking and dragging.

- With the buttons Transformation Orientation and Transform Pivot Point in the 3D view's header, we can also change the rotation point— or pivot point—and the type of transformation such as Global, Local, Normal, etc.

- *With keyboard shortcuts, we can grab or move our object by pressing the key G, rotate it with R, and scale it with S*: We can perform these transformations by constraining them to an axis (X, Y, Z) and modification amount. In addition, we can control by how many units we move the object, by how many degrees we rotate it, and in what proportion we scale it by typing the value of the modification.

For example, with the combination G+Z+1, we move our object of 1 BU (blender unit) position on the z-axis. With R+45+X, we can rotate our object on the x-axis by 45 degrees. If we click Shift instead of the letter of a single axis before typing it, we limit this transformation to the plane determined by the other two axes. For example, by clicking Shift +X, we define the YZ plane modification.

- We can also perform the main transformations in the Transform panel of the Sidebar on the vewport's right. We need to change the boxes' location, rotation, scale, and dimensions with those wanted. We can open and close the sidebar with the shortcut N and choose Item from the side menu.

Now that we have learned to navigate the view, select, and transform objects, let's see what we can do with the Object context menu.

The Object Context Menu (RMB)

Using the left button instead of the right one for the selection in Blender 3.0, we can use the right button for the Object context menu.

In this menu, we find specific actions. It is interactive with the chosen object mode and the type of object we select.

So, the Object context menu in Object mode with a cube selected presents the essential features for that object. Instead, in Edit mode, we can open some subobject features for a vertex, edge, or face.

In Figure 1-31, we can see the Object context menu in Object mode. We can see this by right-clicking the selected object.

Figure 1-31. *The new Object context menu in Object mode*

If we select an object, we have a menu related to the object's characteristics.

For example, if we select a light, the menu will change and have features to modify that light, the same as a camera, etc.

In the Object context menu of an object, we can modify how to visualize the object, switching from Shade Flat to Shade Smooth.

We can convert an object to another, such as a Bezier curve to a mesh.

We can establish the object's origin to the geometry, the cursor, etc. Then, we can copy and paste one or more objects and duplicate them.

We can rename the active object, apply a mirror, perform a snap, or create a relationship with other elements with parent.

Also, we can move one or more entities from one collection to another with the Move to Collection command. Finally, we can insert keyframes to animate the selected objects or delete them with the Delete item.

This section has deepened our knowledge of navigation, transformation, and selection techniques in Object and Edit modes. Then we saw the Object context menu tool: a right-click menu for particular actions for faster and easier workflow.

In the next section, we will see a different way of working with keyboard shortcuts.

Using New Keyboard Shortcuts

Keyboard shortcuts have always been a significant feature in Blender because they allow us to perform many operations directly from the keyboard.

Many tools and modes have been added in the new versions of Blender up to 3.0, but keyboard shortcuts are always crucial because they can speed up the workflow.

We can see, activate, and edit all Blender keyboard shortcuts in the Keymap section of the User Preferences.

Figure 1-32 shows the window Keymap with the main functions and the related shortcuts.

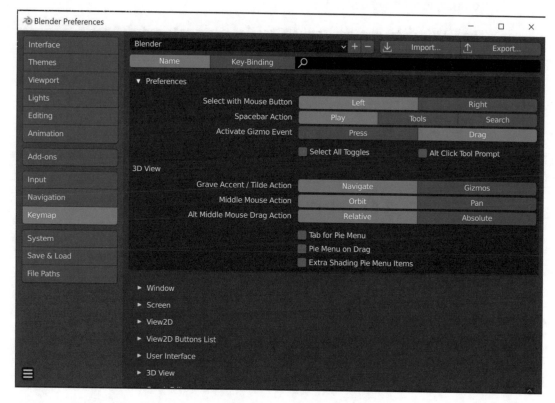

Figure 1-32. *The Blender Keymap window in the user interface*

Let's look at some of the essential keyboard shortcuts shown in Figure 1-32. Of course, the keyboard shortcuts are many.

The following list includes the most important and frequent ones for Windows; generally, we have to use the Cmd key instead of Ctrl on macOS.

- A primary keyboard shortcut is the one that opens the Search window: F3 (Cmd+F on macOS). So, if we don't remember the keyboard shortcut of a tool, we can find it without searching through the various menus.

- The so-called global keys are standard keys used for file operations and essential functions: Ctrl+N to create a new file; Ctrl+O to open an existing file; Ctrl+S for Save, Shift+Ctrl+S for Save as, etc.

- Some keys repeat in each editor: A for Select all; Alt+A for Select none; Ctrl+I for Invert selection; H for Hide selection; Shift+H for Hide Unselected for; Alt+H for Reveal hidden items; T for Toggle Toolbar; N for Toggle Sidebar.

- The 3D Viewport keys such as Tab key also allow us to switch from Object to Edit mode, and the numbers 1, 2, and 3 in Edit mode enable us to turn from vertex to edge to face.

- Other essential keyboard shortcuts are Shift+A to add new objects to the scene and Shift+D to duplicate them.

We can refer to the User Preferences' keymap we have just seen for what is left.

Tip   For comprehensive documentation on keyboard shortcuts, we can also use the online Blender 3.0 Reference Manual, including the Common Shortcuts at `https://docs.blender.org/manual/en/dev/interface/keymap/introduction.html` and the Default Keymap at `https://docs.blender.org/manual/en/dev/interface/keymap/blender_default.html`.

Keyboard shortcuts are fundamental in Blender, and if we want to speed up our production pipeline, it is crucial to learn and use a lot of them.

We've just seen how to use shortcuts, search for them in the interface, and modify them.

In the next section, we'll know how Eevee, Blender's new internal real-time renderer, works using rasterization via OpenGL.

Introducing Eevee

Rendering is a method to create a two-dimensional image or a video from a 3D environment. We need only a few factors: the object and the scene to render, the materials, the lights, the camera features, and the render engine settings.

This section will help us understand the Eevee project and the results of the default rendering engine of Blender 3.0.

The word Eevee is an acronym for Extra Easy Virtual Environment Engine. This real-time PBR Render Engine provides us with all the features we need, more or less the same as Cycles, from ambient occlusion to depth of field, to motion blur, to reflection, to refraction, etc.

Although Eevee still can't get the same realism as Cycles, these renderers have similar features.

Eevee renders very fast, allowing us to see the changes in real time and enabling us to get a preview in the 3D Viewport of our final results with all the render features.

In this way, when working on our models, we can already see textures, lights, shadows, reflections, etc.; then, when it's time to render, we can choose to continue to use Eevee itself or or change to Cycles.

The Cycles renderer uses path tracing, whereas Eevee uses rasterization via OpenGL 3.3. So, Cycles works with light paths, but Eevee renders pixel information, a compressed view of the scene; this is why Eevee is faster than Cycles.

But the new rendering engine is always getting better.

Let's see the main differences between Eevee and Cycles and the materials of both rendering engines: the node-based materials.

Eevee, Cycles, and Cycles X

Blender 3.0 implements Cycles X, the new Cycles version, with new source code that makes rendering faster but keeps the same features and Cycles' default interface.

In version 3.0 of Blender, we can choose the internal rendering engine from a drop-down menu in the Render panel of the Properties Editor, as shown in Figure 1-33.

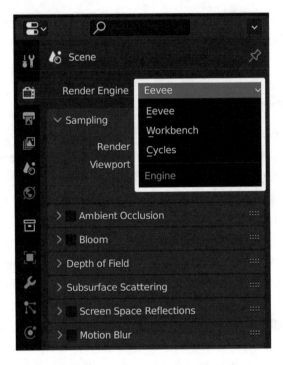

Figure 1-33. *The Render panel drop-down menu*

As we can see in Figure 1-33, we can choose between three engines: Eevee, Cycles, and Workbench. Workbench is used only to give a better display in 3D view for modeling.

In Eevee and Cycles, materials are created and edited directly in the Shader Editor or the Material Properties window of the Properties Editor; the nodes are also almost the same.

Both renderers support the Principled BSDF shader. This shader allows us to obtain various types of material by connecting different textures for each physical characteristic of the multiple elements, as shown in Figure 1-34.

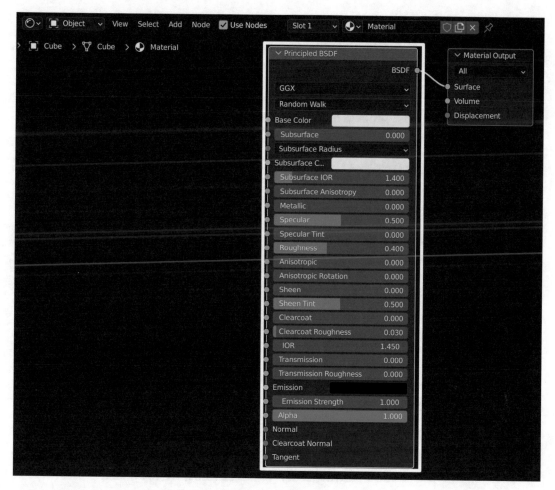

Figure 1-34. *The new Principled BSDF shader*

In Figure 1-34, we can see this particular node; BSDF stands for Bidirectional Scattering Distribution Function. It is a mathematical function that calculates the reflection of a material.

We can control the parameters of both renderers in the Render Properties panel of the Properties Editor; some parameters for Eevee are different from those in Cycles.

Let's see the essential Render Properties in the Properties Editor:

- The Sampling panel (Properties Editor ➤ Render Properties ➤ Sampling), as in Cycles, is indispensable to reduce the aliasing effect: the higher the sampling, in Viewport or Render, the lower the aliasing or the distortion artifacts.

- The Ambient Occlusion panel (Properties Editor ➤ Render Properties ➤ Ambient Occlusion), as in Cycles, contains the parameters to render the environmental occlusion and simulate global illumination.

- Bloom is a post-process effect that simulates glare and blur; we can use it to increase rendering realism.

- The Depth of Field panel applies a post-process effect that controls the focus and the depth of field in the camera settings and produces a defocusing effect like in real cameras.

- Subsurface Scattering simulates natural subsurface scattering.

- Instead, Screen Space Reflection activates refraction in the scene. If we want to reproduce a transparent material, we must enable the Refraction setting in this window. We must also select Screen Space Refraction in the Settings window of the selected material's Material Properties panel.

- Motion Blur blurs the render results by post-processing the image after rendering.

- We use Volumetrics settings to obtain the fog effect and other similar atmospheric effects; in the same window, Volumetric Lighting and Volumetric Shadow activate the respective atmospheric impact.

- Eevee uses Shadows Mapping techniques for shadow rendering; in the Shadows window of the Render Properties panel, we can choose the shadow definition.

- The Indirect Lighting panel defines the number of Diffuse Bounces and the sampling parameters of each bounce expressed in pixels.

We have seen the main features of the Render Properties panel of the Properties Editor regarding Eevee.

Let's now, more concretely, briefly analyze the main elements of our rendering engine based on the nodal system.

Node-Based Materials

The nodal system plays an essential role in Blender, not only for materials. We have to use nodal materials to start working with Eevee and Cycles. Each node has a specific function, and the different nodes have to be combined to achieve and modify effects; thus, they have input, output, and other connection channels.

In Blender 3.0, two nodes work only with Eevee: Shader to RGB and Specular BSDF. Otherwise, nodes are common to both Cycles and Eevee.

We can edit nodes in the Shader Editor, created especially for this purpose.

Materials, lights, and backgrounds are all defined with nodes divided into different categories: Input, Output, Shader, Texture, Color, Vector, Converter, Script, Group, Layout. Each type has its functions specific nodes.

We use these nodes to modify the characteristics of the nodal materials (Color, Contrast, Bitmap, or Procedural Texture) through different systems that we will learn more about when discussing the Materials section in Chapter 4.

In the Shader Editor, we can use the same object's keyboard shortcut of the 3D Viewport: Shift+A to add a new material node.

The primary type of node is the Shader node, which describes the interaction of light with the volume or surface of the object. There are different types of shaders. Currently, we have 16 shaders for Eevee and 20 for Cycles, as shown in Figure 1-35.

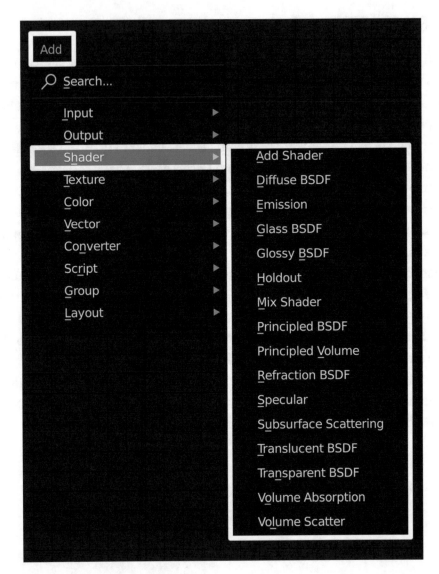

Figure 1-35. *Eevee's shader nodes*

But let's see the most important ones:

- Principled BSDF that we saw earlier is the primary shader that combines different characteristics to create various materials.

- Diffuse BSDF represents the light diffused from the object's surface (reflection, refraction, and absorption).

- Emission represents the emission of light from an object.

- Glass BSDF reproduces the effect of glass.

- Glossy BSDF reproduces the glossiness of the material, and we use it for metallic surfaces or mirrors.

- Mix Shader is for mixing two shaders.

For an in-depth analysis of the nodal system, we can refer to Chapter 4.

This section has seen the main principles of Eevee, which is the renderer that has brought real-time visualization in the 3D Viewport into Blender.

We have seen the main differences between Eevee, Cycles, and Cycles X.

We will develop these concepts in the following chapters.

Summary

In this first chapter, we deepened our understanding of the basics of Blender 3.0 and discussed how to install the stable and experimental versions.

We also started to understand the interface and different working approaches like the various selection systems, the object contest menu, and new keyboard shortcuts. We also had our first encounter with the basics of Eevee.

From the next chapter, we will begin to work more consciously, and we will deal with 3D modeling techniques to build objects in a 3D space: the basis of the whole Blender system.

CHAPTER 2

Modeling Inorganic and Organic Objects in Blender

This chapter will cover 3D modeling, the main feature of any three-dimensional computer graphics. Creating virtual objects gives life to an entirely new world. It is the basis for all the expressive possibilities within Blender.

We will start by creating objects and spaces, analyzing the main modeling methods. Then we will continue by learning other techniques to create three-dimensional objects, from modifiers to sculpting.

Starting in this chapter, we will develop a series of exercises that will demonstrate how to apply the techniques learned in the theoretical part.

In this chapter, we'll cover the following main topics:

- Modeling with meshes, curves, surfaces, and other types of objects

- Sculpting and the basics of modeling in Sculpt mode

- Modeling with modifiers

Preparing to Start Modeling

The main feature of Blender is versatility. We can create practically every digital thing using various available modeling techniques with this software.

Unlike other software born to model only architectural objects—such as SketchUp and Autocad—or specialized in organic modelings such as Z Brush, Blender has sophisticated tools for both inorganic and organic modeling.

In version 3.0, Blender developers added essential modeling tools.

© Gianpiero Moioli 2022
G. Moioli, *Introduction to Blender 3.0*, https://doi.org/10.1007/978-1-4842-7954-0_2

First, Geometry Nodes is a new modifier that introduces a different way of modeling. This tool was introduced in Blender 2.92. Since then, we have had many enhancements from the Blender developer team.

In our software, we can use five main modeling techniques:

- Mesh modeling

- Sculpting

- Modeling with modifiers

- Modeling with armatures and simulations

- Procedural modeling

We will learn about the first three techniques in this chapter and the other two in Chapter 3.

Now let's introduce digital spaces.

Digital Spaces

Before discussing modeling techniques, we will clarify what *digital space* means.

Blender's virtual space uses a Cartesian reference system and the Euclidean space.

Tip   The *point* is the base of Euclidean space. A set of points forms lines, planes, circles, triangles, etc. The Cartesian space provides a system of coordinates. The x-axis and the y-axis create a horizontal Cartesian plane. Joining the z-axis, vertical by convention, we define the three-dimensional space. The three axes, oriented and orthogonal, meet at a single point called *origin* (0.0.0). In this space, we can identify each point with its coordinates. In Blender, we deal with this space.

This world is three-dimensional and gives a precise location and size to our objects because a unit of measure establishes an accurate coordinate for each point of space.

We insert our environments and objects in this space; they are geometric elements defined by functions or algebraic equations. These objects and backgrounds are then, through render engines, transformed into images, videos, or virtual realities.

These elements are the foundation of our worlds in Blender.

Objects, materials, and lights compose a digital space. Virtual objects are Mesh, Curve, Surface, Metaball, Text Object, etc. These objects have different characteristics and details that allow us great versatility and expand our creative possibilities.

First we will learn the primary modeling techniques of Blender.

The essential tool is Mesh. Meshes have more possibilities and options than other objects; for example, some modifiers work only with meshes and not with curves or other elements.

However, as we will see later in this chapter, we can quickly transform a text or a curve into a mesh and vice versa.

Now let's look at adding different types of objects in Blender 3.0.

Add Objects (Shift+A)

By clicking the Add item from the Header menu or using the keyboard shortcut Shift+A, we access a window containing all the objects we can create in Blender.

We can add any objects such as meshes or lights, cameras, etc., from the menu shown in Figure 2-1.

Figure 2-1. *The Add menu*

As shown in Figure 2-1, we can add a lot of different objects.

- In the first part of the window, we find the modeling objects: Mesh, Curve, Surface, Metaball, Text, Volume, and Grease Pencil.

- In the second, we have two animation tools: Armature and Lattice.

- In the third, we have Empty (for transformations) and Image.

- In the fourth are some objects to light the scene: Light and Light Probe (support lights for Eevee).

- Finally, we added Camera, Speaker, Force Field, and Collection Instance objects.

Now let's start to analyze the different types of modeling objects we can add to our scenes.

Mesh

Meshes are the standard tools in most 3D modeling software and are composed of vertices, edges, and faces. A mesh is a grid of subobjects that defines an object in space.

In Object mode, the mesh appears as a single entity.

In Edit mode, the same item presents three types of editable subobjects:

- A *vertex* represents a single point in space defined by its position and three Cartesian coordinates (X, Y, Z).

- An *edge* is a line that connects two vertices and indicates the segments common to two faces of a polyhedron, or the sides of these faces.

- A *face*, instead, is the surface enclosed by edges and vertices. The faces can be triangles (tris), quadrilaterals (quads), or polygons with more vertices (n-gons); quadrangles are preferable to other polygons both for modeling and animation for various reasons.

These subobjects create two-dimensional or three-dimensional objects of different types: the primitives. We can modify these objects to create complex virtual forms similar to the real ones.

The following section will deal with the main modeling objects, starting from primitives, the basic geometric objects.

Add Mesh

Blender 3.0 allows us to create several basic primitives. Primitives are the primary objects of any 3D modeling software. The most basic ones are usually the same in all software.

These objects are the first geometric figures to add from the Add menu scene (Shift+A). The window that opens already contains the most common primitives; we will soon see how to add to the same window more complex objects when we need them.

Meanwhile, in Figure 2-2 highlighted on the right, we see the basic primitives preinstalled in Blender 3.0.

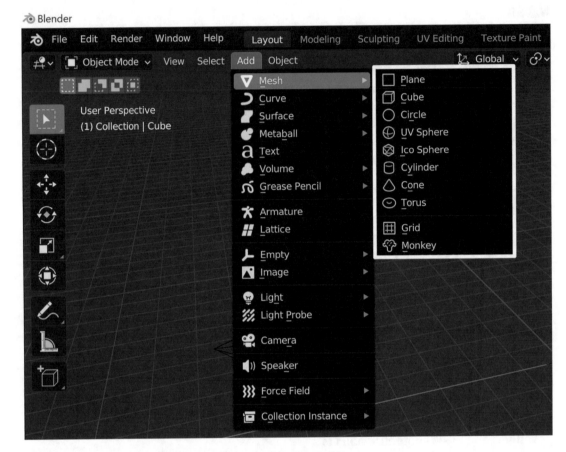

Figure 2-2. *Preinstalled primitives in Blender 3.0*

We can add these objects: Plane, Cube, Circle, UV Sphere, ICO Sphere (the two spheres have different geometries), Cylinder, Cone, Torus, Grid (an already subdivided plane), and Susanne, the mascot of Blender.

We can modify these base shapes in Edit mode to create any desired form of them.

When we add these objects to the scene, a dialog box opens on the bottom left of the screen. We can expand it by clicking the arrow on the left.

Here, we can change the created object's size, position, rotation, and alignment. Finally, we can collapse the dialog box by clicking the down arrow on the left.

This dialog box is available for operation only just after object creation. If we execute other commands, this dialog box vanishes. You can recall it with F9.

Let's look at the other types of objects, starting with the Curve object.

Curve

Curves represent an essential Blender modeling object and can split into two types.

- Bézier curves are mainly suitable for creating tubes, wires, bottles, glasses, texts, logos, etc.

- We can also use them for other purposes, such as animated paths.

- Nonuniform rational B-splines (NURBS) are more suitable for organic and beveled shapes, vehicles, and industrial design objects. Unfortunately, in Blender, this type of object has many shortcomings and is somewhat limited compared to other software such as Maya, Rhinoceros, etc.

The most crucial difference between Bézier and NURBS objects is that while Bézier objects are approximations, NURBS shapes are exact.

Both are modifiable in Object and Edit modes and composed of control points to adjust them.

The computer calculates curves faster than meshes during modeling because they contain less data, but the calculation time could be longer during rendering.

Now we see how to add and edit curves.

Add Curve

We can add a curve from the Add menu or the shortcut Shift+A, as shown in Figure 2-3.

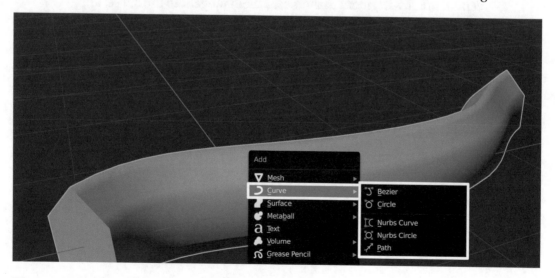

Figure 2-3. *The Add Curve menu in Object mode*

As we see in the menu, we can create two types of Bézier curves.

- Bézier, an open curve

- Bézier Circle, a closed circular curve

Or we can build three different kinds of NURBS.

- Nurbs curve, a 2D open arc

- Nurbs circle, a 2D closed circular curve

- Path, a 3D open curve with five aligned control points

Now let's see the essential characteristics of Curves.

Explaining Splines

The subobject of the curve is the spline, which is composed of control points. We have three types of splines: Poly, Bézier, and NURBS.

Let's look at them.

- *Poly splines* are the simplest, and we do not use them to model.

- We get them by converting meshes to curves, and they don't have control points.

- *Bézier splines* have control points that modify their shape through a central point, a segment that crosses them tangent to the curve, and two handles at the ends, as shown in Figure 2-4.

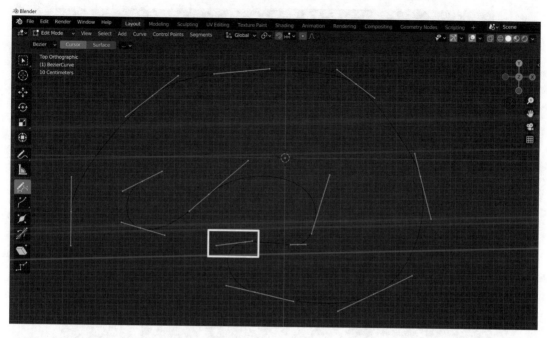

Figure 2-4. *Bézier curves in Edit mode*

Figure 2-4 shows a Bézier curve in Edit mode with various control points selected. The central point moves the segment. The two handles at the end modify the spline curvature.

The Bézier curves have four different handle types to modify the shape of the curve in various ways. We can set them either with the shortcut V or from the Object Context menu by selecting the points we want to modify, clicking with the right mouse button, and choosing the desired type in the window Set Handle Type, as shown in Figure 2-5.

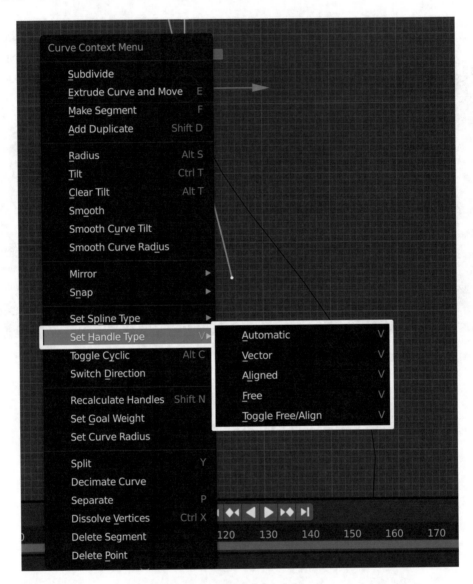

Figure 2-5. *The Set Handle Type options of the Object context menu*

In Figure 2-5, we see five options.

a.   Automatic to get the smoothest curvature

b.   Vector to obtain sharp corners

c.   Aligned to keep the three points in line at all times and maintain smooth curves without sharp corners

    d.   Free that creates vertices with independent handles

    e.   Toggle Free/Align, which changes the vertex from free to aligned

- *NURBS splines* have different control points than the Bézier curves because they do not have the two handles but only the center point. Still, they have a weight option that increases or decreases the influence of the control point on the shape of the curve or surface, as shown on the right of Figure 2-6.

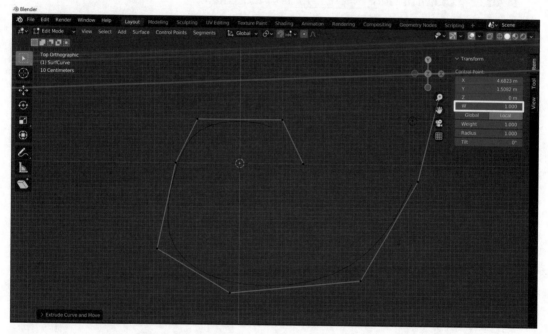

Figure 2-6. *A NURBS in Edit mode*

We can change this weight in the W Number field of the Transform panel of the Sidebar shown in Figure 2-6. If we select a point and bring the W value from 1 to 0, we see that the curve flattens, and the point no longer affects the shape of the curve. If the window is not visible, we can activate it with N.

Now we can start to modify curves.

Editing a Curve

We must create the curve in Object mode (Shift+A ➤ Curve ➤ Bézier) and then add vertices by selecting and extruding them by clicking E in Edit mode.

Finally, back to Object mode; we chose the Geometry window in the Properties Editor ➤ Object Data Properties.

Here we give shape to our curve by changing the Depth value to 0.1 in the Geometry ➤ Bevel panel.

The Toolbar

The toolbar contains the same tools for both Bézier curves and NURBS.

Figure 2-7 shows the most specific tools in Edit mode.

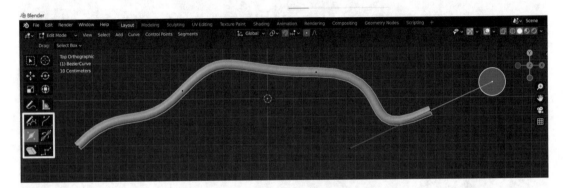

Figure 2-7. *The Bézier curve and the toolbar in Edit mode*

Here are the devices dedicated to Curves to edit them in Edit mode:

- Draw outlines a freehand spline and allows us to create the curve directly, drawing fluidly without extruding one vertex at a time.

- Extrude ejects new vertices from the selected existing ones.

- Radius modifies the thickness of the curves by widening or tightening them at the control points.

- Tilt controls the rotation of the curves.

- Shear inclines selected vertices along the horizontal screen axis.

- Randomize randomizes selected vertices.

We find other exciting tools in the Item window of the Sidebar that we open with N after selecting the control points we want to modify.

For example, for a Bézier curve, Radius modifies the thickness, and Tilt tilts the curve in 3D.

These tools are similar to those in the toolbar but numerically modifiable.

Object Data Properties

This panel of the Properties Editor controls the features of the curve. Figure 2-8 shows that we have several options to modify our objects.

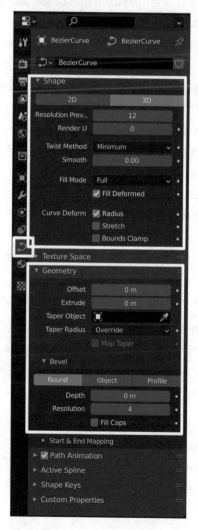

Figure 2-8. *The Object Data Properties of the Properties Editor for Bézier curves*

In Figure 2-8, in the Shape window, the first buttons, 2D and 3D, allow us to control the development of the curve and transform it from a two-dimensional to a three-dimensional object.

The default option is 3D to distribute the curve three-dimensionally in space. However, if we change the option to 2D, we keep the curve development in the two-dimensional space of the XY plane.

Resolution is an essential value because it allows us to control the definition of our curve and its smoothness: the more the value increases, the more the curve will be dense, rounded, and defined.

Thus, Resolution Preview U is the value in the 3D window, and Render U is the value for rendering.

Expanding the Geometry tab, we find various labels with their respective fields to input values.

The Extrude value allows us to extrude the curve on the z-axis, obtaining a ribbon-type shape. After that, we can choose to fill values for the Offset field. With this, we can move the curve parallel to its normal.

The Geometry window also contains the Taper object that controls the thickness of the curve along the path. For example, this tool can thin the curve toward the ends and expand it in the center.

Then, if we expand the Bevel tab, we can give a thickness to the curve modifying some value.

Three options compose this tool: Round, Object, and Profile.

- Round assigns a circular profile to the curve that we can control with Depth and Resolution. By changing the Resolution value, we can alter the smoothness of the angle. We also have the option Fill Caps to fill the curve caps.

- The Object option allows us to add another curve to determine the profile of the primary arc. To assign the thickness, we need to add a new curve and then set it in the Object box of the Bevel window. By modifying the second curve, we interactively modify the profile of the first one.

- Profile instead provides us with a tool to modify the shape of the selected curve through Depth and Resolution options. It also gives us other essential editing tools, including a graph that we can modify by changing the profile of the curve. In addition, by changing the Resolution value, we can alter the smoothness of the bevel. The options Start and End under Start & End Mapping help shorten and lengthen the curve profile, and we can create keyframes to create cool animations of the curve.

Let us now briefly introduce the Surface object.

Surface

Surfaces are the extension of curves in the three-dimensional space. Still, Blender considers surfaces and curves different entities that we cannot join into a single object.

If we create two separate meshes in Object mode, we can select them both and click Ctrl+J to join them in one object.

Instead, if we do the same thing with curves and surfaces, we can't join them.

In Blender 3.0, the only objects we can create as surfaces are NURBS. However, if we need a Bézier surface, as we have just seen, it is possible to obtain it directly from the curve's Object Data Properties.

To add a surface, we must use the same method for meshes and curves, from the Add menu or the shortcut Shift+A.

We have six different surfaces: NURBS Curve, NURBS Circle, NURBS Surface, NURBS Cylinder, NURBS Sphere, and NURBS Torus.

NURBS surfaces have no volume and no thickness. They are only two-dimensional objects, and they have only two interpolation dimensions. The modification systems are similar to those of curves and meshes.

Metaball is another Blender object; it is less known but no less appealing. Let's see its primary tools.

Metaball

Metaballs are strange and simple objects defined by pure mathematical expressions directly inside Blender. Therefore, we cannot modify them in Edit mode as with meshes or curves and surfaces.

These elements influence each other, and a field of interaction surrounds them.

If Influence is positive, they will exert mutual attraction, while if it is negative, they will apply repulsion.

We can use them to create organic elements or basic shapes for natural forms. Finally, we can convert them into meshes via the Convert To button of the Object tab in the 3D View Header menu.

Object mode displays them with a black circle to select them.

While in Edit mode, they don't have either vertices or control points but only two colored rings. The green circle allows us to adjust the stiffness, while the pink one selects the sphere and applies the main transformations.

In the Sidebar, we can change the location, the radius, and the stiffness with numerical values. In this bar, we can also change the metaball type.

Object Data Properties

Also, in this case, we can control the metaball through the Object Data Properties panel of the Properties Editor. As shown in Figure 2-9, we have a few elements to modify our object.

Figure 2-9. *The Object Data Properties of the Properties Editor for metaballs*

In the Metaball window, we find the Resolution Viewport that controls the viewport visualization; the Render box determines the resolution in the render. Lowering these two values increases the resolution. Instead, the Influence Threshold option changes the influence of the entire metafamily of Metaball elements.

Objects in the same family affect each other. So to build separate entities, we need to create different families.

When we duplicate a Metaball object, we must modify the object's name to change its family, as in Figure 2-10.

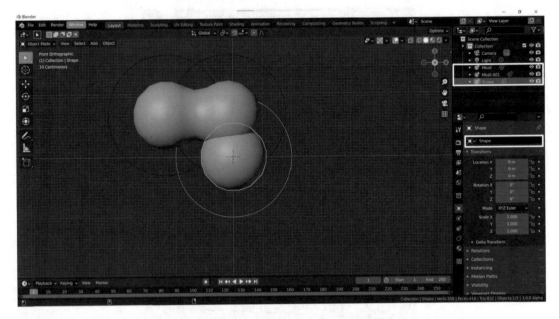

Figure 2-10. *Changing the name and family of metaballs*

We need to change the object name via the Outliner panel in the Properties Editor. Once we change the name, we create another family from this metaball.

Finally, in the Properties Editor, open the Object Data Properties ➤ Active Element window in Edit mode. We can change the primitive shape of our meatball by choosing one of the five Metaball types (Ball, Capsule, Plane, Ellipsoid, and Cube), as shown in Figure 2-11.

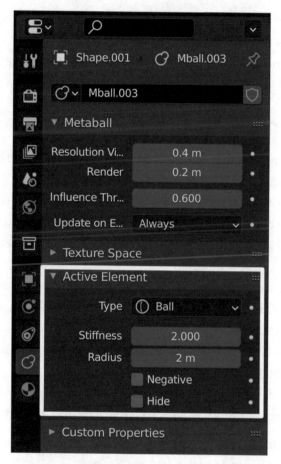

Figure 2-11. *The Active Element window*

Figure 2-11 displays the Type box. Also, we have the same tools of the Sidebar. The Stiffness value controls the influence of the selected metaball. With lower stiffness values, the object is influenced and deformed by the other elements from a greater distance. Instead, the Radius value modifies the object's size.

We now see another helpful object, Text, which is for creating logos, signs, or three-dimensional graphics and animations.

Text

The Text object is composed of mathematically calculated vector data. We use it to create two-dimensional or three-dimensional texts in which the letters are curves filled by surfaces. We write directly in Blender and make words and sentences with this tool.

We can also import text from an external text editor.

We create the Text object in Object mode. Then in Edit mode, we change the letters and write other words as in a text editor.

Finally, we can quickly transform the text into a mesh from the 3D View Header menu; select Object ➤ Convert ➤ Curve/Mesh/Grease Pencil.

Object Data Properties

As in other object cases, an essential edit box for text is the Object Data Properties of the Properties Editor, in which we find many editing tools.

On the Shape tab, we can find the standard Resolution Preview U and Render U values, which determine the resolution of the object in the 3D Viewport and in the render.

The primary text is two-dimensional, but we can give it thickness and make it three-dimensional.

On the Geometry tab, Extrude, Offset, and the other parameters are more or less similar to the Curve Object Data Properties. For example, Offset modifies the text width; Extrude extrudes the text, increasing its depth and making it three-dimensional.

We can also add a Taper object to provide a draft-like appearance such as a Bézier curve to modify the thickness.

With the Bevel tool, we can provide a chamfer feature that enhances the text's look. Three buttons compose this tool as with curves: Round, Object, and Profile.

- Round assigns to text a circular profile. We can control the depth and resolution. We also have the option Fill Caps.

- The Object option allows us to add another object to determine the depth of the text, as with curves.

- Profile instead provides us with tools to modify the text shape through the depth and resolution. It also gives us other editing tools. Moreover, by changing the resolution value, we can alter the smoothness of the bevel.

The Blender Text tool already contains many characters, and it also allows us to import external fonts.

In the Font window of the Object Data, we can click the Folder icon to load new fonts. When we click the icon, a window that contains many preinstalled typographical characters opens. In the same window, the Transform section allows us to change the dimension of our text in the Size box and the inclination in the Shear box.

After these values, we have the Text on Curve box, where we can choose a curve on which to apply the text, as shown in Figure 2-12.

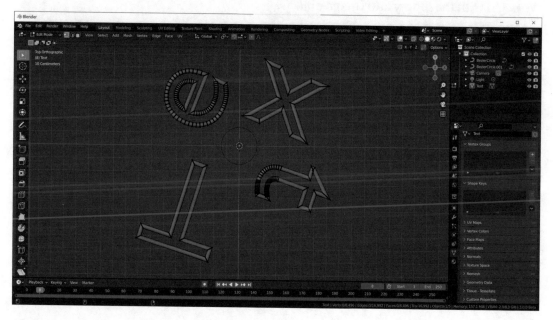

Figure 2-12. *Modified Blender text*

In Figure 2-12, we can see the result of the default Blender text with a Bézier circle applied as a Bevel object in the Bevel window. With this operation, we have given three-dimensionality to a text. We have also changed the text's distribution with another Bézier circle referred to as Text on Curve in the Transform window. Finally, we have converted the text into a mesh with Object ➤ Convert ➤ Mesh.

We can also assign a material to the text in the Materials window of the Properties Editor as we do with all the other objects.

After briefly discussing all the main modeling objects, let's talk about the different elements we can add from the Add window of the main menu or with the shortcut Shift+A.

Other Blender Objects

We have seen modeling objects and the tools to modify them until now.

We can also add other kinds of objects to our scenes.

Let's look at these: the main ones are lights and cameras to light and film our sets, or empties and images useful to help us in modeling.

Empty and Image

We begin with the Empty and Image objects.

Empty is a point in space without geometry. There are different types of empties for various purposes: Plain Axes, Arrows, Single Arrow, Circle, Cube, Sphere, Cone, Image.

We can use an empty, for example, as a reference image for modeling, or, as we will see later, to control the modifications of the modifiers, or it can be related to more objects to modify a group of them more quickly and efficiently.

We can also create an image from the menu Empty ➤ Image that opens by clicking Shift+A. In this way, an empty frame appears in the 3D view displayed in wireframe. So, we can import the image from the Properties Editor in the Object Data Properties window by loading it from the Open button of the Image window.

Instead, the Image item of the Add menu (Shift+A) allows us to import a reference image directly.

For example, we can use an image as a reference for modeling.

We can introduce an image into the 3D view both as a reference and as a background. We can also drag an image from a directory to the Blender's 3D view already aligned with the current view.

The only substantial difference between reference and background is that while the reference image hides in the viewport the objects behind, the background is transparent.

Light

Another object that we create with the Add menu, or with the shortcut Shift+A, is Light (and Light Probe for Eevee), which we use to illuminate the scene. There are four different types of lights (point, sun, spot, and area), each with other characteristics. We will learn about lights in detail in Chapter 4.

Camera

Cameras have the characteristics of real cameras and are used to take photographs or make movies in virtual spaces.

We can add them from the Add menu or with the hotkey Shift+A.

We will see the characteristics of cameras and how to use them in Chapter 4 and throughout the book's exercises.

This section has dealt with the main Blender 3.0 objects to create three-dimensional spaces and virtual elements. Next, we deepen our knowledge of the modeling of the primary type of object: the mesh.

Understanding Mesh Modeling

There are three modeling modes to edit a mesh: Object, Edit, and Sculpt. Object mode is the general processing way of performing the main transformations on the whole object.

Edit and Sculpt instead allow us to modify an object's shape in subobject mode, which means acting directly on vertices, edges, and faces.

So, the Blender modeling modes are as follows:

- Object mode allows us to perform basic operations on entities as follows:

  a. The creation of the object

  b. The translation, rotation, and scale

  c. The union of two or more entities

  d. Other fundamental activities related to visualization, distribution of items in collections, etc.

- We make most mesh editing operations *in Edit mode* by directly acting at the subobject level on vertices, edges, and faces.

- Sculpt mode instead allows us to work on the mesh by sculpting it with brushes. To get good results in sculpt mode, we must have enough geometry to work efficiently with the chisels.

Object Mode

To modify the object's general features in Object mode, we have many tools in the Header menu of the 3D viewport in the Object menu items, as shown in Figure 2-13.

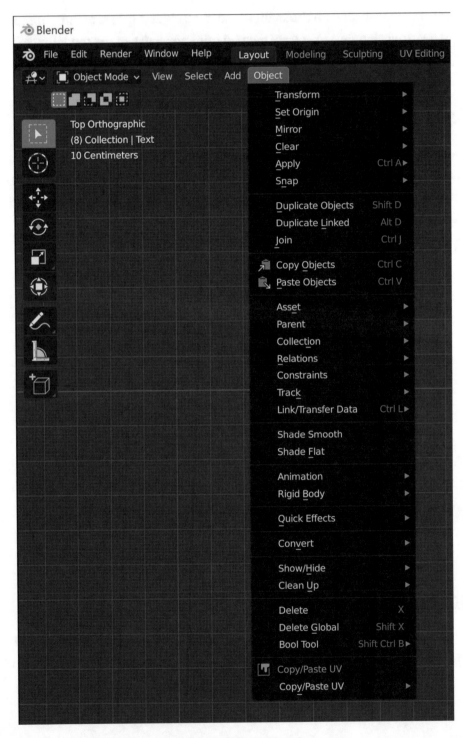

Figure 2-13. *The Object items of the 3D View Header menu*

Let's look at the most important of these devices in more detail.

Transform

We can perform transformations on objects with the Transform button of the Object tab. We've already seen basic transformations in Chapter 1.

Set Origin

This tool sets the origin of the selected object respect to the geometry.

The origin is the orange point that Blender by default places in the object's geometric center; it determines its location in the 3D Viewport.

It is the point of calculation of the main transformations.

Some transformations are more straightforward if the object's origin does not match its geometric center.

We can reposition the origin of our object with Set Origin, using the Object tab of the header menu of 3D view, as shown in Figure 2-14.

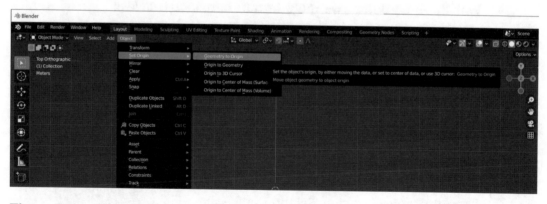

Figure 2-14. *The Set Origin tool of the Object menu*

We can open the window shown in Figure 2-14 to move the object's origin to the geometry, the 3D cursor, or other positions.

Mirror

We can reflect the object's geometry by selecting the entity, clicking the Mirror button of the Object tab or with the keyboard shortcut Ctrl+M, and then pressing the Axis key of the desired transformation (X, Y, or Z).

Clear and Apply

In the Sidebar transform panel, when we create an object in the origin of the Cartesian space (0,0,0) and when this origin corresponds with the object's origin, the location and rotation values are 0 while the scale is 1.

If we move, rotate, or scale the object, the values change with the modifications made.

We can reset the transformations or apply them to the object. That's what the Clear and Apply commands do.

- Clear resets the changes we have done to the object. With this operation, we cancel the transformations, and the item returns to the original values. Also, the location and rotation values return to 0 and the scale value returns to 1 in the panel transform.

  We can perform this operation by clicking Clear from the Object tab or with the keyboard shortcuts Alt+G, Alt+S, Alt+R, and Alt+O.

- With the Apply button, we apply the transformations made to an object.

  We do not cancel the transformations, and our object stays in the position and maintains the modified rotation and dimension.

  Instead, we reset the values of the changes so that Location and Rotation return to 0 and Scale returns to 1.

  We can perform this operation by clicking Apply from the Object voice or the shortcut Ctrl-A. This way we apply the main transformations: Location, Rotation, and Scale.

These two commands of the Object tab are essential when we want to animate an object or sculpt or apply modifiers or constraints. For example, in some cases, if the Scale values of X, Y, and Z are not 1, Blender does not apply some changes correctly. This error happens because it cannot interpret the object's shape if the Scale value is not the default value of 1.

Snap

In Chapter 1, we have already seen that we can snap an object during a transformation. In Figure 2-15, we see a second type of snapping on the Object tab.

Figure 2-15. *The Snap tool of the Object menu*

This type of transformation snaps the selected object or the 3D cursor to a series of given points. For example, we can choose Selection to Cursor and move the center of the selected object to the 3D cursor, or Cursor to Selected and move the cursor to the center of the chosen object Cursor to World Origin, Cursor to Grid, etc.

Duplicate

We can duplicate our objects with Duplicate Objects or Duplicate Linked in the Object tab.

We create a copy of the object untied from the original by clicking Shift+D or Duplicate Objects. This duplication system is proper when, after the duplication, we want to alter one element without changing the other.

Instead, we can create a linked copy with Alt+D or Duplicate Linked. After that, if we modify one of the elements in Edit mode, we also change all the others; on the other hand, the Object mode transformations on one of the items will not alter the others.

Instead, we separate the two objects in Object mode by selecting one and clicking Object ➤ Relations ➤ Make Single User ➤ Object and Data.

Link/Transfer Data

We can also connect separated objects by selecting them and clicking Link/Transfer Data on the Object Header's menu or with the shortcut Ctrl+L and then choosing Link Object Data in the window.

The two items remain distinct but connected, as in the previous case with Alt+D or Duplicate Linked.

Also, in this case, if we want to separate the two objects again, we can click Object ➤ Relations ➤ Make Single User ➤ Object and Data.

The window Link/Transfer Data feature is essential because it allows us to copy data from one object to another in Blender, such as materials, animation data, modifiers, etc., as shown in Figure 2-16.

Figure 2-16. *The Link/Transfer Data window*

This can save us a lot of time. We must first select (LMB) the object where we want to copy the data, then select the second object (Shift+LMB), press Ctrl+L, and choose, in the window that opens, the data we want to copy.

Join

We can join two objects in Edit mode with the command Join or Ctrl+J. However, they must be objects of the same type; for example, we cannot merge a mesh with a Bézier curve.

If we create, with Add or Shift+A, different objects in Object mode, we build separate items.

But if we create the first one in Object mode and then select it and go to Edit mode, making the second, we create a single object.

In reverse, in Edit mode, we can separate two parts of a single object by selecting the elements to separate, pressing P, and choosing Selection in the window that opens.

Convert

With the Convert tool, we can convert one object into another. For example, we can transform a mesh into a curve and vice versa. Likewise, we can quickly transform a mesh or a text into a curve, as shown in Figure 2-17.

Figure 2-17. *Converting a mesh or a text to a curve and vice versa*

In the Header menu under Object, we can select Convert and convert one object into another.

We use this tool mainly to change other objects to meshes.

Show/Hide

If we want to work comfortably in the 3D viewport, hiding and showing some objects is essential.

Blender helps us with the collections. We can put different types of objects on various collections and show or hide them altogether, hiding the whole collection from view by clicking one of the buttons in the outliner, as in Figure 2-18.

Figure 2-18. *The Collections display buttons*

In Figure 2-18, we have highlighted the buttons Hide in Viewport, Disable in Viewports, and Disable in Renders.

For example, in an architecture project, we can separate the environment, the walls, the architectural elements, the furniture, etc., by putting them in different collections, and we can display them separately.

But there is another faster method. We can also control the display of every singular object with the Show/Hide tools. With these commands in the Object panel or with some shortcuts, we hide the selected elements of the scene.

We hide the selected objects with H; we hide the unselected things with Shift+H and show the hidden objects with Alt+H. This method is advantageous when modeling, especially when we have a scene crowded with many things.

Delete

We can delete selected objects from the scene with the command Delete or the shortcut X.

In Edit mode, we can delete vertices, edges, and faces or dissolve them, as we will see in the next session.

We have just seen the essential operations that we can perform in general in Object mode; now, let's deepen meshes and their editing techniques in Edit mode.

Edit Mode

We can modify meshes in Object or Edit mode, as we have already seen.

We do most of the modeling work in Edit mode, where we shape our models with the many modeling tools Blender makes available.

In this modality, we create, duplicate, move, and scale objects at the subobject level with many different tools to control with the keyboard shortcuts, the 3D View Header menu, and the Object Context menu.

The subobject level involves modifying vertices, edges, and faces with their specific editing tools that we can find in the menu of the 3D view header.

We can also recall three items that contain the tools related to each subobject with three keyboard shortcuts:

- Face tool menu (Ctrl+F)

- Edge tool menu (Ctrl+E)

- Vertex tool menu (Ctrl+V)

Before proceeding with mesh editing at the subobject level, let's look at mesh visualization tools.

Mesh Visualization

In Edit mode, we have the tools for correct visualization of the meshes.

We must orient the face's normals in the right way to correctly visualize an object.

Normals

Normals are the lines perpendicular to the faces. 3D modeling software uses them for the correct visualization of objects. Any 3D modeler visualizes surfaces with the normals directed toward the observer; it does not display those pointing in the opposite direction.

In the Viewport Overlays panel in Edit mode, as shown in Figure 2-19, we can visualize the direction of the normals of vertices, edges, and faces.

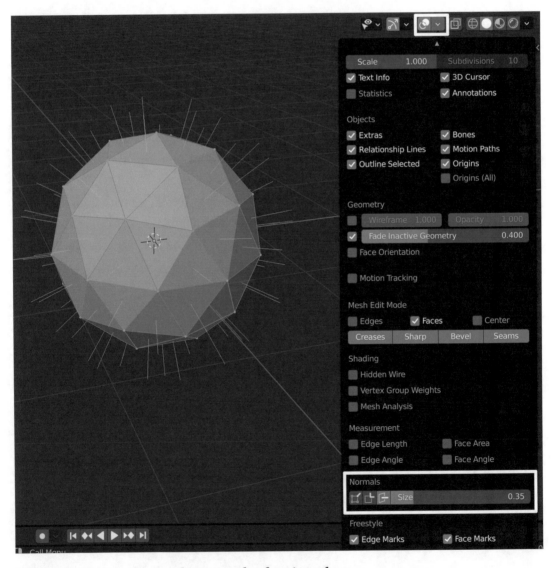

Figure 2-19. *Displaying the normals of an icosphere*

We select the object and click Tab to switch to Edit mode. Then, in the 3D View Header, we click the arrow next to the Show Overlays button, and in the window that opens, we go down to Normals and click the icon of the normal we want to display.

Normal Configuration

Normals can be reconfigured with tools and keyboard shortcuts on selected faces in Edit mode.

In Figure 2-20, we see the Normals menu for modifying the normals.

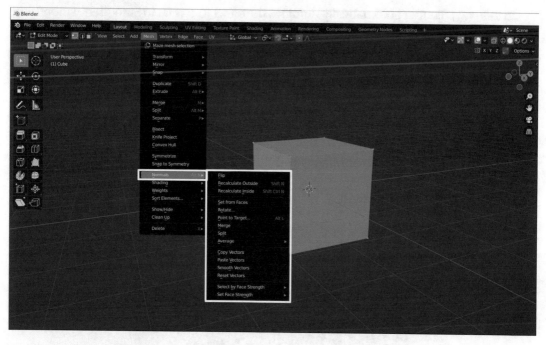

Figure 2-20. *The Normals window of the 3D View Header menu*

We can open the Normals window in Edit Mode, in the 3D View Header menu with Mesh ➤ Normals or the shortcut Alt+N. Here we find all the normal editing operations.

For example, with Shift+N, we can Recalculate Normals Outside, and with Ctrl+Shift+N, we can Recalculate Normals Inside. We can also use the Flip key inside the window to reverse the direction of the selected Normals.

Auto Smooth

In the Object context menu, as we saw in Chapter 1, we can choose between Shade Flat and Shade Smooth for the shading of the chosen object.

Instead, if we want to render an object with defined edges and curved parts and we have to put together flat and smooth faces, we can use Auto Smooth. We can achieve auto smoothing by selecting the objects in the 3D View. After that, we go to Object Data Properties. Then, scroll down to the Normals tab. Click the arrow to expand and select the checkbox marked Auto Smooth to enable it.

In this way, Blender automatically modifies the effect from Flat to Smooth by smoothing the edges of faces according to the face's inclination. By default, the angle is set to 30 degrees.

Using the Angle tool in the Normals window, we can control this angle to leave the sharp corners between the faces above this value.

These results affect the visualization and not the geometry of the objects. So if we have to 3D print an object, we must change the geometry, and we can do this by adding a Bevel modifier to add more defined edges to the thing.

Now let's see how to edit subobjects with the toolbar.

The Toolbar in Edit Mode

Figure 2-21 shows the toolbar in Edit mode.

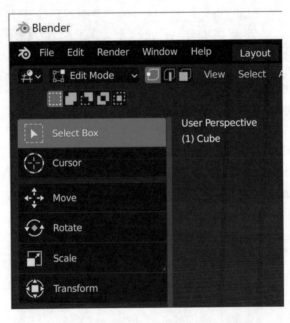

Figure 2-21. *The first part of the toolbar in Edit mode with the main transformations*

Let's take a look at the tools:

- In the upper part, we have the select box. By clicking and holding down the arrow at the bottom-right corner of the button, we open a submenu that contains the various selection methods: Tweak, Select Box, Select Circle, and Select Lasso. We can choose any of these based on the requirement to select objects in 3D view.

- The next button below is Cursor. We can position the cursor anywhere in the 3D view. When we click the Cursor button, its background is highlighted in different colors (depending on the selected theme). We can then left-click anywhere in the 3D view, and we can observe that the cursor goes where we click. It is super easy to place any object in a new position.

- Then we have different sets of buttons, the Move, Rotate, and Scale options. With them we can move, rotate, or scale any vertex or selected set of vertices, any edge or set of selected edges, and faces or selected sets of faces. When we click and hold the mouse on the bottom-right corner of the Scale button, there is one more option: Scale Cage. We can select Scale Cage for scaling objects from a particular point or axis.

- Next, we find Transform, the tool to perform the three main transformations by clicking the manipulator of the desired transformation on the 3D view. The value of this option is that we can combine all three options in one module. This thing is handy for speeding up the modeling work.

We can see the second part of the toolbar for the mesh in Edit mode in Figure 2-22.

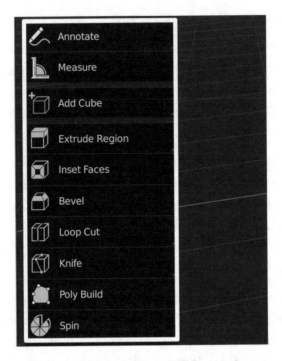

Figure 2-22. *The second part of the toolbar in Edit mode*

First, we have the buttons Annotate and Measure.

- Annotate is a tool to write and draw freehand in 3D view. By clicking and holding down the arrow at the bottom-right corner of the button, we open a submenu that contains various tools for annotating: Annotate, Annotate Line, Annotate Polygon, and Annotate Eraser.

- The Measure tool is also essential in geometry creation, especially in the mechanical and architectural industries. This device allows us to measure objects in the 3D view. We can clear the measurement lines by selecting one of the measured ruler ends and pressing X or Delete on the keyboard. We can also measure angles, thickness, etc.

  Instead, if we click and expand Overlays in the 3D View header in Edit mode, we will find particular measurement settings such as Edge Length, Edge Angle, Face Area, and Face Angle.

Then there are other essential modeling tools:

- Add Mesh allows us to add Cube, Cone, Cylinder, UVSphere, and IcoSphere objects by clicking and dragging directly on the 3D view, snapping on the grid or the object's surface.

- We have the tool Extrude to extrude vertices, edges, and faces, creating new geometry (see Figure 2-23). With the shortcuts E for extruding and Alt+E for the extruding menu, we can perform all the options of this operation. If we want to extrude a subobject, we must press E and move the mouse. We can press, for example, E ➤ Z+1 and extrude the selected object (a vertex, an edge, or a face) on the z-axis of a unit of measure. Instead, by pressing E ➤ Shift+X, we extrude on the ZY plane.

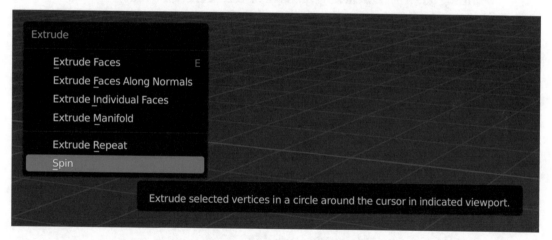

Figure 2-23. *The Extrude menu (Alt+E)*

After pressing Alt+E, we can see the various instruments for the Face subobject in Figure 2-23. In the Extrude menu, we find several items with different extrusion possibilities according to the selected subobject: Extrude Faces, Extrude Faces Along Normals, Extrude Individual Faces, Extrude Edges, Extrude Vertices, Extrude Repeat, and Spin.

Tip   If we want to extrude in Edit mode vertices, edges, or faces quickly, we can Ctrl+RMB click where we want the extrusion. With the same method, we can duplicate an object in Edit mode.

- Another tool that adds geometry to a selected face by creating a more internal face is Inset Faces, and we can activate it from the toolbar.

- Then we have Bevel, which allows us to create new geometry by inserting new loops in the selected elements by chamfering and rounding edges and corners. We can select Bevel in the toolbar and move the yellow widget that appears to create a bevel or chamfer, or we can use the shortcut Ctrl+B.

- Instead we add new loops with the Loop Cut tool of the toolbar or by clicking Ctrl+R and turning the mouse wheel to increase or decrease the number of loops.

- Knife and Bisect allow us to add geometry by activating the tool and cutting faces by left-clicking an edge or vertex and then dragging the mouse on another edge or vertex and clicking again. When we want to apply the modification, we have to press Enter to exit knife mode (if we're going to leave without applying the cuts, we have to use the Esc key); passing through other edges will add vertices at the contact points between the wound and the crossed edges. The Knife shortcut is K.

- Then we have Poly Build that can create meshes extruding with just the cursor's movement. To create a shape, delete the base cube and make a plane. Then enter Edit mode, click Poly Build, and get closer to the edges or vertices; when they turn blue, we can create new faces by clicking and dragging the LMB.

- Clicking and dragging the blue highlighted edge we create a face with four vertices. Instead, if we drag the mouse while pressing the Ctrl key, a unique triangular face having three vertices is created.

- The ultimate tool in this part is Spin, which extrudes the selected elements (face or edge or vertex), rotating around a specific point and axis. By default, the Spin tool has no keyboard shortcut. However, we notice a dialog box appearing just below the 3D View header after pressing the Spin tool. It consists of three settings: Steps, Orientation axis X or Y or Z, and the Drag tools. With these three tools, we control the options. For example, we can select the required orientation axis during the Spin operation.

  Nearby the object, we can observe a widget showing two plus signs at the ends. We can move this widget to the required position then applying the transformation.

  In the third and last part of the toolbar, we find another instrument category, as shown in Figure 2-24.

Figure 2-24. *The third part of the toolbar in Edit mode*

- Smooth/Randomize is the first tool in the menu from the top.

  Smooth blunts the selected object, making it concave and convex.

  The Randomize device instead moves the vertices of the chosen object randomly. Both tools need geometry to be effective, so if we have to apply them to the base cube, before we have to select everything in Edit mode, right-click, and subdivide the cube.

- Edge and Vertex Slide move an edge loop or a group of vertices in the mesh.

- Shrink/Fatten scales the selected vertices, edges, or faces depending on their normal. We can use it by choosing the required subobjects and pressing Alt+S or clicking the menu icon. After that, we can drag the mouse based on the needed scaling: shrink or inflated.

- Push/Pull instead will push the selected elements (vertices, edges, or faces) closer together or pull them further apart. We open this submenu by clicking and holding down the arrow at the bottom-right corner of the of the Shrink/Fatten button. This movement occurs from the center by the same distance. We can control this distance by dragging the yellow handle up or down.

- Shear and To Sphere are in the same menu, and, respectively, the first one tilts the selected subobjects along, and the second moves the selected vertices, gradually transforming the object into a sphere.

- Rip Region or the shortcut V and Rip Edge, respectively, rip regions and vertices.

Now let's look at other mesh modeling tools in Edit mode.

Other Modeling Tools in Edit Mode

The toolbar doesn't collect all the most critical mesh editing tools at the subobject level. We can access other tools via keyboard shortcuts or search them in the various menus.

Duplicate (Shift+D)

Just as we can duplicate objects in Object mode, we can duplicate subobjects in Edit mode from the Mesh ➤ Duplicate menu or the shortcut Shift+D.

Fill: Make Edge/Face (F)

With this tool, we create faces from already existing vertices or edges. For example, if we have three or four vertices or two already existing edges, we automatically generate a face by selecting them and clicking the shortcut F.

We can use this method also to create N-Gons, faces with more than four vertices. However, if we have to build a face with more vertices, it is preferable to use Poly Build on the toolbar we have covered earlier in detail.

Deleting & Dissolving (X)

With these tools, we remove or dissolve subobjects. We can access them from the usual Header menu under Mesh or from a menu that appears by typing the X hotkey.

We have two possibilities.

- Delete cancels vertices, edges, and faces or only edges and faces and keeps vertices or deletes only faces and keeps vertices and edges.

- Dissolve removes the selected elements, keeping the shape intact.

Merge Vertices (M)

We use the Merge tool to merge several vertices into one. We can access the various options from the mesh item in the header menu or shortcut M.

We have a few possibilities: At Center, At Cursor, Collapse, At First, At Last. We can choose where to put the vertex that remains with these options. For example, At First merges all the vertices with the first selected.

Then we find Merge By Distance that joins all the vertices at a certain distance from each other. We choose the length by typing the value in the Merge Distance space in the window that appears on the left side of the screen.

Separate (P)

We separate selected from unselected subobjects with this tool, creating two different objects. To operate it, in Edit mode, we choose the part of the object we want to separate and press P, choosing Selection in the window that opens. Then, in Object mode, we have two separate entities. We select them all in Object mode and press Ctrl+J to bring them together again.

Bridge Edges Loops

We use this device to connect two or more edge loops or edges across a surface, creating interconnected faces.

We can apply it from the header menu by clicking the Edge item and then clicking the Bridge Edge Loops button in the window that opens.

From the creation window on the bottom-left corner of the screen, we can also decide the number of cuts, twist the selection, and check the profile created from the Profile Factor value and the shape from profile shape.

Triangles to Quads (Alt+J)

This tool converts selected triangular faces to square faces, and we can activate it from the Header menu under Face ➤ Tris to Quads or with the shortcut Alt+J.

Now that we know about Blender's default mesh objects, we will introduce specific mesh add-ons.

Add Mesh Add-Ons

As we saw at the beginning of this chapter, the Blender default Add menu (Shift+A) allows us to add a limited number of objects to the 3D Viewport.

From the add-ons panel of the User Preferences, we can add many more objects and, in particular, many other types of meshes to the Add menu.

We can add, for example, some shapes created directly with mathematical formulas, architectural modeling objects, or mechanical items.

If we want to add these objects to the Add menu, we have to activate the respective add-ons in the User Preferences by checking the boxes for the type of mesh we want to enable (Topbar ➤ Edit ➤ Preferences ➤ Add-ons).

There are add-ons in Blender activable in two different ways:

- By enabling the preinstalled script by checking the equivalent box in the Add-ons window of the User Preferences

- By downloading the installation files from the internet and clicking the install button of the User Preferences

In Figure 2-25, we can see the Add-Ons section of the User Preferences window.

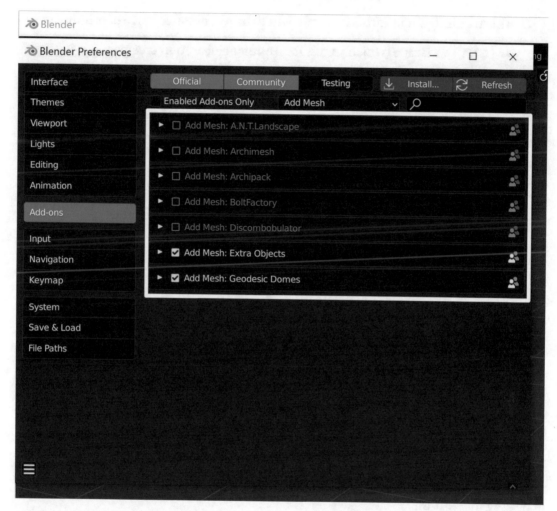

Figure 2-25. *The Add Mesh preinstalled add-ons*

In Figure 2-25, we have visualized and highlighted all the Add Mesh add-ons preinstalled in Blender 3.0.

By adding these tools, the number of primitives we can create in Blender increases exponentially.

Let's see quickly some add-ons we can add to have a broader range of primitives:

- ANT Landscape (which stands for Another Noise Tool) creates landscapes and planets controllable with different parameters.

- Archimesh is an architectonical tool containing many building elements, such as doors, windows, arches, columns, and walls.

- The Bolt Factory allows us to create bolts and nuts with many editing options. This add-on is also handy for 3D printing. We can develop suitable screws and bolts. With this tool, we can also add a nut and a bolt to the objects we print in 3D to assemble them with other elements.

- The Discombobulator enables us to modify the surfaces of an existing object and create panels for science-fiction environments.

- The Extra Objects add-on is complex and adds several heterogeneous primitives collected in various groups, as we will see shortly.

- The Geodesic domes add-on joins geodesic objects we can modify from a window that opens on the left of the screen at the moment of creation and controls many parameters.

Let's take a closer look at the features of the Extra Objects, which are Add Curves: Extra Objects and Add Meshes: Extra Objects.

Figure 2-26 highlights the variety of object categories we can add to the Add menu by activating this add-on.

Figure 2-26. *The Meshes categories of the Extra Objects add-on*

We can add the following types of objects with this add-on:

- The Rock Generator helps us to add easily editable rocks to the scene.

- This algorithm creates an infinite variety of procedural rocks; when creating objects, a window opens on the left of the screen.

- The Single Vert object adds a single vertex to the scene.

- The Round Cube adds a beveled cube to the 3D Viewport.

- Then we've got Torus objects, which adds different types of torus.

- With Math Function, we add many exciting function-controlled surfaces that offer us many possibilities. We can add them by pressing Shift+A and selecting Mesh ➤ Math Function ➤ XYZ Math Surface.

- With the primitive gears, we can create gear- and worm-shaped mesh objects.

- With Pipe Joints, we can add different types of pipes, pipe joints, or tubes with angles.

- The Diamonds menu adds diamond-shaped meshes.

- The Extras menu adds several exciting objects, such as Wall Factory, that allows us to create stone or brick walls but has many options that we can use to create surreal and science-fiction sets.

- Finally, we have Parents to Empty, which adds an empty as a parent of the selected mesh.

Many external add-ons can be downloaded from the Internet and installed in Blender. Some of these are free; for others, we have to pay small amounts.

We can find many of them on this site:

`https://blender-addons.org/advanced-boolean-tool-abt-addon/`

In Chapter 3, we will study other interesting mesh editing add-ons such as Edit Mesh Tools, Bool Tool, etc.

After learning more about the main mesh modification methods in Object mode and Edit mode in this section, we go on with a completely different and more intuitive modeling system: sculpting.

Sculpting

Sculpting is a modeling system much more intuitive than that studied until now.

It is a potent tool that already allows us to obtain professional results and that the Blender Foundation is continuing to develop.

In Edit mode, we work with technical and specific tools at the subobject level.

In Sculpt mode, we model with brushes on a very dense mesh, changing the topology directly. Indeed, we need a lot of vertices to sculpt our objects.

We model like in reality: we shape a sculpture with virtual materials such as clay.

When we select Sculpt mode in the Object mode drop-down window on the left of the 3D view header, the interface and the tools change radically, as shown in Figure 2-27.

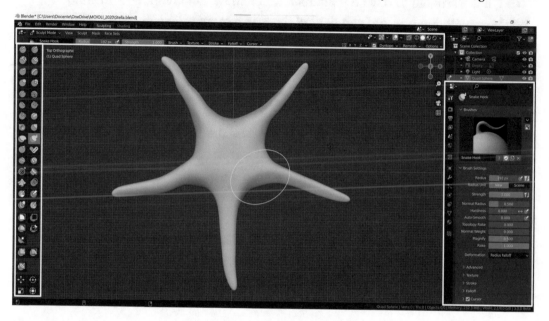

Figure 2-27. *The interface of Blender 3.0 in Sculpt mode*

On the left, in the toolbar, we have all the brushes or chisels, masks, and tools for the main transformations. The cursor turns into a brush represented by a blue, red, or yellow circle depending on the chisel type.

Also, the Tool Settings on the top of the 3D view, the toolbar, and the Active Tool and Workspace Settings panel of the Properties Editor allow us to modify the characteristics of brushes, masks, and tools inherent to the virtual sculpture.

In digital modeling, we use virtual chisels to edit shapes like working with real instruments; let's see more closely what they are and how they work.

Brush Settings

Sculpt mode has many features in Blender 3.0. This digital modeling system is becoming more and more critical in open source software like Blender.

Let's start to model.

Tip   It is essential to have a pen tablet for painting, sculpting, and drawing because, with the pen, we can control the brush more efficiently, even with tip pressure.

First, we must distinguish between tools and brushes. The tools are on the toolbar and have general settings; instead, brushes are our tools saved with the customized settings. We can keep our brushes and find them on the Tool Settings of the 3D View header. We create our brushes based on the tools present by default.

We build our own set of brushes starting from the existing ones, modifying their characteristics, and then saving them in the Properties Editor's Active Tool and Workspace Settings tab.

So, we select the desired brush in the toolbar, click the Add Brush button in the Active Tool and Workspace Settings tab, and name it. Finally, we modify its characteristics in the Tool Settings of the header of the 3D Viewport.

We can find it whenever we need it in the window that opens by clicking the Browse Brush button in the Tool Settings.

The cursor turns into a brush represented by two circles in Sculpt mode. The smaller circle depicts the force, and the larger one displays the radius. The dot represents the point of action.

The default chisel is Draw, which moves outward vertices within the brush radius.

Holding Ctrl, we obtain the opposite effect pushing the affected vertices inward; instead, we smooth the vertices and flatten the surface holding down Shift.

By pressing F, we scale the dimension of the brush, and by pressing Shift+F, we change the strength of the tool. We can obtain the same result with the Radius and Strength values in the Settings tool of the 3D Viewport header.

In the Active Tool and Workspace settings window of the Properties Editor, we can find all the values to modify the characteristics of the selected brush: Radius, Strength, Direction, Normal Radius, Hardness, and Autosmooth.

Now let's start modeling some simple shapes.

Preparing the Object

We can start modeling quickly by creating a new file from the Topbar menu by selecting File ➤ New (Ctrl+N) and choosing Sculpting from the drop-down menu.

We are in the Sculpting workspace with a spherical object ready to sculpt.

This way is the quickest to start modeling.

But we can create shapes to model with several other methods.

We can build any primitive and subdivide it to add vertices.

We can model the general shape with several separate primitives in Object mode and join Ctrl+J in a single mesh to create a more complex object. Of course, meshes must have closed forms. We can also use the Boolean modifier, as we will see later in this chapter.

Then we go to Sculpt mode and add more and more details to model more organic shapes. So, let's create our form. We start with a cube and switch to Edit mode with Tab.

Then we right-click the object to open the Object context menu. In the Object context menu window, we click Subdivide to create more geometry; we change the number of cuts to 40 and increase the Smoothness value to 1.00.

Let's go back to Object mode, right-click the smoothed Cube, and choose Shade Smooth. Then we add a Subdivision Surface modifier to our object and set Levels Viewport and Render values to 2.

Then we apply the modifier.

We can also use the Multiresolution modifier and set the number subdivision to 3.

Please see the "Modeling with Modifiers" section of this chapter to see how they work.

If we want to change the scale of our element, enlarging or shrinking it, it is essential to apply the transformation with the shortcut Ctrl+A and then select Apply ➤ Scale.

This shape is my favorite, ready to sculpt everything, starting from a smoothed cube.

We have prepared the object to model. Now we set the interface to sculpt.

Preparing the Interface

We can switch directly to the Sculpting workspace, already set for this type of modeling.

Let's set the toolbar as a dual-column row to have all the instruments available simultaneously in the interface. When the mouse is on the right edge of the toolbar, a double-sided arrow appears. If we click the left mouse button and move it to the right, we arrange the instruments in two vertical lines. If we continue to drag the mouse, the name will be displayed next to the brush.

We find the Properties Editor's Active Tool and Workspace Settings to the right of the interface.

Now we're ready to sculpt, and we can learn about Blender's various digital sculpting tools.

Sculpting Tools

Let's look at the essential modeling tools of Blender's Sculpt mode. We have many instruments available, divided into a few categories and identified by the color assigned to them in the interface.

We first encounter the blue tools, as shown in the toolbar in Figure 2-28.

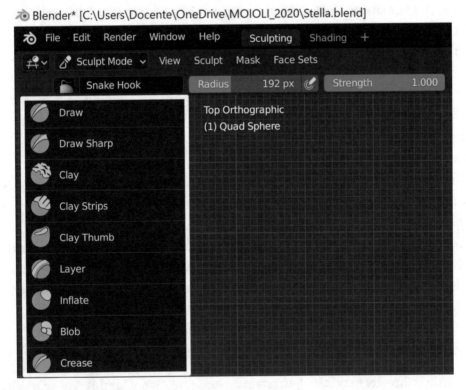

Figure 2-28. *The toolbar in Sculpt mode with the Blue tools*

These are the essential tools of Sculpt mode that add or subtract volume; let's look at them one by one:

- Draw (X) is the default brush that moves the vertices inward or outward following the vertices' normals. You have to press Ctrl to dig the surface instead of extruding it.

- Draw Sharp digs into the surface and is essential to define the details; it acts more precisely than Draw, with a sharper falloff to delineate the shape exactly. By pressing Ctrl, we reverse the effect, and we rise vertices up from the volume. In other words, since this is more precise than Draw, we can consider this as a finishing operation during sculpting.

- Clay (C) is similar to Draw but smoother and more precise in defining the plans. It looks like modeling clay, but virtual clay. This tool combines the Draw brush with the Flatten brush.

- The Clay Strips brush is similar to clay but with more defined brushstrokes. The effect is like modeling with a flat shape rather than the more rounded Clay chisel shape.

- Clay Thumb is another tool that we can use to reproduce digital modeling. It creates fingermarks on the surface, like when you model natural clay with your thumbs.

- The Layer brush (L) creates flat surfaces extruded from the base surface and generates several overlapping surface layers. As long as we hold down the left mouse button to sculpt, it extrudes a single surface, while when we interrupt and resume a new session, this brush resets and creates a new layer.

- Inflate (I) inflates the sculpted surfaces softly and irregularly. This instrument is similar to Draw but softer and more rounded.

- The Blob brush acts like Inflate, creating more decisively spherical surfaces. It also allows controlling the connection points between the existing surface and the spherical surfaces it makes.

- Crease (Shift+C) creates square indentations by digging the mesh.

The second tool group comprises red brushes that increase or decrease the contrast; we can see them in Figure 2-29.

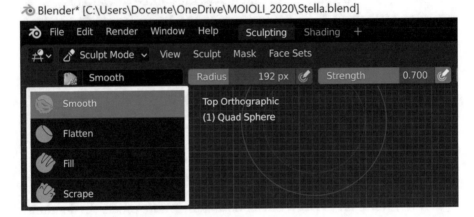

Figure 2-29. *The toolbar in Sculpt mode with the Red tools*

They are as follows:

- Smooth (S) blunts the surfaces and flattens the irregularities, making the shape softer and smoother.

- Flatten (Shift+T) flattens the volume by setting an average height between the vertices of the area of influence. When using Ctrl when working, we reverse the effect and increase contrast.

- The Fill brush acts as the flatten brush by flattening the surfaces, but more decisively, and by filling holes or grooves between them. When using Ctrl instead, we increase the surface contrasts and define more precisely the details.

- Scrape flattens the surface leaving a mark similar to that of clay modeling spatulas. In addition, it increases the contrasts of hollowed-out parts.

The yellow brushes grab the surface of the sculpted object. Let's see them in Figure 2-30.

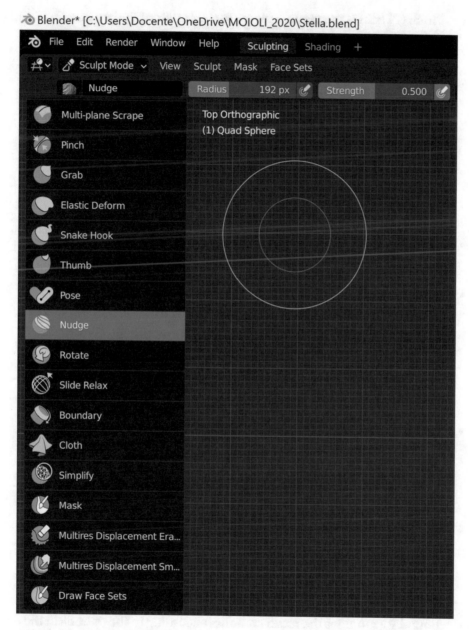

Figure 2-30. *The toolbar in Sculpt mode with the Grab tools*

- Multiplane Scrape scrapes the mesh surface with two inclined planes, creating an angle with a sharp edge in the center. The Plane Angle option increases the angle between the two planes, making it brighter and more defined. Holding Ctrl reverses the corner.

- Pinch (P) brings the vertices closer to the center of the brush. Pressing Ctrl activates the option Magnify that moves vertices away.

- Grab (G) does not add vertices to the shape but drags the existing ones in the direction of the mouse pointer.

- Elastic Deform is similar to Grab but smoother and softer in dragging the vertices while maintaining a regular shape.

- Snake Hook (K) is similar to Grab but creates more defined and thinner shapes. It pushes the form in the direction of the brush and allows us to develop snake-like forms.

- Thumb is similar to Grab but with flatter and thinner surfaces. It flattens the mesh by moving it in the direction of the cursor.

- Pose moves the selected part of the mesh as an armature. Blender calculates the point of rotation considering the dimension of the brush. By clicking Ctrl during the transformation instead of the rotation movement on the pivot, the selected shape rotates perpendicularly to the form itself in the direction of the mouse movement.

- Nudge rotates the vertices in the direction of the mouse movement.

- Rotate, like Nudge, rotates the vertices in the direction of the mouse movement in a much more defined and accentuated way to create vortices.

- Slide Relax flows the mesh's topology in the direction of the mouse movement, trying to preserve its volume. This tool enters the Relax mode by pressing Shift and creates a more uniform distribution of the faces without deforming the mesh volume.

- Boundary modifies the mesh contours according to the options in the Deformation drop-down menu of the Brush Settings window of the Active Tool and Workspaces Settings: Bend, Expand, Inflate, Grab, Twist and Smooth.

- Cloth allows us to simulate cloth physics interactively on the mesh we are editing. It mimics fabric folds. It is preferable to use brushes of small size.

- To use the Simplify brush, we must activate dynamic topology. This tool simplifies the geometry concerning detail size in the Dyntopo window.

- Mask (M) is an essential tool. It allows us to mask the mesh parts not to change the brushes. The mask is represented in 3D view by grayscale tint. To select the parts we don't want to edit, we must paint them dark gray. The lighter parts will remain editable with the tools. Holding Ctrl we change the brush into an eraser and clicking Shift with Mask we switch to Mask smoothing mode.

- To deactivate the mask, we must press Alt+M or paint with the same tool selecting the minus sign (-) in the Header Tool Settings of the 3D Viewport. By pressing Shift with the Mask tool active, we switch to smoothing mode.

- Multires Displacement Eraser erases changes made in the offset of a sculpted object. To get an effect, we need to apply a Multiresolution modifier and then modify the object's shape with other brushes before acting with this tool.

- Multires Displacement Smear modifies the offset of a sculpted object.

- To get an effect, we need to apply a Multiresolution modifier and then vmodify the object's shape with other brushes before acting with this tool.

- Draw Face Sets modifies the visibility of the mesh by changing the color of the selected faces every time we click the left mouse button. We use it, as we will see shortly, with Edit Face Set.

Then we have other different tools, as we can see in Figure 2-31.

Figure 2-31. *Mask, Hide, Filter, and other Blender 3.0 sculpt tools*

Let's look at them.

- Box Mask, Lasso Mask, and Line Mask give us different masking possibilities to prevent object modification.

- Box Hide hides the mesh parts we click and drag with the left mouse button; of course, the tools do not modify them. Then, with Alt+H, we bring everything back into view.

- Box Face Set and Lasso Face Set are the same as Draw Face Sets, but while the latter has a brush painting mode, the first ones have methods of selecting the faces to be painted by Box and Lasso.

- Box Trim and Lasso Trim allow us to cut the object with Box and Lasso modes.

- The Line Project tool cuts the object following a straight line. We draw this segment by clicking and dragging the cursor in the 3D viewport. The shady part of the mesh is cut off.

- Mesh Filter applies a deformation to the entire object through a filter.

    We can choose different filters in the Tool Settings or the Active Tool and Workspace Settings panel.

    Filters in Blender 3.0 include Smooth, Scale, Inflate, Sphere, Random, Relax, Relax Surface Sets, Surface Smooths, Sharpen, Enhance Details, and Erase Displacement.

    These filters modify the shape by applying their algorithm to the whole object; for example, Smooth smooths the form, and Inflate expands it.

- Cloth Filter applies the same modifications as the Cloth brush to the whole object.

- We use the Edit Face Set tool with Draw Face Sets, Box Face Set, or Lasso Face Set. This tool modifies selections made with the previous tools by enlarging them, shrinking them, etc. It currently provides the following devices: Grow Face Set, Shrink Face Set, Delete Geometry, Fair Positions, and Fair Tangency. We find them in the Properties Editor's Active Tool and Workspace Settings panel.

Finally, we have the standard tools for the main transformations: Move, Rotate, Scale, and Transform, followed by the Annotate tool group.

Now let's see how to work on a mesh by adding geometry with different tools.

Adding Resolution

We have three different ways of working in the Blender Sculpt mode with high-resolution model objects and can get excellent high-definition results:

- The Multiresolution modifier adds geometry to the mesh by making it denser. This tool is not specifically for Sculpt mode, but we can use this modifier effectively when sculpting.

- Remesh is useful when we want to standardize the level of detail of our objects and decide their density.

- The Dynamic Topology option adds and removes details interactively while we work.

In the next section of this chapter, dedicated to modifiers, we will see the Multiresolution modifier.

Next, we will learn about two systems to make a denser polygons mesh, dedicated expressly to the Sculpt mode: remesh and dynamic topology.

Remesh

We apply Remesh to the object after the sculpting. We can achieve uniform geometry and modify its density as we like.

Dynamic Topology instead is interactive and allows us to add geometry in the exact moment we sculpt.

These tools are effective and will enable us to define details of the modeled object as we want.

We can start from a basic shape created with other sculpting techniques.

In this case, we can combine different primitives to form a primary object and then go into Sculpt mode.

When we want to standardize the geometry of different shapes or increase the mesh density to edit it into sculpt mode, we can use Remesh.

Of course, this tool will not work if we have Dyntopo active simultaneously.

This technique automatically rebuilds the form with a more uniform topology; in this case, we can control the voxel size resolution and generate a better topology, as shown in Figure 2-32.

Figure 2-32. *The Remesh options*

We access the Remesh window from the Remesh button in the Tool Settings of the header of the 3D window, and we click the Remesh button.

This way, we create a mesh from the geometry with a correctly distributed topology without any shape change.

Editing the object in Sculpt mode, we move the vertices and modify the mesh's geometry. For example, using the grab brush, we drag the vertices. Then, switching to edit mode, we see that the mesh is less dense where we have worked with this brush because sculpting has moved the vertices away. Remesh helps us make the geometry of our object more homogeneous, retopologizing and unifying the density of the vertices.

Dyntopo

Dynamic topology is interactive and helps us create new geometry when we need it while sculpting.

So, we don't have to start from a high-defined mesh in this case.

We add geometry and change the object's topology during the sculpting. Thus, we can model interactively without adding too much geometry to the base object when we activate this tool.

We enable this tool by checking the Dyntopo box in the Tool Settings tab of the 3D window header by choosing Subdivide Collapse as Refine Method and Relative or Constant Detail as Detailing. We can also decide the topology resolution with the Detail Size value from the same window, as shown in Figure 2-33.

Figure 2-33. *The Dyntopo options*

We can toggle Dyntopo with the checkbox in the Tool Settings, as we have just seen, or with the Ctrl+D shortcut.

Most brushes will subdivide the mesh with dynamic topology active during the stroke.

We have seen how to sculpt with Blender 3.0 and interactively with Dyntopo; now, let's see how to model by applying different algorithms to objects: the modifiers.

Modeling with Modifiers

Modifiers are an essential part of Blender's structure and involve different software functions, from modeling to animation to physics.

They are efficient modeling tools in many cases.

They are separate algorithms applied to objects that are not directly part of the object and modify the mesh, so we assign them nondestructively.

So we can modify the object by changing the modifier values at any time. We can apply them when we have obtained the desired result or delete them if we decide they are not necessary. If we delete the modifier, we cancel every effect exerted on the object.

We can add to a single object all the modifiers required with different functionalities until we obtain the desired result. If we want to apply the modifiers all at once, we can do so from 3D view's header menu by selecting Object ➤ Convert ➤ Mesh.

We add modifiers from the Properties Editor by clicking the Modifier Properties icon and then using the Add Modifier drop-down menu to choose what we need, as shown in Figure 2-34.

Figure 2-34. *The header of the Modifier Properties window in the Properties Editor*

In Figure 2-34, we can see the following:

- The Add Modifier button. It allows us to choose and add the modifiers.

- The modifier stack. It is the list of all modifiers applied to that object. If we have added multiple modifiers, we can reorder them as per our requirements before applying them.

- The three buttons to display the modifier in Edit mode, Viewport, and Render mode.

- Next to the buttons, we see the arrow that opens the menu to apply, duplicate, and move the modifier in the modifier stack.

- With X, we can instead delete the modifier to cancel the modifications from the object.

We add each new modifier at the bottom of the list; the changes performed by modifiers are calculated from top to bottom.

We can modify their position so that each time we get the layout we need.

For example, if we want a reflected and smoothed shape, we must have the mirror modifier at the top of the stack for a correct effect.

The blender modifiers are divided into four groups, as shown in Figure 2-35.

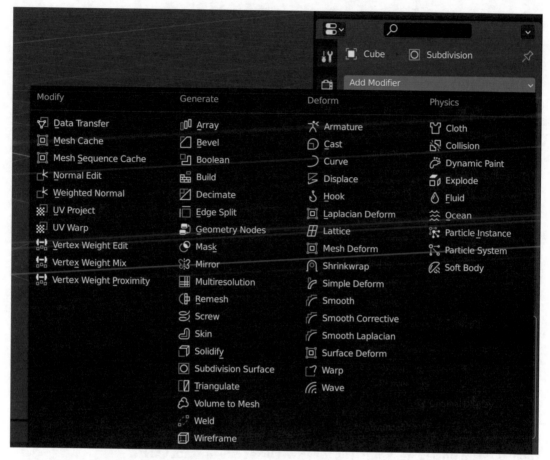

Figure 2-35. *Blender's modifiers*

Let's take a look at each category in detail:

- The Modify category checks the object's data. For example, the Data Transfer modifier transfers data from one mesh to another.

- The Generate group creates new geometry or modifies the existing one. For example, the Mirror modifier mirrors the mesh, or the bevel modifier smooths the angles of the objects by adding new edges.

- The Deform group modifies the object's shape without changing the object's geometry or creating new geometry.

- The Physics category groups the modifiers that affect the physical effects, and Blender automatically adds them when applying a physical simulation to an object.

This chapter will only discuss some of the modifiers useful for object modeling.

However, Blender supports several other modifiers for modeling and many other functions.

But let's take a closer look at the ones we are most interested in for modeling.

Generate Modifiers

As we've just said, there are four groups of modifiers.

In this chapter, we deal with two types: Generate and Deform. These categories are the most suitable for modeling.

We will look at the Geometry Nodes modifier, which Blender 3.0 implemented to edit objects' geometry and create procedural modeling.

Let's start with the Generate modifiers, adding geometry to the object or modifying it significantly.

Array

We can use the Array modifier to create groups of objects to develop complex scenes with repeated elements.

It builds an array of copies of one element.

We can determine the number of instances with the Count value. Then, we can shift them with an offset determined as Relative Offset or Constant Offset.

We can also move, rotate, or scale the array concerning a reference object with the Object Offset option.

The reference object can be an empty, and we must choose it in the Object Offset box. This empty replaces the offset table's numerical values. It controls the transformations series of objects reproduced by the modifier, so it is sufficient to translate, rotate, or scale this object to modify the arrangement of the repeated elements in 3D view.

We can also add more than one array modifier to the same object to multiply the element with different spatial distributions on the various Cartesian planes.

By selecting Merge, we merge the vertices of each copy according to the Distance value; also, selecting First Last, we join the vertices of the first with those of the last if they are in the distance range we set.

Bevel

The Bevel modifier bevels the edges of the object and allows us to control the width type of the angle, the amount or percent, and the number of segments. We can also modify the bevel shape with the Profile option.

We have five options that control width types: Offset, Width, Depth, Percent, and Absolute.

If we click the Vertices button, the effect is applied only to the vertices and not the edges.

At the same time, under Geometry tab intersections, Clamp Overlap prevents new geometries from intersecting and overlapping the existing ones.

By changing the Profile value, we modify the shape of the beveled profile.

We can choose between a default profile and a customizable one.

Miter Outer and Inner are functional in the Geometry window when two beveled edges meet at an angle. Still, one last important option in the same window is Intersection Type that controls the intersections at the vertices. It can be adjusted as Grid Fill to maintain a smooth continuation of the bevel profile or Cutoff that creates a cutoff face at the vertices.

Several other options allow us to solve even the most complex cases that we won't see in this book.

Boolean

The Boolean modifier is a simple-to-use tool that combines two objects to create a single entity with the possibility of making the two meshes interact in three ways: Intersect, Union, and Difference.

With the first operation, we keep the intersection of both objects. With the second, we obtain the union of both meshes in a single element.

With the third operation, we subtract from the first object the part in common with the second.

We can also apply the modifier to more than one object simultaneously by choosing a collection as an operand type instead of just one entity.

Let's see how to use this modifier.

We need two meshes: select the first one, add Boolean from the modifier stack, and choose one of the three available interaction types. Then we add the name of the second object in the Object box or click it with the eyedropper.

We must select Wireframe for the objects in the Viewport Display section of the Object Properties window to see the geometry changes in real time. To better view the creation process, we can also enable Toggle X-Ray.

Once we finish this operation, applying the modifier and deleting the second object is essential because Blender does not automatically delete it.

In many cases, it is convenient to replace this modifier with the Bool Tool add-on.

With this add-on, we can directly edit objects, simplifying the application process. We will see this tool in Chapter 3.

Decimate

The Decimate modifier allows us to reduce the number of polygons of an object as much as possible without changing its shape. We use it, for example, to simplify the geometry of objects modeled in Sculpt mode. But, too exaggerated reductions can also heavily modify the object's geometry until it is unrecognizable.

We have three different types of simplification available.

- The Collapse feature combines the vertices progressively, and the value that controls the changes is Ratio. The value 1.0 keeps the original mesh, while 0 annihilates the geometry.

- Un-subdivide is more or less the opposite of Subdivide that we have seen among the mesh editing tools to add geometry to the object. Therefore, we must use it mainly for meshes with grids-based topology.

- Planar is particularly useful on shapes composed mainly of flat surfaces. The value to reduce the geometry is Angle Limit, where we can choose the angle to minimize the geometry.

At the bottom of the window, there is the Face Count setting, which is the number of faces after the reduction.

Geometry Nodes

This is a fundamental tool for creating and modifying geometry and procedural modeling. So, we can't help but dwell a little bit longer on it.

The Geometry Nodes modifier has been part of Blender since version 2.92 in early 2021, and new nodes have been added continuously since then.

Now in Blender 3.0, we are starting to see the first results.

It's a complex system that is getting bigger and bigger, and in this book, we only have time to introduce the basic concepts.

This modifier allows gathering, through a nodal system, all the Blender modifiers to edit the object's geometry.

This specific nodal system has been built the Geometry Node Editor, a particular editor for creating and modifying geometry. Moreover, Blender developers introduced the workspace shown in Figure 2-36.

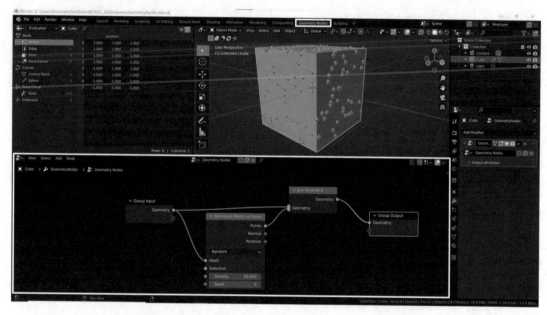

Figure 2-36. *The Geometry Nodes workspace*

At the top of Figure 2-36, we see the button for activating the Geometry Nodes workspace. This workspace comprises the Spreadsheet Editor on the top left, the 3D Viewport, and the Geometry Nodes Editor at the bottom, highlighted by the white box. Then, as usual, there are the Outliner and the Properties Editor on the right.

At the top of the Geometry Nodes Editor, there is the button New to create the nodal system and some nodes to create the simple object that we can see in the 3D Viewport.

The Group Input and Group Output nodes appear in the Geometry Nodes Editor by clicking the New button.

In addition, a Geometry Nodes modifier appears in the Modifier Properties of the Properties Editor.

In this case, we have applied a Point Distribute node to the cube to distribute points on its surface. The Join Geometry node allows us to visualize the cube and the distributed elements togheter.

The points and their distribution in space are the fundamentals for the geometry nodes.

The Geometry Nodes workspace spreadsheet displays all the geometric information of the objects in the left window. Figure 2-37 displays all the cube's vertices and their positions.

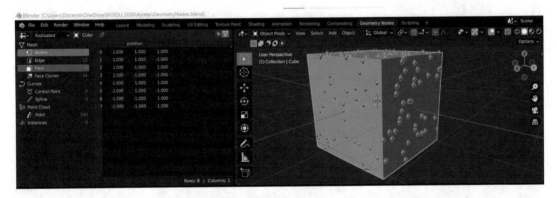

Figure 2-37. *The Cube vertices in the spreadsheet*

The geometry nodes modifier works on this information.

But let's see step-by-step how to create our first geometry nodes.

1. Open Blender and create a new file.

2. Select the Geometry Nodes workspace in the Topbar to open the nodal modeling interface.

3. Delete the default cube and create a plane (Shift+A ➤ Mesh ➤ Plane). Then, scale the plane (S ➤ 4) and apply the transformation (Ctrl+A ➤ Scale).

4. Create a new modifier by clicking the New button in the middle of the Geometry Node Editor window. Then, a Geometry Nodes modifier appears in the Modifier tab of the Properties Editor.

   You can also add the modifier directly from the modifier panel of the Properties Editor by clicking Add Modifier and then on Geometry Nodes in the section "Generates."

5.   Add a Point Distribute node (Shift + A ➤ Search ➤ Point
     Distribute), distributing points on the plane's surface and creating
     a cloud of points instead of the plane itself. These points are
     displayed in the spreadsheet, as shown in Figure 2-38.

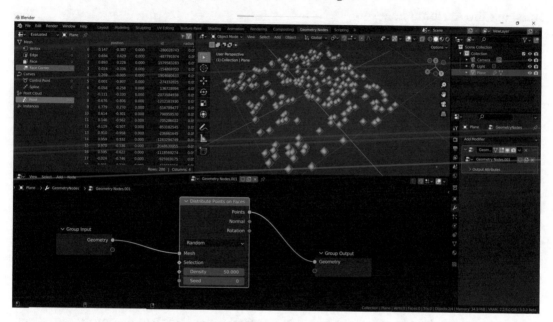

Figure 2-38. *The Point Distribute node*

But let's take another elementary example of modifying the geometry of an object.

1.   In the Topbar, select the Geometry Nodes workspace.

2.   Create a new modifier by clicking the New button in the middle of
     the Geometry Node Editor window.

3.   Let's delete the Group Input node and add an IcoSphere node
     from the Mesh Primitives menu to create a primitive object and
     connect it with the Group Output node.

4.   By adding a Transform node from the Geometry menu and
     inserting it between the two existing nodes, we can modify the
     geometry of the icosphere by moving, rotating, and scaling it.

In this way, starting from the basic geometry, by adding nodes, we can quickly create objects and environments with complex geometries and control them through a nodal system.

There already are a lot of nodes. If, for example, we want to act on single points, we must use the Attribute node, etc.

These simple principles create a complex node system that represents a new way to approach 3D modeling, including other Blender add-ons such as Sverchok and Sorcar that we will see in Chapter 3.

Let's continue with the other nodes and analyze the Mirror modifier.

Mirror

In many cases, symmetry is indispensable for modeling organic, mechanical, or artificial objects.

The Mirror modifier allows us to model only half of the element and reflect changes on the other half with real-time shape updates during modeling.

If we want to introduce asymmetries in the object, we must first apply the modifier.

This tool reflects the object on the x-, y-, and z-axes, and usually, the reference point for the mirroring is the entity's origin.

We can also take as a reference point an external object, such as an empty.

To do this, we must select the name of the object we want to use as a reference in the Mirror Object selector.

We can also add more than one Mirror modifier to a single object.

Multiresolution

The Multiresolution modifier allows us to subdivide the geometry of the selected object, adding subobjects and blunting its shapes, similarly to Subdivision Surface, which we will learn about in a moment.

Once we add the modifier to the object, we must click a few times on the Subdivide button to add geometry.

Multiresolution allows us to switch from one definition level to another easily with Level values.

It has one more advantage: Sculpt mode can also edit the new subdivided geometry without applying the modifier.

We must first subdivide the surface with the Subdivide button, and then, to see the results, we can switch from one definition level to another in Level Viewport, Sculpt and Render.

We can use this modifier in Sculpt mode by checking the box Sculpt Base Mesh.

Remesh

The Remesh modifier is similar to the tool we've already seen in Sculpt mode.

It allows us to create a new mesh topology and transforms all faces into quads, or faces with four vertices.

We can choose between four different types of Remesh.

- The Blocks option has no smoothing.

- The Smooth type smooths the surface entirely.

- Sharp instead eases the surface while maintaining a higher definition of edges and corners adjusted by the Sharpness option.

- Voxel is the last option added. It generates a shape similar to the selected one, allowing us to modify its density with the voxel's Size value; by decreasing it, we reduce the size of the voxels and increase the mesh density.

The mesh must have a thickness and a closed shape for this modifier to act correctly.

For flat surfaces, we add the Solidify modifier above Remesh to give a volume to the mesh.

Skin

This modifier creates a volume from a set of vertices and edges. The shape obtained is mainly composed of quads and some triangular surfaces at the intersections.

In Edit mode, we can scale the single parts of the object by left-clicking and then pressing Ctrl+A and moving the mouse. There is also the ability to develop an armature for the generated form with the Create Armature button. A Blender armature is like a skeleton composed of bones related to the corresponding parts of the mesh. When these bones are moved or rotated, the associated form moves and deforms similarly. So, we can also quickly animate the shapes created with this modifier.

Solidify

It adds thickness to meshes. The Thickness option controls the width in the unit of measure we are using in the file. To get the correct result, we must first apply the transformations and ensure that the Scale values are 1.

Two different algorithms are available to add thickness within this modifier:

- Simple mode is simpler and faster. In Simple mode, the modifier extrudes the geometry but does not work well where edges have more than two adjacent faces.

- Complex mode is a more complex but more precise and sophisticated method.

If we want accurate results, we have to use the Complex mode with Constraints Thickness mode. This solution for 3D printing is advantageous, but it is still necessary to check the thickness with Blender's internal add-ons for 3D printing or other external tools.

Subdivision Surface

The Subdivision Surface modifier subdivides the mesh faces, adding more definition and geometry to the mesh.

We can use two different subdivision algorithms with the Catmull-Clark and Simple buttons: the first subdivides and smooths the surfaces, while the second divide them without blunting.

With the Levels Viewport and Render values of the window, we can increase the number of subdivisions both in render and in the 3D Viewport; with the Quality value of the Advanced window, we control the precision of the vertex positioning. These values define the mesh section: the higher they are, the more subdivided the mesh.

To keep some sharp edges less blunted, we have to add edge loops or select the Use Creases option.

Subdivision surface does not allow us to edit the new subdivided geometry without applying it in Sculpt mode.

In this case, we must use the multiresolution modifier.

Now let's go on with another type of modifiers for modeling: the deform modifiers.

Deform Modifiers

These modifiers change the object's shape, but they do not alter its topology, unlike the Generate modifiers we have just seen.

We will deal with only two of these: Displace and Wave, but others like armature or lattice, although not specific for modeling, can be essential to modify objects, or others like shrinkwrap, useful to reproduce or simplify already created things.

Displace

We move the mesh's vertices using a texture, either an image or a procedural one with Displace modifier.

This tool needs a dense geometry to work well.

So to get good results, we have to subdivide the mesh. Then we must add a subdivision surface modifier with a subdivision value of 3 or 4.

We can add Displace first and then the texture to create a vertex displacement, as shown in Figure 2-39.

Figure 2-39. *The Displace Modifier window*

If a texture is already present in Blender, we add it by clicking the small arrow next to the chessboard shown in the figure; if we have to create a new one, we must click the New button. Then clicking the button to the right in Figure 2-39, we go to the texture window to edit it.

From this window, we can add different types of textures: Image, Blend, Clouds, Distorted Noise, Magic, etc.

In the interface of Figure 2-39, we have two more essential buttons to adjust the results: Strength, which controls the power of the movement of the displacement, and Midlevel, which checks the application level of the modifier.

Wave

Finally, we introduce a modifier that brings movement into our scene. Wave applies wave motion to the object, and we can use it on meshes, lattices, curves, surfaces, and texts.

Also, this modifier needs geometry to work, so to see the effect, we must perform the procedure seen with Displace and Create, for example, a plane of 10 meters with 100 subdivisions.

The Motion buttons control the orientation of the wave on the x- and y-axis. With the Time window, we can manage the animation.

We have just seen modifiers and deepened the essential ones for modeling.

This section closes the theoretical part of this critical chapter about the different modeling techniques.

Now let's move on to the part dedicated to practicing the theoretical notions learned until now.

Exercises: The Mad Hatter's Tea Party

This book aims to split each chapter into two parts: theoretical and practical sections.

The first chapter and the first part of this second chapter introduced the various tools about the essential concepts and the different modeling techniques of Blender 3.0. From this section, we start to practice those concepts with some exercises.

We will refer to an art and design exhibition held at Spazio Temporaneo Gallery in Milan 2000, shown in Figure 2-40.

Figure 2-40. *Albertini and Moioli, the Mad Hatter's Tea Party, exhibition in Milan, 2000*

There is some information about the exhibition in the presentation brochure "The Mad Hatter's tea party," which we find in at `https://issuu.com/giampieromoioli/docs/mad_hatter`.

In this book, we will re-create some of those objects.

We will examine several important topics that we can now summarize in the following points:

- Model some of the objects: practicing architectural and organic modeling.

- Create the surrounding environment by modeling and import some external elements.

- Create ambient lighting and apply materials to things and the environment.

- Easily create some characters for the scene with Make Human.

- Render the scene with Eevee and Cycles.

Now it is time to put the theoretical notions we have learned so far into practice. In the first two exercises, we will start by modeling a teapot and a glass.

Exercise 1: Modeling a Teapot

First, let's create a teapot modeled from a mesh; we can use several techniques and modeling possibilities. We have chosen to start from a primitive, a sphere, and apply the Multiresolution modifier. In this first exercise, we will learn our first operations in Blender: movings, rotations, extrusions, scaling, etc.

However, the user can still utilize a different method for creating objects, environment elements, etc.

Follow along with Exercise 1 step-by-step. The final result is in the Teapot.blend file that is available in the downloads for the book.

Setting the File

Let's start setting up the Blender file to model our objects easily. This step seems bland, but it's vital for a good start.

1. Create a new Blender file by selecting File ➤ New ➤ General. Next, save the file with Ctrl+S as **Teapot** in the local computer drive; from the main menu, select File ➤ Save ➤ Save Blender File, as in Figure 2-41.

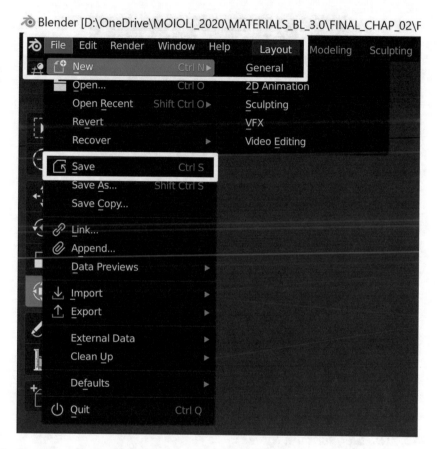

Figure 2-41. *Creating a new Blender file and saving it*

2. Set the unit system of the scene. Go to the Scene Properties window of the Properties Editor and open the Units window. From here, set Unit System to Metric and Length to Centimeters, as shown in Figure 2-42.

Figure 2-42. *The Blender Unit System*

3. Delete the cube with X ➤ Delete, as in Figure 2-43.

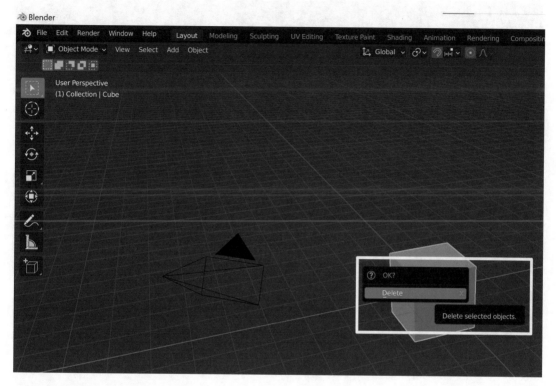

Figure 2-43. *Deleting the cube*

Creating the Base Shape

Now let's create the basic shape for our teapot. In this exercise, we will work starting from the object's volume. Let's begin by importing a reference drawing, creating a sphere, and giving it the dimensions of a real thing.

1. Go to the Right Orthographic view by pressing 3 on the Numpad; import the reference drawing for the teapot by dragging and dropping it in the 3D viewport or with Shift+A (Shift+A ➤ Image ➤ Reference ➤ Select Teapot and click Load Reference Image), as in Figure 2-44.

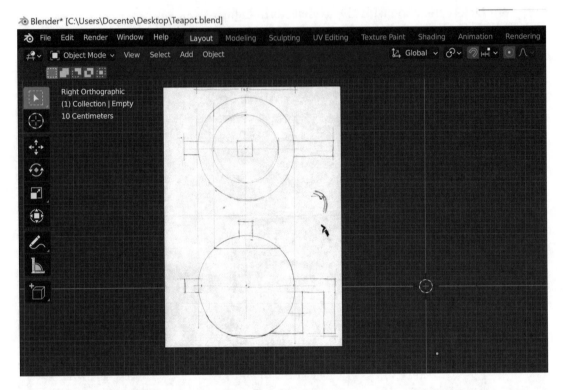

Figure 2-44. *The reference drawing for the teapot*

2. Create a sphere by using the Add menu item or by pressing
    Shift+A ➤ Mesh ➤ UVSphere.

3. Change the sphere's size by setting the Sidebar dimensions to
    14.5 x 14.5 x 14.5 centimeters, as in Figure 2-45. Then apply the
    dimension's changes with Ctrl+A ➤ Scale.

4. Modify the reference drawing of the sphere by selecting it, clicking
    S, and reducing it until it corresponds with the sphere's shape, as
    shown in Figure 2-45.

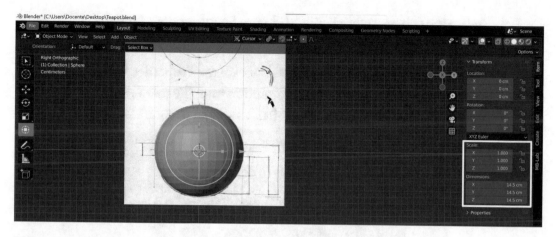

Figure 2-45. *Creating a sphere, changing its dimensions, and adapting the reference drawing*

5.   Duplicate the Reference Image (Shift+D) and rotate it -90 degrees on the y-axis (R ➤ Y ➤ -90). Then align the drawings with the sphere shape, as shown in Figure 2-46.

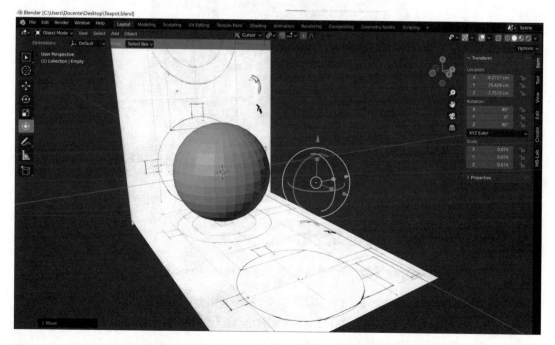

Figure 2-46. *The reference drawings for the Teapot model*

6. Select the sphere, right-click, and choose Shade Smooth from the menu that appears.

7. Then go to the Modifiers Properties panel of the Properties Editor, click Add Modifier, choose Multiresolution from the menu, and click the Subdivide button three times, as shown in Figure 2-47.

Figure 2-47. *Adding the Multiresolution modifier*

Creating the Handle and Spout

Then, we create the teapot's spout, lid, and handle through extrusions and scaling.

1. Press Tab and go to Edit mode. Go to the Right Orthographic view, select and adjust the loops for the extrusion of the handle and spout as in Figure 2-48, and scale them to maintain the spheric shape of the teapot.

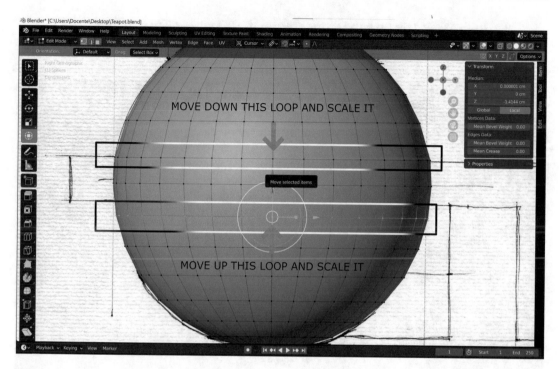

Figure 2-48. *Adjusting the loops vertically for the extrusion of the handle and spout*

2. Change the Transform Pivot Point setting from Median Point to 3D Cursor, as shown in Figure 2-49.

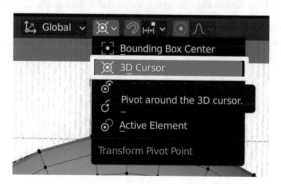

Figure 2-49. *Changing the Transform Pivot Point to 3D Cursor*

3. In this way, you turn the loops around the 3D cursor. Then, rotate the circles on the Top Orthographic View, as shown in Figure 2-50.

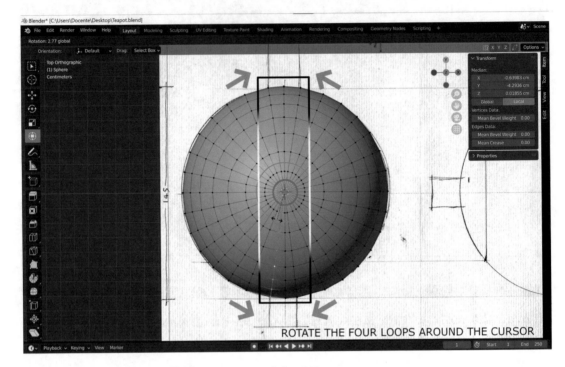

Figure 2-50.   Turning the loops around the 3D cursor

4. Then go to Front View by clicking 1 on the Numpad, go to Face Select by pressing 3, and select the four front faces of the spout, with Alt+LMB as shown in Figure 2-51.

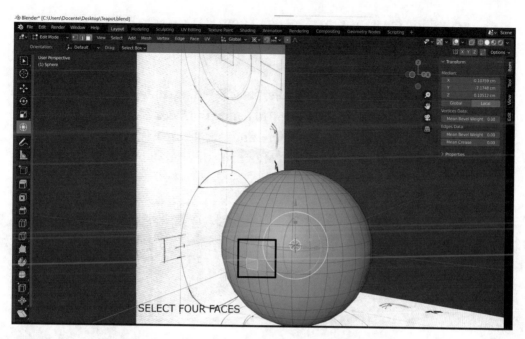

Figure 2-51. *Selecting the faces of the spout*

5.   Press 3 on the Numpad to go to Right View and extrude with E ➤ Y
     the spout following the drawing trace, as shown in Figure 2-52.

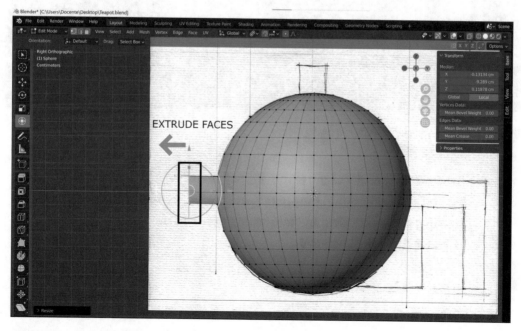

Figure 2-52. *Extruding the spout*

6. Reposition the transform pivot point from 3D Cursor to Individual Origins and then, with the faces selected, click S ➤ Y ➤ 0 and scale on the Y-axis to flatten the faces.

7. Select the four faces of the handle, press E ➤ Y, extrude the handle, and then press S ➤ Y ➤ 0 to flatten the faces. Next, extrude on the y-axis again and continue modeling the handle, following the drawing, until you obtain the desired shapes, as shown in Figure 2-53.

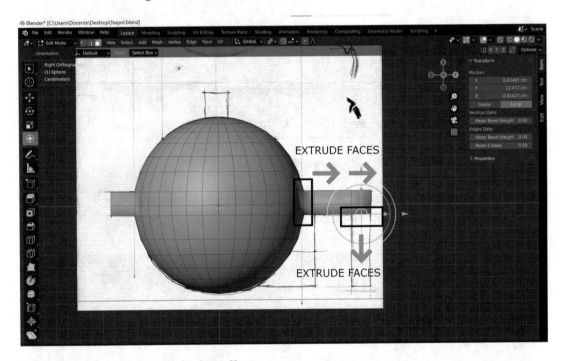

Figure 2-53. *Extruding the handle*

8. To create the handle of the teapot lid, select the vertices at the top and scale them until they match the profile on the reference drawing; then, extrude them and scale to zero on the z-axis (S ➤ Z ➤ 0), as in Figure 2-54.

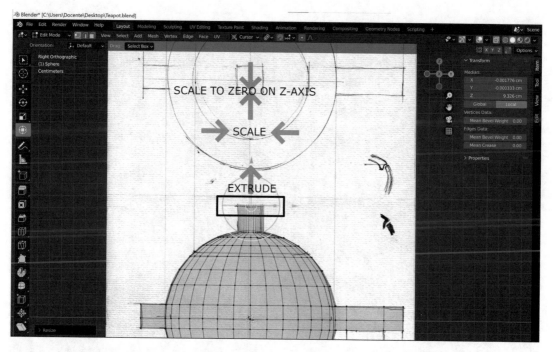

Figure 2-54. *Extruding the teapot lid*

Now transform the lid into a box.

9. Press 7 to go to Top Orthographic View, and then click Toggle
    X-Ray to see all the handle vertices. Type B for Border selection
    and drag to select 9 + 9 vertices on the top as in Figure 2-55. Then
    scale them on the y-axis to 0.

    Repeat the same operation on the bottom vertices.

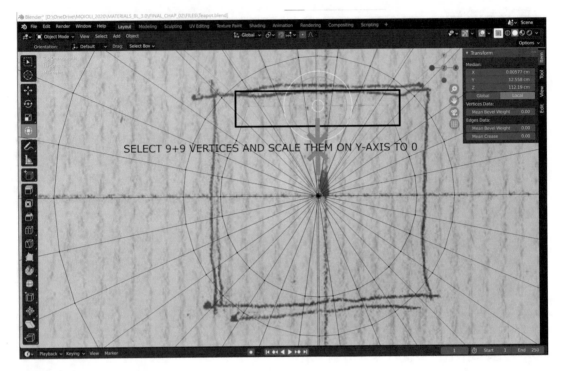

Figure 2-55. *Squaring the lid handle*

10. Then scale the right and left sides vertices of the lid handle to zero on the x-axis.

11. After clicking 2, go to edges selection and select the handles and spout edges, as shown in Figure 2-56.

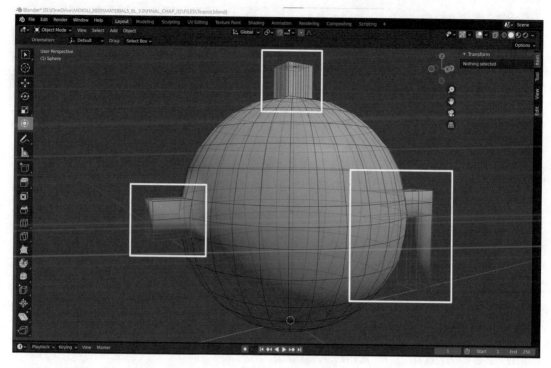

Figure 2-56. *The creased handles and spout edges*

12. Give them a Crease to make them angular (Shift+E ➤1).

    Go to object mode and see the result.

We can select the Autosmooth box in the Normals window of the Object Data Properties of the Properties Editor for a more defined edges visualization. We leave the Autosmooth angle at the default setting of 30 degrees.

Separating the Cover

Now we create the division between the lid and the teapot.

1. Type 3 on the Numpad to go to Right Ortho view and select the loop next to the lid division with Alt+LMB, as shown in Figure 2-57; make it coincide with the drawing and then click V ➤ ESC to detach the vertices of the selected circle.

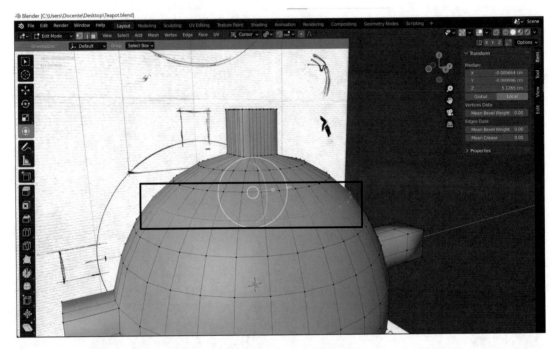

Figure 2-57. *Selecting the loop to separate the lid*

    2.   Deselect All by pressing A twice; then go with the mouse on the lid, and press L+LMB click to select the whole top with the linked selection. Next, move the cover a bit up.

Creating the Teapot Base

Finally, we create a stable base for the teapot continuing with extrusion and scaling.

    1.   Delete the single vertex at the teapot's base.

    2.   Select the loop cut at the teapot's base (Alt+LMB) and extrude it with E ➤ Z, as shown in Figure 2-58.

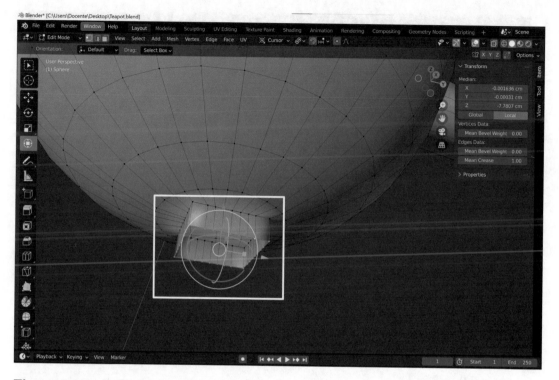

Figure 2-58. *Deleting bottom vertice to create the teapot base and scaling the loop cut*

3. Then extrude it, holding the new vertices in the same position as the previous ones with E ➤ ESC, and scale them with S ➤ Shift+Z.

4. Extrude the selected vertices on the Z-axis again (E ➤ Z), extrude again (E ➤ ESC), and scale (S ➤ Shift+Z) to close the base, as shown in Figure 2-59.

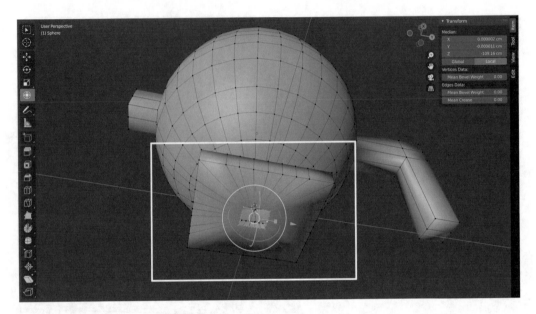

Figure 2-59. *Extruding the teapot base*

5. Finally, select all the base's angular vertices and crease them
    (Shift+E ➤ 1).

    You can see the teapot in the 3D Viewport in Solid shading, as in Figure 2-60.

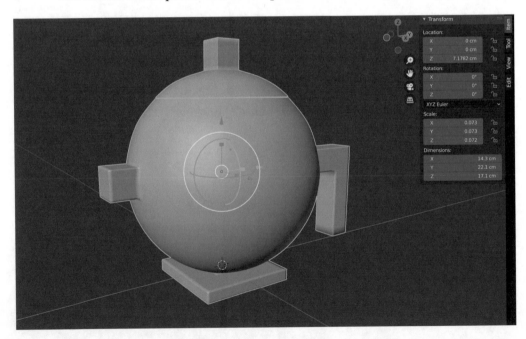

Figure 2-60. *The teapot in solid shading in the 3D viewport*

Since we've learned about the mesh modeling in Edit mode in this exercise, we will investigate other techniques by rotating a profile with the screw modifier.

Exercise 2: Creating a Glass

Now let's make a glass; several techniques and modeling possibilities exist.

Since we started from a volume in the first exercise, this time we will begin from a single vertex and extrude a profile and apply the Screw modifier. This method allows us to practice Blender's essential subobject modeling techniques.

The final result is in the `Glass.blend` file that accompanies the book.

Follow along with Exercise 2 step-by-step.

Setting the File

Also, in this second exercise, we start by setting up the file to model our objects easily.

1. Repeat steps 1, 2, and 3 of this chapter's Exercise 1.

    Save the file as Glass.blend on the local computer's drive from the main menu and select File ➤ Save ➤ Save Blender File or press Ctrl+S.

    If you don't want to repeat these steps every time you can save a custom startup file from the main menu and select File ➤ Defaults ➤ Save Startup File, as shown in Figure 2-61.

    This way, when you create a new file, it will have the settings you have given it now.

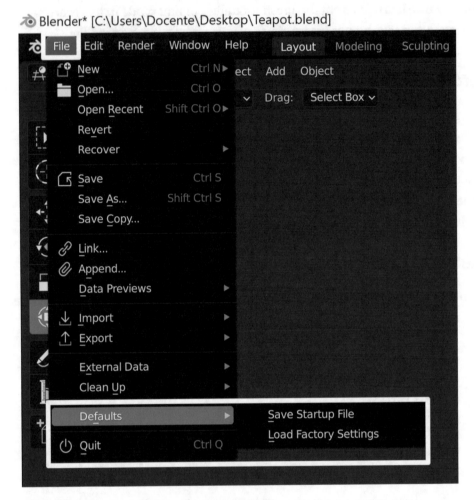

Figure 2-61. *Creating a customized startup file*

2. Prepare the scene by selecting the light and the camera, and
    pressing M. In the window that appears, click New Collection and
    create another collection called *scene*. In this way, you have a layer
    containing the light and the camera, as shown in Figure 2-62.

Figure 2-62. *Moving the light and camera in a new collection*

3. In the Outliner Editor, click the eye to the right of the scene
    collection and hide the objects it contains in the 3D view.

Preparing the Basic Object

Now let's create a reference object to give accurate measurements to our glass. Then we
import an image to help us model its profile.

1. Go to the Front Orthographic View by pressing 1 on the Numpad.
    Then, create a plane by using the Add menu item or by pressing
    Shift+A ➤ Mesh ➤ Plane, as shown in Figure 2-63.

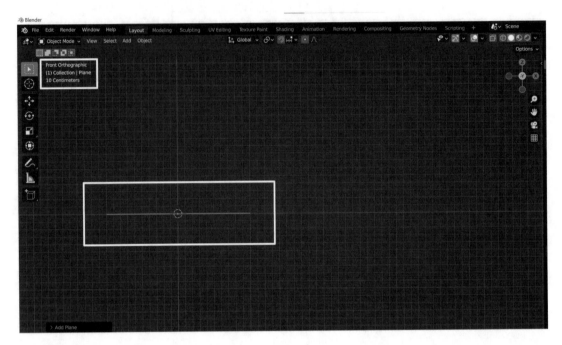

Figure 2-63. *Creating a plane*

2. In the Outliner Editor, when we click the eye to the right of the Scene collection, we can hide or show the objects it contains in the 3D view by toggling the eye symbol on and off, as shown in Figure 2-64.

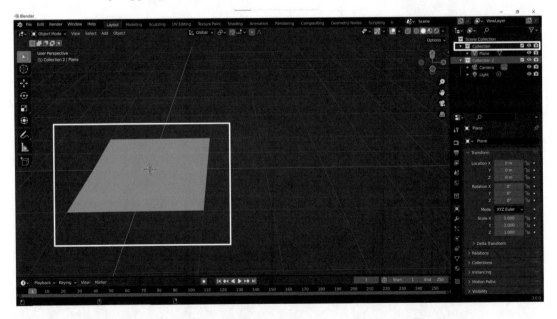

Figure 2-64. *Controlling the object's visualization with the collection*

3. Select the plane and go to Edit mode by pressing Tab. Select the four vertices if they are not yet selected. Then merge them by clicking M and choosing At center, as shown in Figure 2-65.

    This way, the four vertices will join in the center, and there will be only one left.

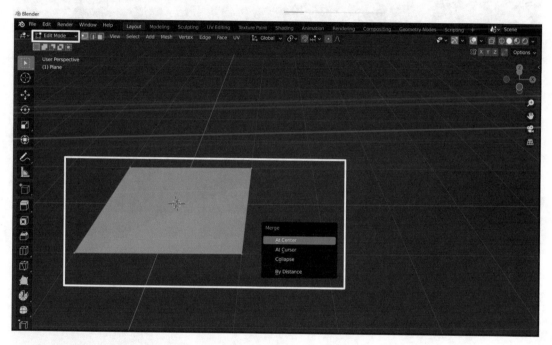

Figure 2-65. *Merging four vertices into one*

4. Select the vertex, select the Plane object in the Outliner, and rename it Glass by double-clicking the Plane name, typing the new name, and pressing Enter to apply it.

5. Go to Edit mode, press B for Border Selection, and drag the left button, selecting the vertex. Then click E ➤ Z ➤ 20 and get a 20-centimeter vertical edge, as shown in Figure 2-66.

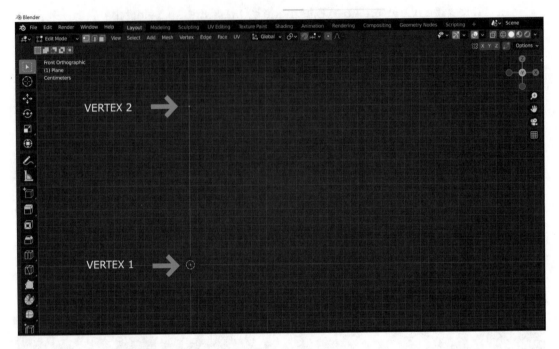

Figure 2-66. *Creating the edge for reference*

6. Clicking B again selects both vertices, and clicking E ➤ X ➤ 20 creates a 20 by 20-centimeter plane that serves as a reference for your model's height. The glass is 20 centimeters high.

7. Now press Tab to return to Object mode, press 1 in the Numpad to go to Front Orthographic View, and drag and drop the image Glass, as shown in Figure 2-67.

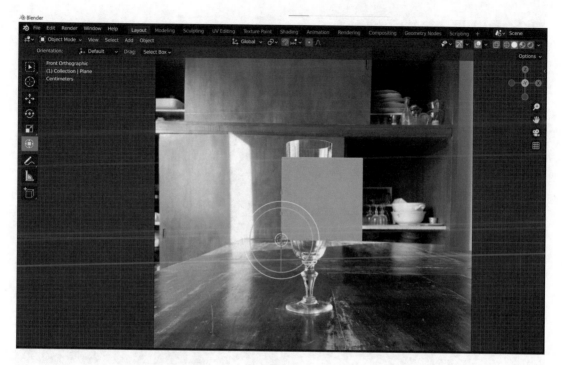

Figure 2-67. *Creating the reference plane*

8. Then select the reference image, move it with G, and shrink it with
    S such that the height of the glass from bottom to top will be 20
    cm, as Figure 2-68.

    Pan and zoom the view with the mouse's central wheel and use
    the shortcut Shift when necessary.

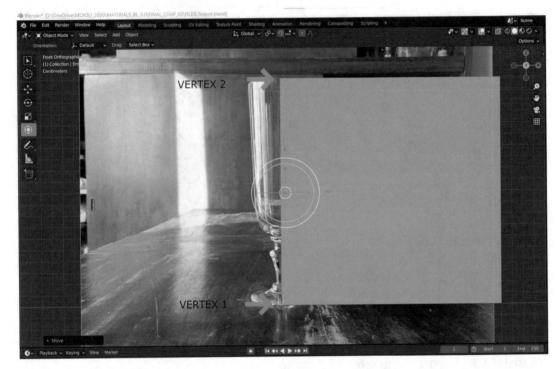

Figure 2-68. *Positioning the reference image and giving the actual size to the glass*

We also could have followed much quicker processes. For example, we could have directly created a plane 20 by 20 centimeters and positioned it frontally in the Front Horthographic View. Nevertheless, the procedure we have chosen, surely more complex, has introduced some essential concepts of the Blender Edit mode.

Creating the Profile and Screwing It

Finally, we keep only one vertex, extrude it in Front Orthographic View to get the profile of the glass, and apply a Screw modifier to create the volume. A second Subdivision Surface modifier will help us round and define the shape precisely.

1. Make sure that you still have Glass selected and go to Edit mode.
    Keep only the bottom vertex, and delete the other three by clicking
    X and choosing Vertices from the drop-down menu.

2. From the Front Ortho view, move the vertex to the right and select
    and click E several times to extrude it following the shape of the
    glass until you get a profile like the one in Figure 2-69.

Figure 2-69. *The profile of the glass to screw*

3. In the Properties Editor's Modifier Properties window, apply the
    Screw and Subdivision Surface modifiers. Then for the subsurf
    modifier, change both the Render and Viewport values to 2 or also
    3; finally, in this way, you will get the shape of the glass shown in
    Figure 2-70.

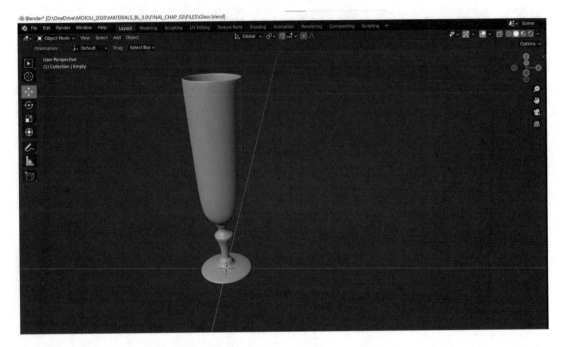

Figure 2-70. The final glass shape

4. Now apply the Screw modifier first and then Subdivision Surface by clicking the Apply buttons in the Modifiers Properties panel of the Properties editor.

5. Finally, press 1 to enter Vertex mode, select the loop cuts at the bottom of the glass by pressigning Alt, left-click a loop edge, and press F. This creates a face that closes the bottom of the glass.

6. Repeat for the other loop that remains open at the base.

We have started to practice the theoretical information studied until now with these first exercises, and we've set a solid foundation for our future work with virtual modeling.

Summary

In this chapter, we learned about the main objects and the fundamental 3D modeling techniques of Blender 3.0. We first studied the modeling objects such as Mesh, Curve, Metaball, etc. Then we analyzed the leading modeling systems: object editing, subobject editing, sculpting, and modifiers. This chapter also showed us the essential techniques of 3D modeling.

In the next chapter, we will see how to create spaces and deal with architectural modeling.

CHAPTER 3

Building a 3D Environment

It is time to build an environment to insert the elements we've created.

Blender provides several add-ons for architectural and environmental modeling. It's also possible to import three-dimensional environments from Blend Swap, TurboSquid, and BlenderNation. This chapter will lay the foundation for architectural and precision modeling and procedural and parametric creation. We will create architectural and urban spaces using both manual and automatic techniques. Finally, we'll define in more detail our environments by inserting objects, furnishings, and people.

In the second part of the chapter, the exercises will show how to build an architectural environment and some characters and objects to populate it.

The following are this chapter's main topics:

- Modeling for architecture

- Character modeling for architecture

- Blender 3.0 add-ons for architectural modeling

- Procedural and parametric modeling

- Modeling and importing furniture

Modeling for Architecture

This section deals with modeling for architectural spaces. We need virtual environments for movies and video games and virtual scenarios for films and so on.

© Gianpiero Moioli 2022
G. Moioli, *Introduction to Blender 3.0*, https://doi.org/10.1007/978-1-4842-7954-0_3

Virtual architecture is becoming more and more critical in today's industries. We are talking about a type of architectural representation beyond just images and videos. Virtual spaces are becoming interactive, and we want to create digital versions of architectural objects as close to reality as possible.

Architectural modeling involves precision in measurements and proportions. Therefore, even for a video game or a virtual environment, we must respect the actual dimensions of objects and environments. Otherwise, the result of our work will not have the necessary realism to engage users.

So, we must analyze the tools that allow us to respect the measures of the project. Let's see how to use these methods in Blender.

Precision Drawing

When we are going to create a real or virtual architectural project, it is essential to draw accurate proportions and measures. Blender helps us a lot with this. Even if it is not software for architectural and parametric drawing, it offers many technical and precision drawing tools.

We will learn about some computer-aided drawing (CAD) and model measurement tools, but first, we learn how to import the external material from CAD files into Blender.

Importing and Exporting CAD File Formats

The most popular file formats for architecture are AutoCAD DWG, AutoCAD DXF, and 3Ds. So, even if we use Blender, we must learn how to deal with these files formats so we can import them into Blender.

In fact, customers who commission our work might provide us with source files for our project in these formats. Moreover, there are many valuable materials available online that Blender does not directly support.

AutoCAD's native format is DWG, which stands for "drawing" and remains a proprietary Autodesk format that has never released its specifications. Instead, the most common exchange format for CAD files is AutoCAD Drawing Interchange Format (DXF) (or Drawing Exchange Format).

The DXF file format is also for CAD files, developed by Autodesk to exchange data between AutoCAD and other programs. Autodesk has published specifications for this format so that every user or programmer, having the source code available, can create tools for importing and exporting this file format.

Blender does not allow us to import the DWG format directly, but it enables us to import and export DXF files easily. It also supports another open source format for vector drawing: Scalable Vector Graphics (SVG).

Blender 3.0 does not yet directly import 3D Studio Max files, but we can import 3Ds files into Blender 3.0 with a small trick.

This chapter will teach how to perform these file imports; now, let's quickly look at CAD software programs.

CAD Drawing Tools

To import CAD files into Blender or speed up two-dimensional drawing work, we can use some CAD drawing tools such as AutoCAD. There are many alternative open source software options to AutoCAD at a much lower cost or even free of charge.

FreeCAD

FreeCAD is an open source, multiplatform, and customizable parametric modeling application that works on Windows, Mac, and Linux, allowing us to design objects of all kinds, both mechanical and architectural.

It does not read DWG but allows us to import and export many formats compatible with Blender and other platforms such as DXF, SVG, Obj, etc.

The workflow is logical and starts with a 2D shape to obtain three-dimensional objects, even complex ones. The software keeps track of all the steps performed in creating elements and allowing us to modify their parameters.

It has many exciting features that intersect and complete the Blender tools.

QCAD

QCAD is a two-dimensional cross-platform open source application for CAD to create technical drawings for architecture and engineering. It offers a full version at a bit of cost.

It has an intuitive and easy-to-use interface and helps draw mechanical parts, plan for buildings, and import Blender or FreeCAD drawings into DWG format. In addition, it can open DWG files and export them in the various DXF versions. Blender does not support DWG, but it can quickly import DXF, so QCAD can efficiently act as a bridge to import DWG in Blender.

ODA File Converter

The ODA file converter is a simple interface that allows us to transform DWG to DXF files and vice versa. In addition, it provides many versions of DWG and DXF files, enabling a complete correspondence between the two formats, and is useful to import DWG files into Blender.

We can also work directly inside Blender by activating tools and add-ons for measuring and precision drawing.

Let's see them in detail.

Blender 3.0 Measuring Tools

Blender itself comes with numerous tools and add-ons for precision drawing.

Let's start with Annotate and Measure, the two toolbar tools we didn't analyze in the previous chapter. Then let's see how to activate the Measurement tools in the interface. Finally, let's take a look at the MeasureIt add-on.

Annotate

The Annotate tool helps draw or write three-dimensionally in the viewport or other editors. To use it, click the Annotate icon in the toolbar and start writing or drawing in 3D view.

We have four drawing options; to make them appear, we have to left-click the Annotate box and hold the button until the window with the options appears, as in Figure 3-1. Then select the one we want.

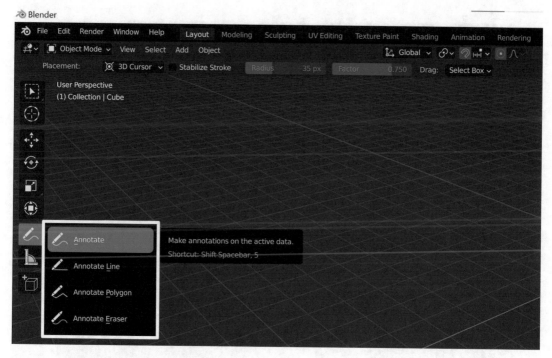

Figure 3-1. *The Annotate tools*

But let's consider the features of these four options:

- **Annotate** tracks freehand lines.

- **Annotate Line** draws straight lines by clicking and dragging the left mouse button.

- **Annotate Polygon** allows you to create polygons.

- **Annotate Eraser** instead erases the drawn lines.

Finally, from the Overlays window in the 3D view Header, we can control the display of our annotations by checking the Annotations box, which shows and hides the strokes of this tool.

Measure

The Measure instrument allows us to measure angles and distances. We can activate it from the toolbar by clicking the Measure icon shown in Figure 3-2 and then clicking and dragging in 3D view with the left mouse button. In this way, we can create a ruler with the distance measurement.

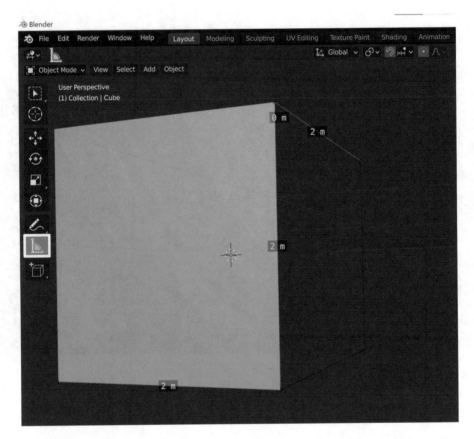

Figure 3-2. *The Measure tool*

Releasing the button and clicking and dragging on another part of the 3D Viewport creates another ruler. If we click and drag on a ruler when a cross appears, we make an angle by creating a new vertex. Instead, when the cross appears, we press X to delete the ruler. We can freely move the segment's vertex by clicking one end of the ruler when the four arrows appear.

If we click Ctrl, we enable the snap at the vertices, edges, and faces; in this way, we can accurately measure all distances in the three-dimensional space.

We can also activate the precision measurement by pressing Shift when the four arrows appear and dragging on a created ruler. We measure the object's thickness. With Ctrl+C, we can copy the value of the selected ruler to the clipboard.

Measurement

We can also activate the Blender 3.0 Measurement tools. These instruments are simple but very useful for precision drawing.

We can see the options in the white highlighted box in Figure 3-3.

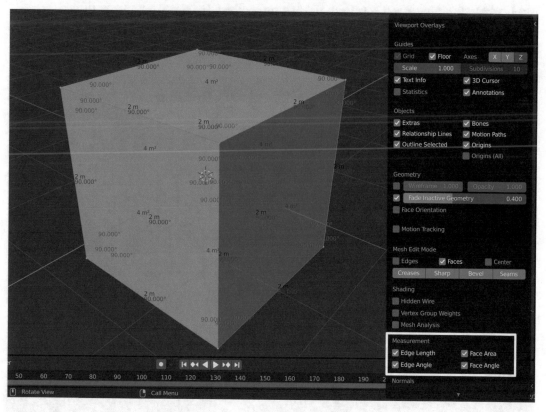

Figure 3-3. *Measurement tools*

In Edit mode, we click the arrow next to the Show Overlays button in the 3D view header to find the Measurement panel, highlited in Figure 3-3. Then, we select Edge Length, Edge Angle, Face Area, and Face Angle; immediately in the selected object, the measures appear.

This tool is handy, especially for mechanical and architectural drawing. It allows us to model and see the measurements in real time. However, it displays them only in Edit mode; they disappear when we go to Object mode.

If we want to see the measurements in Object mode, we must activate MeasureIt.

MeasureIt

MeasureIt is a preinstalled add-on, and we use it to visualize the dimensions of the objects in 3D view in both Object and Edit modes.

Like all other add-ons integrated with Blender, we activate it in the User Preferences by checking the MeasureIt box in the Add-ons section. (in the Topbar, use the main menu to select Edit ➤ Preferences ➤ Add-ons ➤ MeasureIt).

We can work with it in the View tab of the Sidebar, as shown in Figure 3-4.

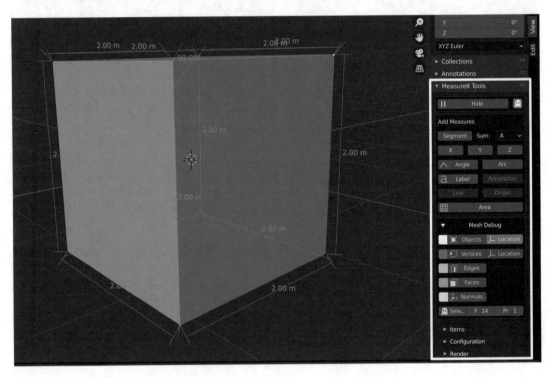

Figure 3-4. *The MeasureIt add-on*

There are six panels, as listed here:

- Show and Hide displays or hides measurements.

- Add Measures lets us add the measures, for example, the dimensions of segments, angles, arcs, and areas.

- By clicking the Mesh Debug button, we open a panel containing many valuable options to identify the subobjects' index numbers and display their data.

- The Items panel allows use to choose the measurement colors; we can see it only after adding at least one size.

- The Configuration panel allows us to modify the font settings.

- The Render tab controls the render settings.

We covered precision drawing in Blender, interoperability of file formats, and measurements. Next, we will learn about the architectural modeling add-ons in Blender.

Blender 3.0 Add-ons for Architectural Modeling

As we have already seen, add-ons are scripts in Python that extend the functions of Blender.

Several types of add-ons help us in architectural modeling. The three main types are as follows:

- *Preinstalled add-ons*: They need to be activated in the User Preferences.

- *Free add-ons*: We install them by downloading the code from the Internet.

- *Paid add-ons*: These can be downloaded from the Internet for a fee.

We can activate directly the preinstalled add-ons in the Add-ons section of the User Preferences. Instead for all other add-ons we must first download the installation files from the Internet before activating them. So we open the User Preferences from the Blender main menu's Edit ➤ Preferences items and install the add-ons with the Install button.

Finally, we must activate the add-ons we need in the Add-ons window of the User Preferences.

Let's take a closer look at the main add-ons for architectural design.

Preinstalled Add-ons

This section covers the first type of add-ons, the ones preinstalled in Blender but not yet activated.

We enable them in the User Preferences by clicking the Add-ons button and looking in the list for the ones we want to install. This system helps to keep the software as light and high-performing as possible. In this way, users activate only the add-ons they need.

Let's take a look at this set of tools.

Edit Mesh Tools

This exciting add-on activates, in Edit mode, a set of modeling tools not directly available in Blender's default interface, speeding up mesh editing.

We can access these devices from the Sidebar by pressing N, clicking Edit on the vertical menu, and then clicking Mesh Tools, as shown in Figure 3-5.

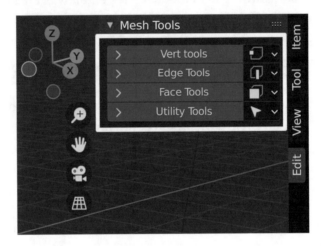

Figure 3-5. *The Mesh Tools add-ons menu*

In the Sidebar, we can see the tools divided into four groups: the first three contain the operations according to each subobject, and the fourth one contains utilities.

Let's see them.

- Vertices Tools, of course, works on vertices and contains Chamfer, Extrude Random, and Bevel.

- Edge Tools works on edges and includes Offset, Fillet, Edge Roundify, Set Edge Length, Edges Floor Plan, Extrude, and Bevel.

- Face Tools allows editing of the Face subobject and contains the Face Inset Fillet, Cut Faces, Multi Extrude, Split Solidify, Face Shape, Inset Faces, and Extrude Individual Faces tools.

- Utility Tools provides the tools Subdivide, Merge by Distance, Limited Dissolve, Flip Normals, Triangulate Faces, Tris to Quads, and Relax.

- We also find the icon to change the subobject selection tools on the right of each section.

These tools make the work faster and easier, so it's worth activating this add-on.

Precision-Drawing-Tools (PDT)

PDT is built for CAD designers to draw two-dimensionally with precision.

It helps when we use Blender for mechanical or technical and architectural drawing.

The goal of PDT is to make a precision drawing easier in Blender, especially when combined with MeasureIt for highlighting measurements during drawing.

PDT builds CAD models starting from a plane.

It contains numerous tools for the precision drawing; this GitHub page describes it in more detail: https://github.com/Clockmender/Precision-Drawing-Tools/wiki.

Scatter

The Scatter add-on allows us to create instances of a selected object by painting its arrangement on a flat or spherical surface.

We activate it by checking the Object: Scatter Objects box in the Add-ons window.

We first select the object we want to reproduce and then the surface on which we want to place it; finally, we click F3, type **Scatter**, click Scatter Objects, click with the left mouse button, and drag.

This is how to paint the duplicates of the object on the surface. When we have finished, we press Enter.

The Properties Editor's Active tool and Workspace settings window can modify different parameters: Density, Radius, Scale, Randomness, Rotation, Offset, and Seed.

Tiny CAD Mesh Tools

TinyCAD combines several scripts for precision CAD drawing. First, we activate it in the usual way. Then, we use it in Edit mode by right-clicking the object and opening the context menu. We'll find the following six functions:

- **VTX |AUTO** allows us to extend, project, or intersect two edges on the same plane.

- **V2X | Vertex at the intersection** creates a vertex at the intersection of two edges.

- **XALL | Intersect selected edges** adds a vertex at the meeting of each edge.

- **BIX | Bisector of two planar edges** generates the bisector of two selected edges.

- **CCEN | Resurrect circle center** creates a circle from three selected vertices and moves the 3D cursor in its center.

- **E2F | Extend edge to face** extends a selected edge to the intersection with a selected face.

These particular tools can be helpful. Now let's see another exciting tool for mesh editing.

Bool Tool

With Bool Tool, we can directly edit objects with Boolean modifiers to simplify the application process. It is an excellent add-on.

We must activate Bool Tool from the User Preferences by selecting the Object: Bool Tool checkbox. In this window, we can select Display as Wireframe to modify the visualization of these objects in the viewport and work more efficiently.

We access it from the Edit menu in the Sidebar or by pressing the keyboard shortcut Ctrl+Shift+B.

We select first the object we want to remove or add and then the main one from which to add or subtract.

Then we click the button for the modification we want to achieve on the panels highlited in Figure 3-6.

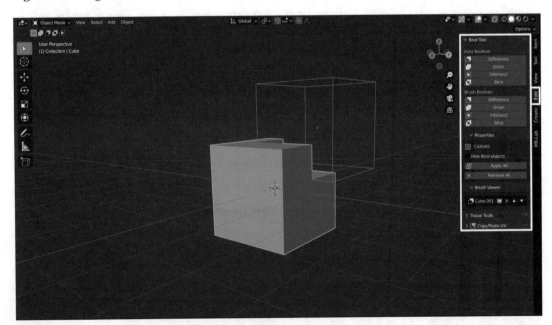

Figure 3-6. *The Bool Tool add-on panels*

As we can see in the figure, there are two panels:

- Auto Boolean immediately applies the transformation.

- Brush Boolean allows us to move the object to subtract or add until we find the proper position. It enables us to do a nondestructive operation until we click the Apply All button and finally apply the modifier. Using the Boolean brush, we can directly see the result because it visualizes the shape to subtract or add in the wireframe.

For the functioning of the various options, we can refer to the Boolean modifier covered in Chapter 2.

Sapling Tree Gen and Modular Tree

Sapling Tree Gen is one of Blender's tools for generating trees. It creates trees from Bezier curves that are lighter than meshes. Instead, the leaves are meshes. Several options allow us to modify the basic types offered by the tool and customize them as we like.

Tip An essay by Jason Weber & Joseph Penn, "Creation and Rendering of Realistic Trees ", deals with the topic more theoretically and presents images of the types of trees we can generate. We quickly find this text online by using a search engine.

We activate this tool on the Add-ons tab and select the Add Curve: Sapling Tree Gen box. Once activated, we can add a tree from the header menu of the 3D view by selecting Add ➤ Curves or the keyboard shortcut Shift+A.

Then we can start to customize it in the window that appears on the bottom left of 3D view when we create the object.

If we exit creation mode by clicking another object or the same tree, the window disappears and no longer allows us to modify the parameters. We find all the options in the Geometry menu shown in Figure 3-7.

Figure 3-7. *The Geometry options of the Sapling Tree Gen add-on*

We can divide the Settings window into eight different interfaces that serve to control the various characteristics of the tree we are creating.

- Geometry changes the general geometry of the tree.

- Branch Radius controls the branch radius.

- Branch Splitting contains the tools for forming and splitting branches.

- Brunch Growth checks how the branches grow.

- Pruning prunes the branches, almost like a real tree.

- Leaves can create and control the shape and distribution of the leaves.

- Armature allows us to add an armature to the tree so that we can later animate it.

- Animation contains the tools to animate the tree.

Instead, from the Load Preset window at the bottom-left corner, we can choose one of the new tree types available and modify its characteristics. We have many editing possibilities through the parameters of the eight windows. We can also change the plant's shape in Object mode or enter Edit mode and change the characteristics of the branches using the control points of Bezier curves.

Another possibility for tree creation is a modular tree. This add-on uses an entirely different technique and the nodal system to create trees divided into three parts: the Trunk node, the Branch node, and the Tree Parameters node.

After getting to know the internal add-ons, let's look at the significant external add-ons for architectural modeling.

External Add-ons

Now let's look at some of the add-ons that are not preinstalled in Blender. We must install them by downloading the files from the Internet.

QBlocker

This add-on is similar to the new Add Object tool in the Blender 3.0 toolbar.

With this tool, we can add primitives easily in the viewport.

Furthermore, QBlocker allows us to create objects with a few clicks and edit them interactively to quickly create complex scenes starting from planes, cubes, and spheres. We also can use different types of snaps and interactively orient objects as we make them.

We download it from Gumroad first. Then we click the Install button in the Add-ons section of the User Preferences and search in the file browser for the zip file we just downloaded. We access it from the Add window (Shift+A) and choose QBlocker. Once we have created our objects, we can modify their parameters on the right of the 3D view from the QBlocker Properties section of the Object Data panel of the Properties Editor.

We can also change the mesh type even after creating our objects.

Blender GIS

This add-on is an exciting and sophisticated Geographic Information Systems (GIS) that is effortless to use.

It includes several tools to import directly into Blender's 3D view for terrain geometry and satellite imagery. In particular, it mainly allows us to do the following:

- Import GIS data files, including the most popular GIS data formats such as OpenStreetMap XML, raster images, Shapefile vector, and GeoTIFF DEM

- Import directly from web geodata and visualize dynamic web maps in 3D view with the help of OpenStreetMap and NASA SRTM Mission

It is crucial for architecture to import entire cities from different sources with minimal effort, either with satellite images or with open source maps and 3D models from OSM data. OpenStreetMap is a world map that we can use freely with an open license. We can import satellite images and transform them into three-dimensional land, buildings, streets, etc.

We must first download the installation files from GitHub, as in Figure 3-8.

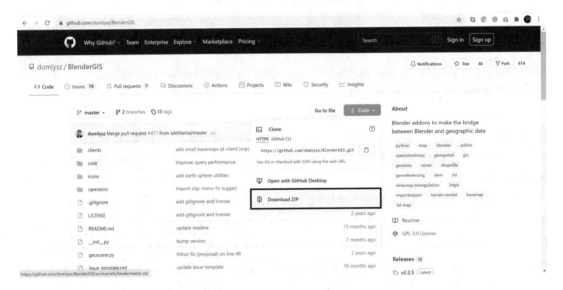

Figure 3-8. *Downloading the Blender GIS add-on*

We can go to `https://github.com/domlysz/BlenderGIS`, click Download ZIP, and choose the file folder to save the zipped file.

Then we open the User Preferences and install this add-on with the Install button.

Again in the User Preferences, we enable the add-on and select a temporary cache folder in the Basemap window to find a temporary file save path.

Now we can find all the available tools in the added GIS item in the menu of the 3D view header, as shown in Figure 3-9.

Figure 3-9. *The BlenderGIS menu*

We can open the Basemap window from GIS ➤ Web Geodata ➤ Basemap; leave the Google and Satellite options and click OK. The map of the world we can navigate in the 3D view appears as in Figure 3-10.

Figure 3-10. *The Blender GIS add-on Basemap*

To zoom the view, we can rotate the mouse wheel. We can also search for a location (for example, Milan) by typing its name in the box that opens by pressing the G button.

Let's go to the viewport to the area we are interested in and frame it in the 3D view. Then we can press E to import the whole area. In this case, we have imported a two-dimensional image of the space.

Now we import the land and the buildings and everything else. So, we select the plane and go again to GIS ➤ Web geodata ➤ Get Elevation SRTM; in this way, we import the SRTM elevation of the terrain.

Then we must import the three-dimensional models. In GIS ➤ Web geodata ➤ Get OSM, we select all the items: building, highway, landuse, leisure, natural, railway, waterway.

Finally, we select the "Elevation from object" box. After a short waiting time, we see the three-dimensional models of streets, buildings, and everything else materialize, as in Figure 3-11.

Figure 3-11. *An area of Milan imported into Blender*

We can see an area of Milan imported into Blender with the Blender GIS add-on in Figure 3-11.

The final result is in the BlenderGIS.blend file that accompanies this book.

This first section has deepened our knowledge of architectural modeling and software extension through Blender 3.0 add-ons.

We will introduce procedural and parametric modeling in the next section.

Procedural and Parametric Modeling

Procedural modeling uses mathematical functions or *algorithms* to create complex shapes faster and in more detail. This method is developing constantly. It was initially introduced to create textures for objects; then, these techniques have expanded rapidly to include animation and modeling. We can deepen the understanding of procedural techniques in texturing, modeling, and animation by reading the exciting book "Texturing & Modeling: A Procedural Approach", edited by Morgan Kaufmann in 2003. [1]

Currently, this topic is widening even more with the study of artificial intelligence's implications on 3D modeling. With artificial intelligence (AI) in computer graphics, we can extend the modification possibilities of our entities and expand our creativity and productiveness.

The procedural generation makes it possible to create complex shapes and multiply them infinitely by applying parametric variations. We already saw an easy example with the Geometry Nodes modifier in the previous chapter.

Generative design is a programming-based approach to design. It helps designers and architects build large quantities of geometrically complex shapes with less effort.

We realize procedural generation through data entities of various types, such as geometries, materials, textures, sound, and much more. We can produce all these through a sequence of instructions rather than a static data block. This way, we can introduce all the parameters we need separately in our work.

Procedures provide parametric control in this system.

Therefore, we can differentiate between procedural modeling and parametric modeling.

- We create a system that allows us to achieve our objectives with procedural modeling. Moreover, we can reuse this chain endlessly by making the changes we need to obtain always different results.

- We use parameters and create something we can edit endlessly with parametric modeling. This method speeds up modeling work and reduces the need for computer resources.

The tools for introducing procedural techniques in Blender are the nodal systems.

---

[1] David S. Ebert; F. Kenton Musgrave; Darwyn Peachey; Ken Perlin; Steven Worley. *Texturing & Modeling: A Procedural Approach.* Morgan Kaufmann, 2003.

Blender 3.0 is evolving to use these techniques more and more extensively for geometry with geometry nodes, materials, textures, animation, physics, etc.

There are also many add-ons available for parametric and procedural modeling. However, we will see only some of those that seem more important to us, from Archimesh to Archipac to Mesh Maze Addon, and so on.

But let's see in practice what Blender 3.0 provides us with for parametric and procedural modeling.

Add-ons for Procedural and Parametrical Modeling

As we have already said, Blender is sophisticated software that is continuously evolving.

It was not created for parametric modeling, but the Blender Foundation and Blender communities are developing many tools that help us use it for parametric modeling.

These tools are, in many cases, handy and very flexible.

The last of these tools is the Geometry Nodes modifier, but let's see what is at the base of the current procedural tools and crucial for the future development of our software.

Internal Add-ons

Let's see some specific add-ons for procedural modeling. The first is a long-time internal Blender add-on and is typically used for parametric architecture: Archimesh.

Archimesh

Archimesh allows us to build parametric architectural elements.

First, we activate Archimesh in the User Preferences by checking its activation box: Add Mesh: Archimesh.

Then we add parametrical objects from the add window or by pressing Shift+A and then selecting Mesh ➤ Archimesh. We can also add the entities to the scene directly from the Archimesh panel of the Sidebar.

Once we have created the object, we can modify its parameters in the Sidebar.

It is a simple but helpful tool to set architectural scenes quickly and effectively. We can create different objects, structural elements, and furniture such as rooms, doors, rail windows, panel windows, cabinets, shelves, columns, stairs, roofs. In addition, a separate menu called Decoration Props contains books, lamps, roller curtains, Venetian blinds, Japanese curtains.

We can insert the templates in the cursor position to control their insertion point.

We can also precisely control the parameters we need to create the object from the Sidebar, as shown in Figure 3-12.

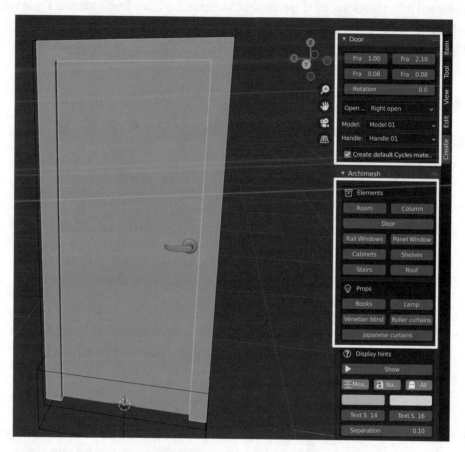

Figure 3-12. *The Archimesh add-on*

Figure 3-12 shows a door; we can see the parameters to modify it in the Sidebar by selecting Create ➤ Door window. The lower window contains the objects we can create.

Since a few parts compose it, we click its name in the Outliner in the Properties window to select this object. Then, to delete it, we choose the name in the Outliner, right-click it, and choose Delete Hierarchy.

This chapter will show us how to add doors and windows with Archimesh in Exercise 3.

Tissue

Tissue contains a set of tools for computational design objects.

We install it by checking the box Mesh: Tissue in the User Preferences. Then we find the tools in the Sidebar by selecting Edit ➤ Tissue Tools.

This tool provides us with different types of devices grouped into these three categories:

- Tissue Tools includes the following:

    a.   Tessellate, which distributes the first mesh on the surface of the second

    b.   Dual mesh, which duplicates the first mesh to edit the active object tessellating it

    c.   Refresh, which we use to apply the changes to the mesh when we modify it

    d.   Rotate Faces, which serves to move the order of the vertices of the selected faces

- Weight Tools contains tools to distribute the shapes using Weight Paint. We access it by going to Weight Paint mode and searching for it in the Sidebar on the right.

- Color Tools convert vertex colors to vertex groups.

Tessellate, for example, allows us to distribute the first mesh, the Component object, on a second mesh, the Base object, or Generator with different control options.

To use it, we can create two meshes; or we can make the first one, select it, and then click the Dual Mesh button in the Tissue tools in the Sidebar.

The Base object will become the surface where the shapes of the first one will be distributed, as in Figure 3-13.

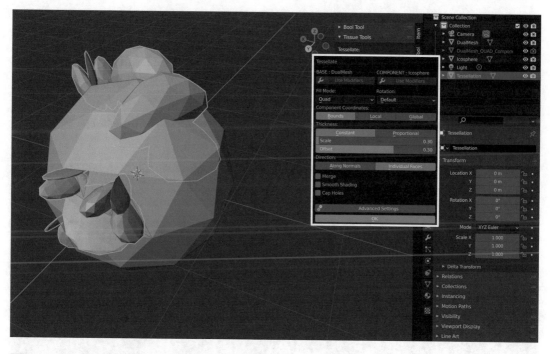

Figure 3-13. *The Tissue add-on window*

We created the first IcoSphere and selected it. Then we clicked Dual Mesh in the Tissue tools in the Sidebar; this duplicates the object and generates a similar mesh with a particular component tessellation.

Next, we selected the original mesh and then the one created by Dual Mesh, clicked Tessellate to open the window, and then modified the options in the panel.

We modified Proportional in Constant, changed the Scale and Offset values to 0.30, and then modified Along with Normal in Individual Faces. Then we clicked OK to display the add-on effect in the 3D view and got the result shown in Figure 3-13.

Tissue is a good tool for architectural and product design and is helpful and easy to use.

Mesh Maze

Mesh Maze is a simple add-on to build labyrinthine shapes from any mesh. It can be helpful to create different kinds of complex objects in a short time and with great ease.

We can install Mesh Maze by downloading the `.zip` file from the GitHub repository here: `https://github.com/elfnor/mesh_maze`.

We install it from the Install button in the User Preferences. Then we activate it by selecting the box in the same window.

Let's start with a mesh, for example, a plane. First, let's create it and scale it five times by pressing S+5 and then Enter. Then we go to Edit mode and subdivide it 40 times to make faces.

We go to Object mode, apply the scale by pressing Ctrl+A and then clicking Scale, and go back to Edit mode.

Then, in the header of 3D view, we click Mesh after selecting all the faces and then "Maze mesh selection," as shown in Figure 3-14.

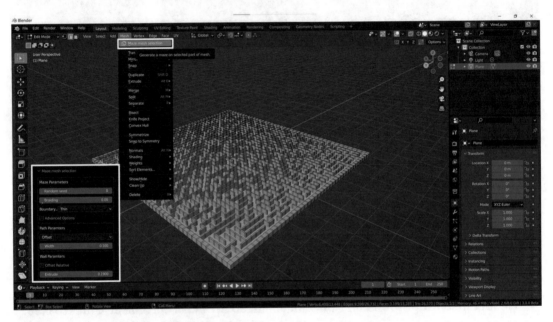

Figure 3-14. *The Mesh Maze add-on interface*

In the window on the bottom left, we modify the values according to the result we want to obtain. In this case, as shown in Figure 3-14, we modify the path parameters from Offset to Width. Then we set the width to 0.03 and Extrude to 0.2. Here we have used a simple plane, but we could also use more intricate shapes and experiment with the effects that this straightforward tool creates.

We have seen many interesting internal add-ons of parametric modeling; now, we will learn about external add-ons that are useful for procedural and parametric modeling.

External Add-ons

For external add-ons, we must download the zipped installation file.

Archipack

Archipack builds simple but effective parametric architectural objects such as windows, doors, stairs, fences, trusses, roofs, floors, and walls. Two versions are available: 1.2.85, a free one, and 2.X, a for-fee version downloadable from the site.

Archipack has been an internal add-on for a long time, but it is no longer included among the internal add-ons of version 3.0, as BlenderKit.

We will briefly look at the free version, which has various exciting features and is extremely easy to use.

It contains several primitives specific to architecture, the possibility to modify the parameters of the objects in real time, and the opportunity to maintain complete control of the elements at any time.

We install it by downloading the installation files from the Download ZIP button of this page: `https://github.com/s-leger/archipack/wiki/Setup`. Then, in Blender, we click the Install button in the Add-ons section of the User Preferences and search in the file browser for the zip file we just downloaded.

To create the objects, we must activate the button Activate Render Presets Thumbs in the User Preferences window so that we can see everything in a window in the Blender interface at the top of 3D view at the time of creation.

Then we can modify and customize objects from the Sidebar by clicking Create on the right of 3D view.

Archipack gives us excellent flexibility for modifying objects. For example, with this tool, we can create complex things that we can modify at any time by clicking the Manipulate button in the Sidebar's Archipack window. In addition, we can also modify the objects interactively by changing their measurements in the 3D Viewport, as shown in Figure 3-15.

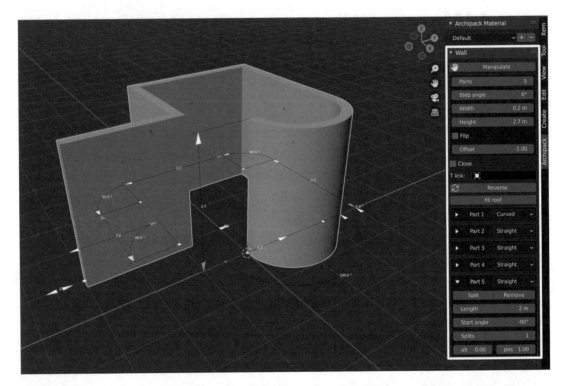

Figure 3-15.   *The Archipack add-on's Manipulate window*

In Figure 3-15, we can see the creation of a wall object. We can modify the parameters directly in 3D view by dragging and dropping the white arrows and squares. We can also adjust the dimensions numerically in the Manipulate window in the Sidebar on the right.

Archimesh and Archipack are two Blender tools for quickly creating architectural objects.

Sverchok

Sverchok, the Russian word for "cricket," is a parametric add-on inspired by Houdini or Grasshopper for architects and designers. It is a complete tool specially developed for parametric object creation. This add-on allows us to program without knowing how to program.

We create and modify shapes and visualize geometry through nodes without knowing any programming languages. It uses Blender's nodal system to build geometry and it is very similar to Blender Geometry Nodes.

Each node is a script; several linked scripts create a chain. Setting more nodes together builds a nodal system that we can use to generate materials, textures, geometries, and much more. The advantage of using a nodal system is that we can modify each node individually at any time and control the final result much more accurately.

Each node in Sverchok represents a modification of the blockchain.

We download the zipped file from `https://github.com/nortikin/sverchok` in the GitHub repository.

Then, as usual, we install and activate it from the Blender User Preferences; in this case, we must first download the zipped file (Edit ➤ Preferences ➤ Add-ons ➤ Install).

This is a fantastic add-on that gives us about 600 nodes if we also include the extra nodes of the Sverchok Extra extension, another Blender add-on designed to extend Sverchok itself. We find the GitHub repository here: `https://github.com/portnov/sverchok-extra`.

Figure 3-16 shows a simple exercise of procedural modeling from a single cube, which in Sverchok is called *Box*, from a matrix of plane vertices.

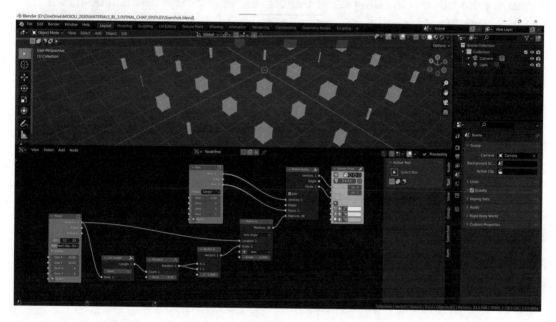

Figure 3-16. *The Sverchok add-on interface*

We open Blender 3.0 and install Sverchok. Next, we modify the Blender interface by dragging up the line that divides the 3D Viewport from the Timeline, enlarging this editor. Then, from the Editor Type button of the Timeline, choose the Sverchok Node editor.

We can add a new node tree by clicking the New button in the center of the editor.

Then we start adding nodes with Shift+A. Viewer Draw is the viewing node; Plane and Box are the input nodes. Finally, we use the other scripts to create a nodal chain whose result is the set of boxes we can see in the 3D Viewport of Figure 3-16. It should be the beginning of a city's creation!

We'll take a closer look at Blender's nodal system in Chapter 4. At that time, we will also better understand how Geometry Nodes, Sverchok, and Sorcar all function. We'll also go deeper into Blender's nodal system for materials and textures.

We can use Blender's internal nodal system to create and edit objects. Let's look at another example by installing another add-on that uses Blender's nodal system to create and edit geometries.

We will work with the Sorcar add-on.

Sorcar

Sorcar is a procedural modeling add-on similar to Sverchok that uses a node-based system within Blender through the Python API.

It is a visual programming environment inspired by Houdini to model meshes with nodes.

We can access its instruments through a customized node editor with nodes dedicated to modeling and starting from Blender meshes. Thus, we can quickly create 3D models with Sorcar and use node parameters to generate limitless nondestructive variations. Furthermore, it allows a real-time modification of objects through node parameters at each process stage.

As with Sverchok, we can download the add-on from GitHub; see `https://github.com/aachman98/Sorcar`.

Then, from the add-ons window of the Blender User Preferences, we click Install and choose the zipped folder and load it (Edit ➤ Preferences ➤ Add-ons ➤ Install). Finally, we activate the software by selecting Node: Sorcar.

Now let's see how to create and modify an object with Sorcar.

1. Open Blender and delete the default cube.

2. Enlarge the Timeline by dragging and dropping upward the line that separates it from 3D view. Then, from the Editor Type button, transform the Timeline into a Sorcar Node Editor.

3. Create a new node tree in the Sorcar Node Editor by clicking the + New button.

4. Press Shift+A to open the "Add node" menu, and from the Input menu, add a Create Plane node, and then click the Set Preview button in the node window. At this point, the plane appears in 3D view.

5. Add a Subdivide node and connect the socket object of this node
    with one of the Subdivide modifiers. Then, increase the Number
    of Cuts option to 20 and click Set Preview.

6. Add a Displace modifier, create a texture in the Texture Properties
    panel of the Properties Editor, and add it in the dedicated box of
    the node.

With this simple nodal system composed of three nodes, we obtain the parametrical
shape shown in Figure 3-17.

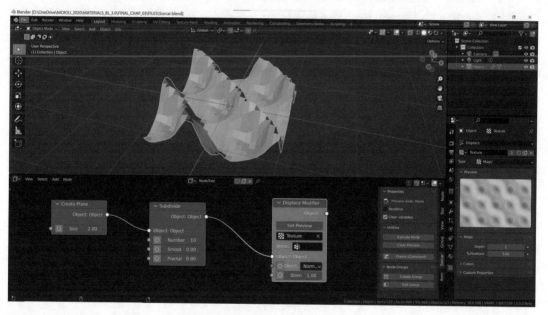

Figure 3-17.   *The Sorcar add-on and some nodes*

We can see the final object and the nodal system in Figure 3-17. We have achieved
the same results that we would have obtained with 3D modeling but with the advantage
that we can edit the parameters of each node interactively. This means we can modify
the result.

For its part, Sorcar is an excellent add-on.

- It allows us to do visual programming easily or program with scripts through nodes.

- It provides us with more than 200 nodes divided into the following categories: Inputs, Curves, Arrays, Noise, Transform, Selection, Deletion, Component Operators, Object Operators, Modifiers, Constants, Utilities, Flow Control, and Settings.

- It maintains a nondestructive workflow. Thus, we can modify each node without any problem at any time.

- It allows real-time updates. In fact, by modifying each parameter, the modification is reflected on the object in the 3D view immediately.

- It allows the automation of operations by automating the changes of values simply.

- It can iterate and randomize the shapes to which it is applied. It allows automatic random effects that speed up the workflow by directly performing operations that, if performed manually, would slow down the workflow.

After understanding the basics of procedural modeling with the tools provided by Blender and its internal and external add-ons, we learn how to import 3D objects into Blender through online sites and libraries.

Modeling and Importing Furniture

The details for a realistic representation of the scene are crucial, so if we want to represent a scene realistically, it is essential to build our objects.

Still, it is necessary to integrate them with proper-quality, ready-made objects downloaded from the Internet.

Many platforms offer a lot of high-quality materials for free or for a small fee. It's not only for furniture. For example, the most common sites where we can find suitable quality materials are as follows:

- https://www.turbosquid.com/

- https://sketchfab.com/

- https://archive3d.net/

- https://www.syncronia.com/en/3d-bim-cad-models-bathroom-furniture/itlas/murano?downloadfile=/en/download-file/79266

- https://archiup.com

- https://3dsky.org

- https://www.reno-reno.pl/modele-3D/

Some templates are free, and some cost money.

We can improve our scenes without much effort and make our work pipeline more productive using these elements.

However, most files are in different formats than Blender's native ones. Instead, there is a lot of stuff in formats such as AutoCAD's DWG and 3D Studio Max's 3Ds. So we need to import them into Blender to use them in our scenes. Earlier in the chapter we saw how to import the DWG file format into Blender.

We can also import the 3DS format with a trick. First, we import the file into the 2.79 Blender version. Then we can copy and paste it into the 3.0 version.

You'll find many objects in this file format on the Internet. Figure 3-18 shows a sofa.

Figure 3-18. *The sofa from the native 3D Studio Max format imported into Blender 2.79*

This object just brought into Blender is Walter Knoll's Prime Time sofa, imported from a 3Ds format in Blender 2.79 and then copied with Ctrl+C and pasted with Ctrl+V in version 3.0.

So, importing this format into Blender is easy. Then, of course, we have to work a little on materials, but we can find exciting furniture and design objects.

In this way, we can download and use many objects like the sofa we just downloaded from `https://archive3d.net/`.

Moreover, we can enrich our projects with realistic elements and details with an Internet search. In addition, we can find ready-made items available in many cases, also free of charge. With these objects we can create libraries that we can reuse in all our projects.

Asset Libraries in Blender

Asset management is one of the changes introduced in Blender 3.0 to speed up the direct importation of objects and create custom parametric libraries.

An asset management system is a tool allowing us to easily access the objects and drag and drop them directly into the scene from other Blender files.

We can create, edit, use, and share our assets with this device.

We can turn the Timeline at the bottom into an Asset Browser Editor, as shown in Figure 3-19.

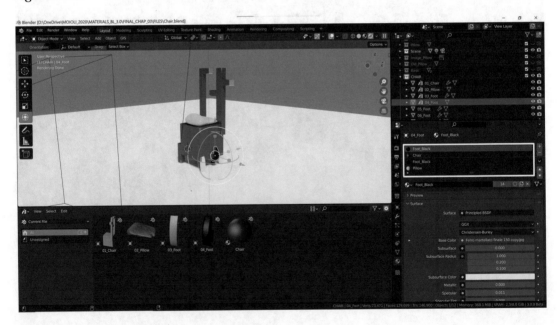

Figure 3-19. *Blender 3.0 Asset Browser*

As shown in Figure 3-19, we can directly import scenes, animations, objects, collections, shading, images and sounds, environments, and others.

To insert a material, click the Active Material Index of the Material Properties, highlighted in the white box in Figure 3-19; then right-click and choose Mark Asset. Then, we have added the material to the Asset Browser Editor.

Instead, if we want to add an object, we must select it in the Outliner Properties, right-click its name, and select Mark as Asset.

To put the asset in the default library and have it available whenever needed in Blender, we only need to save it from the main menu with File ➤ Save Copy in the Default Asset Library.

We can choose to add the asset in the Current File or in the User Library.

We can define asset libraries in the path File ➤ User Preferences ➤ File Paths ➤ Asset Libraries tab. Here we can create new libraries by clicking on the Plus button, and assigning them a Name and a Path.

Then, from the Asset Browser, we can insert every type of object from our libraries directly in the scene by dragging and dropping it in the 3D viewport.

If we want to insert three-dimensional objects, we snap them directly on the surface we want to put them.

With this tool, we can quickly reuse our content or any other object by dragging and dropping the content from the Asset Browser to the 3D view. It is a handy feature provided in Blender 3.0.

An example of these libraries is BlenderKit, an online database of materials, brushes, add-ons, and models. BlenderKit is an add-on that allows us to import objects or upload them directly from the Internet with an interface located in 3D view, as in Figure 3-20.

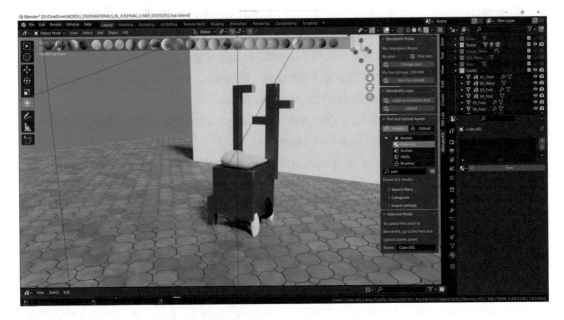

Figure 3-20. *The BlenderKit add-on*

Some materials, brushes, and three-dimensional objects are free, while the rest is for a fee. Currently, there is a library of about 13,500 assets available at https://www. blenderkit.com/.

It was for a long time an internal Blender add-on, but the Blender Foundation did not include it in Blender 3.0. We can download the add-on from https://www. blenderkit.com/get-blenderkit/ and follow the installation instructions on the site.

After activating it in the User Preferences of Blender (Preferences ➤ Add-ons ➤ 3DView: BlenderKit online asset library), we need to create an account. Then we can click Login in BlenderKit Login on the Sidebar directly in Blender or log in from the BlenderKit website.

We have learned how to create and import objects, materials, and textures so far. Then, to add realism and credibility to our architectures, we populate the scene and learn how to create characters that can be animated to make movies or interactive virtual environments.

Character Modeling for Architecture

To make realistic architectural scenarios, we must populate them by inserting people.

Character modeling is a technique for creating virtual human beings. With Blender, we can create digital characters, and it also provides many tools to rig and animate them. But, if we want to make our characters directly in Blender, we must learn how to model them somehow; also we have to create an armature, associate the mesh, and then animate it. All this takes a great deal of time.

Instead, we can quickly make a human being in Make Human, import it directly into Blender, and animate it if necessary.

There is also MB-Lab, another Blender add-on to create characters we can download from `https://github.com/animate1978/MB-Lab`. For this plug-in, we can also find a collection of clothing assets here: `https://github.com/animate1978/MB-Lab-DemoAssets`.

In this book, we will learn how to use Make Human, which is easy, free, and open source and allows us to create an almost infinite number of three-dimensional virtual human beings that we can then import directly into Blender.

Modeling a Character with Make Human

Make Human is integrated with Blender effectively.

In Make Human, we give birth to human beings and modify them. Then we can import these models directly into Blender via the MHX2 format with these easy steps:

1. First, download the installer of Make Human from `http://www.makehumancommunity.org/content/downloads.html` and install it.

2. Create a human and modify it.

3. In the Blender User Preferences, activate the plug-in to import the human directly from Make Human. You can download the add-on to connect the two software from `http://www.makehumancommunity.org/content/plugins.html`.

4. Finally, enable "Accept connections" on the Community tab in Make Human, as shown in Figure 3-21.

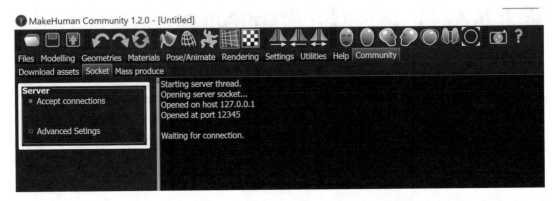

Figure 3-21. *Enabling "Accept connections" in Make Human*

5. In the Make Human interface in Blender, click Import Human, and you will see your Make Human character appearing in Blender.

We can also export from Make Human to Collada (Dae) or Stereolithography (Stl). Then import the file inside Blender from the main menu by selecting Import in the Topbar.

When creating the character in Make Human, we must not forget to add the skeleton; otherwise, we couldn't animate our character.

In Exercise 3 of this chapter, we will see how to create characters in Make Human and import them into Blender.

This section has populated our scenes in Blender through Make Human.

Now we practice the concepts developed so far by performing some exercises and adding elements to our project.

Exercises: Creating an Environment

We will continue with the practical training started in the second chapter by modeling more complex objects and preparing an environment to exhibit them more effectively.

We have developed these exercises with what we believe are methods used in the industry as best practices. However, obviously the users can still utilize other methods for creating objects, environment elements, etc.

Exercise 3: Modeling a Living Room

Let's start getting familiar with architectural spaces by modeling a living room. This way, we will learn how to model architectural spaces. The idea is to import the required reference image drawing that contains the plan view. Then we choose one reference dimension from the plan and create one plane having the size of that particular reference dimension.

After that, we scale the drawing image to match the plane's size.

This way, we will achieve the drawing size matching precisely with the Blender selected units. After that, we use the Extrude commands in X and Y directions to create an exact layout plan.

Finally, we can extend the z-axis plan to build the wall structure. Then we can use the already installed Add-on, Archimesh, to create windows and doors.

A starting example in the `LivingRoom.blend` file is attached to the book.

Creating the Walls

First, we import a reference drawing. Then we start to build the architectural structure: walls, floor, windows, doors, and ceiling.

1. Open Blender, delete the default cube, and save the file as `LivingRoom` in the computer's hard disk.

2. In the Properties Editor's Scene Properties, go to the Units panel, and make sure Unit System is set to Metric and Length is set to Meters.

3. Select the camera and light, create a new collection, press M, select New Collection, and rename it as **Scene**. The camera and light will be located directly in this collection.

4. In the Outliner Editor in the upper-right corner of the interface, click the icon Hide in Viewport next to the Scene collection; in this way, you hide in 3D view the objects you don't need during modeling.

5. Select the second collection and rename it **Walls**.

    It is vital to create collections and store objects in an orderly
    manner to easily find them in the Outliner. In this exercise, there
    are few elements, so this method is not extremely useful. Still, it's
    good to use it when managing many objects and collections.

6. Import the drawing of the room you want to make: press Shift+A
    ➤ Image ➤ Reference to import the image.

    You can also go to the top orthographic view by pressing 7 on the
    Numpad and dragging and dropping the image directly into the
    viewport to align it with the top view.

    The drawing in Figure 3-22 will be the reference for modeling the
    living room.

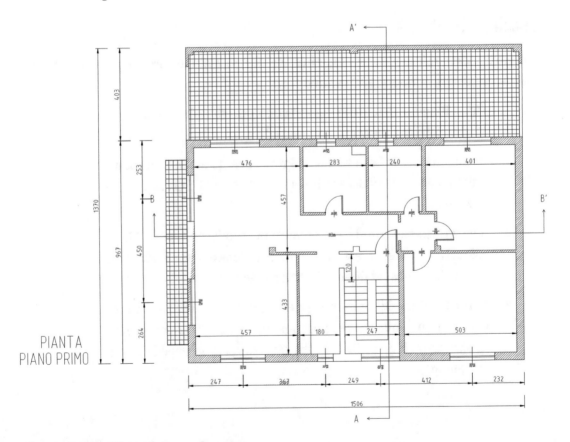

Figure 3-22. *The reference drawing*

7. Create a plane and name it **Wall**.

   Give it the measure of a drawing element. In this example, you can choose a 200-centimeter window and keep the default Plane measure of 2 meters.

8. With the plane selected, go to Edit mode, click the arrow next to the Show Overlays button, and select the Edge Length box in the Measurement panel. This way, when you model, you can see the measurements of the selected edges in real time in 3D view in Edit mode.

9. Back to Object mode, change the plane display in the wireframe by pressing Z ➤ Wireframe, or click the Toggle X-Ray button in the 3D view header to activate it. In this way, the plane becomes transparent, and you can see the drawing below and keep it as a reference for modeling.

10. Move the plane to the center of the window frame. Move the cursor at the plane's center by clicking Object ➤ Snap ➤ Cursor to Selected.

    Next, choose the 3D cursor in the Transform Pivot Point drop-down menu of the 3D view header.

    These operations allow you to scale the drawing corresponding with the 3D cursor to control the transformation and execute it precisely. This way, you can easily fit the plane with the window's width as in Figure 3-23 without continuously moving and zooming the view.

11. Select the drawing, press S, and change the size of the picture until it matches the cube's width, as in Figure 3-23.

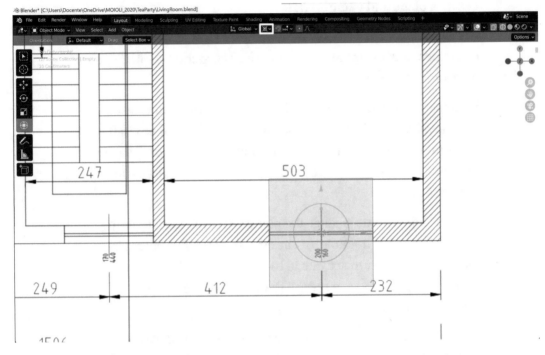

Figure 3-23. *Resizing the drawing*

There is a correspondence between reality, the actual drawing dimensions, and the model we create.

12. Return to Median Point in the Transform Pivot Point drop-down menu of the 3D view header.

13. Put the plane back in solid view by typing Z ➤ Solid; then move the plane in the top-left corner between two walls and give it the size of a pillar (0.33 by 0.33 meters). You can do this by changing the X and Y Dimensions values of the same panel of the Transform window in the Sidebar. Then apply the scale of the plane (press Ctrl+A and then select Scale).

14. Start creating the perimeter walls of the room. First, go to Edit mode and select the two bottom vertices of the plane (B ➤ LMB drag and drop on the vertices), and extrude them with the E key (E ➤ Y ➤ 1.20) to create the first part of the perimeter walls. Extrude again (E ➤ Y ➤ 2) to get the window's width.

You can extrude precisely by pressing Ctrl+Shift for extrusions of 1 centimeter and Ctrl for extrusions of 10 centimeters. To see the correspondence with the drawing, click Z and switch from the solid view to the wireframe view, as Figure 3-24.

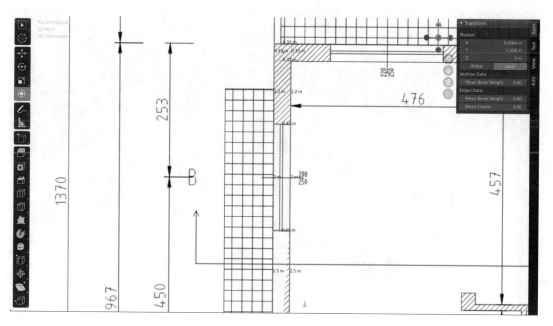

Figure 3-24. *Starting to define the perimeter walls*

15. Go on extruding until you get the whole perimeter of the room.

    Use the formula E ➤ X ➤ extrusion value to obtain the x-axis extrusion.

16. Always remember to press Alt+A or left-click a space on the viewport to deselect everything before selecting the two vertices to extrude.

17. Check the correctness of the measurement by selecting all the walls by clicking the A button. Then check the dimensions of the reference drawing with those displayed on the model.

18.   Then start to extrude on the z-axis to construct the vertical walls; select all the perimeter excluding the French windows openings, as in Figure 3-25, and press E ➤ Z ➤ 0.9 to extrude up to the windowsill height.

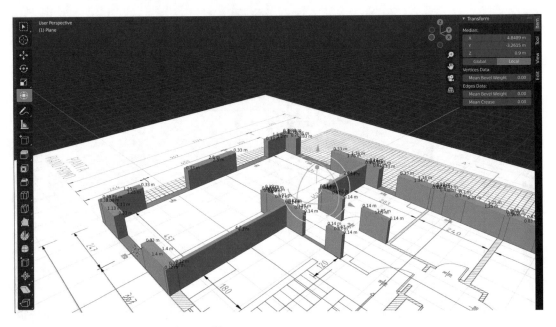

Figure 3-25.   *Extruding the walls*

19.   Now create spaces for the 2.5-meter-high French doors by extruding another 160 centimeters (E ➤ Z ➤ 1.6). Then extrude 0.5 meters more to obtain the total height of the ceiling that is 3 meters.

20.   Delete the faces of the spaces above the French windows to build architraves by selecting them and pressing X ➤ Faces. Then create the window beam of the French windows, as shown in Figure 3-26.

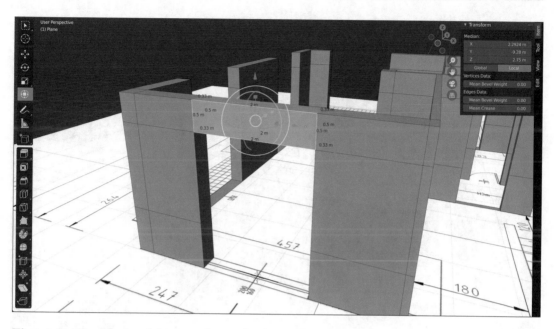

Figure 3-26. *The architrave above the French window*

To do this, go to edge selection mode by pressing 2; select the two top-side wall loop cuts of the architrave with Alt+LMB to choose the first one and Shift+Alt+LMB to add the second one to the selection. Next, click the Bridge Edge Loops button from the 3D view header menu's edge or press Ctrl+E and select Bridge Edge Loops.

Now generate the ceiling and the floor. First, select in Edit mode a plane, duplicate it (Shift+D), separate it from the rest of the mesh by typing P for the Separate tool, and click Selection. Then go to Object mode and select the new object. Next, enter Edit mode's Vertex Select (pressing Tab and then 1) and activate Snap to Vertex in the 3D view header. Next, create the room ceiling by selecting one vertex at a time and building a plane corresponding to the room's perimeter, as shown in Figure 3-27.

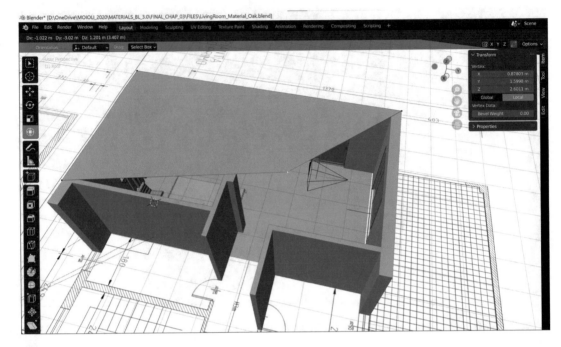

Figure 3-27. *Sizing the ceiling*

Starting from this plane, build the room's ceiling. Click 3 to go to Face select and select the face just created and extrude it by 20 centimeters on the z-axis (E ➤ Z ➤ 0.2).

When creating new faces in Edit mode, we must verify that their perpendiculars point in the right direction, i.e., toward the outside of the object. Otherwise, the faces remain invisible and can create problems with the object visualization in the 3D Viewport and the render. To verify the normals' right direction, in Edit mode, press A, select all the faces, and select Display Normals by opening the Viewport Overlays window with the Overlays button in the 3D view header. Next, press Shift+N to activate the Recalculate Normals tool to recalculate the normals. Then, check that all the blue lines come out from the faces of the created polygon.

21. Finally, create the floor of the room by copying the ceiling: return to Object mode, duplicate the polygon, and snap it to the base of the wall perimeter.

After building the structure of the walls, we will now create the windows and the French windows using the Archimesh add-on that allows us to construct different architectural elements and adapt them to the dimensions of our models through parametric adjustment.

Creating the Windows

As we saw earlier, we can activate some tools from the User Preferences that facilitate and speed up the work in Blender. One of these is Archimesh, with which we will now proceed to create windows and doors for our interior.

In addition, with Archimesh, we can easily insert other architectural elements such as stairs, roofs, books, etc.

1. Activate Archimesh in the User Preferences (Edit ➤ Preferences ➤ Add-ons ➤ Archimesh). Now you can add objects from the add window by pressing Shift+A and selecting Mesh ➤ Archimesh, and you can edit them in 3D View in the Sidebar and select Create ➤ Archimesh.

2. Select the Walls object and hide everything else by pressing Shift+H.

Creating Windows

Follow these steps to create windows:

1. Go to Edit mode, go to Face select by pressing 3, and then LMB-click the lower horizontal face of the window space.

    From the header menu, select Mesh ➤ Snap ➤ Cursor to Selected to place the cursor in the center of the selected face of the window.

    In this way, you indicate to Blender the place to put it.

2. Now create the windows. Go back to Object mode, press Shift+A, and select Mesh ➤ Archimesh ➤ Panel Window. Create a window that is 250 x 200 and adapt it to the window space, which is 220 x 160 centimeters.

Click Create in the Sidebar. This opens the Archimesh panel. Then slide down the Sidebar to the Window Panel section and adjust the dimensions in Figure 3-28.

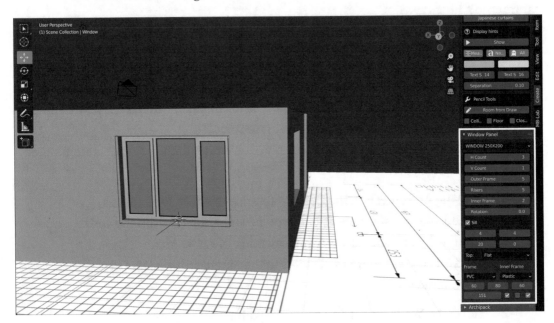

Figure 3-28. *The Window Panel section*

Adjust the window size to the window compartment. Finally, press 1 on the Numpad to go to the front orthogonal view and, selecting Window_Group in the Outliner, align the window to the compartment space.

Creating French Windows

Then, with the same method, create the three French windows. Follow these steps:

1. Go back to Object mode, press Shift+A and select Mesh ➤ Archimesh ➤ Rail Window, and create the window door.

   Create the first one measuring 200 x 250 centimeters. Rotate it in the rotation panel 90 degrees to adapt it to the orientation of the wall and then adapt its measurements to the compartment.

2. Duplicate it and move to the second compartment with the same dimensions.

3. Finally, press Alt+H to make all the objects reappear in 3D view.

The objects created by Archimesh already have essential Cycles materials that later we can improve.

For example, in the windows, we have different materials such as glass, window frames, windowsill, etc.

We can see the result in Eevee after applying some simple plaster and floor materials, as shown in Figure 3-29.

Figure 3-29. *The architectural structure with the windows rendered with Eevee*

We've completed the architectural structure and rendered it with Eevee; now, let's start furnishing and populating the room.

Importing Furniture

Now let's set interior design for the living room, as we learned earlier in the chapter. Again, we have found numerous furniture objects in the 3DS format.

First, we must import these files into Blender 2.79 because version 3.0 does not directly support importation from 3D Studio.

So we import the file into Blender 2.79. Then we copy with Ctrl+C and paste it with Ctrl+V into the 3.0 version.

But let's see how to do it precisely.

1. Install the Blender 2.79b version for your operating system from
    `https://download.blender.org/release/Blender2.79/` and
    open it.

    Then download a file of the furniture from the Internet. For
    example, we have downloaded the Barcelona Pavilion chair by
    Mies Van Der Rohe from Archive 3D. You can download it from
    `https://archive3d.net/?a=download&id=ff63820f`.

2. Download the file and then unzip it.

3. Open Blender 2.79; delete the default cube, light, and camera; and
    import `Chair.3DS` (File ➤ Import ➤ 3D Studio 3Ds).

    In this way, Blender should import the object with materials
    and textures. If not, refer to Chapter 4 to create the two chair's
    materials.

4. Next, select all the chair elements with A and copy with Ctrl+C,
    paste them with Ctrl+V into a Blender 3.0 file, and name it
    BarcelonaChair.

5. Delete the default cube, light, and camera; select the horizontal
    chair's cushion; and press A to select all the elements that make
    up the chair.

    Next, press Ctrl+J and combine them into a single object. Then
    delete $$$DUMMY.Group02 in the Outliner.

6. Center the object's origin on the geometry by selecting the
    chair and choosing Geometry to Origin from Set Origin in the
    Object menu.

7. Finally, let's scale the armchair. The height is 80 centimeters:
    modify the Z dimension in 0.8 meters from the Sidebar ➤
    Transform ➤ Dimensions.

Copy the Scale value of the z-axis with Ctrl+C and paste it with Ctrl+V in the Scale values of width and depth for the x-axis and y-axis. Apply the scale by pressing Ctrl+A and Scale and change the Location values of X, Y, and Z to 0.

8. Then import the chair in the LivingRoom file with File ➤ Append ➤ BarcelonaChair ➤ Object ➤ Mesh03 and place it where you want.

9. You can download and import the sofa, a carpet, and a curtain from the same site and place them in the scene.

After placing the furniture, we also insert some figures in the scene.

Exercise 4: Populating Our Environment

This exercise will deepen the connection between Blender and Make Human for us and show how to create different characters in Make Human to export to Blender. There are some examples of characters in the Humans.blend file accompanying the book.

First, let's take a look at the main features. A few simple elements in Make Human interface allow us to modify the characters. For example, we adjust the principal characteristics of our figure in the Main panel of the Modeling menu: gender, age, muscle, weight, height, etc.

In the other panels of the Modeling menu, we can modify the characteristics and measures of the body.

We add clothes or other body parts in the Geometries menu, such as eyes, hair, etc. We already have some default items, and we can search for many more in the Community menu.

In the Materials menu, we can change the skin and eyes of the character. Instead, through the Pose/Animate menu, we can add an armature for animation. We can find various types of them: from the simplest with 31 bones to the most sophisticated with 163 bones that allow us to animate the fingers and toes.

Now let's see how to connect Make Human with Blender.

1. Download the release of Make Human from `http://www.makehumancommunity.org/content/makehuman_120.html`.

2. Unzip it into a new folder.

3. Open Make Human. Create a human and modify it as you like.

4. In the Make Human Community menu, in the Socket window, activate Accept Connections.

5. Open Blender, create a file, and name it **Humans**.

    Then from the Edit item in the main menu, open the User Preferences and activate the Make Human plug-in MakeHuman: MH Community from the Add-ons window.

6. From now on, you can create your characters in MH and import them directly into Blender by opening the MakeHuman window in the Sidebar on the right side of 3D view and clicking "Import human" and Sync with MH, as shown in Figure 3-30.

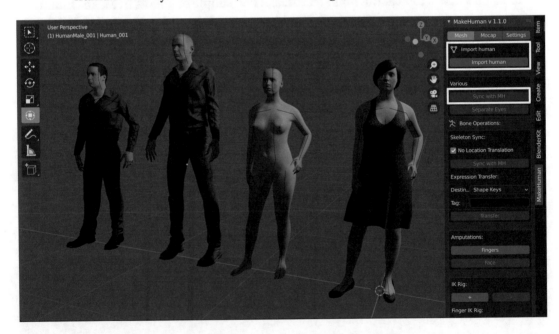

Figure 3-30. *Characters imported directly from Make Human*

Another way to import virtual human beings from Make Human to Blender is to export files in Collada or Stereolithography format and import them directly into Blender. When we export the file in Collada, we create the mesh, a .dae file, and a folder with the textures that allow us excellent flexibility in controlling the materials.

7. Populate your project's scene by inserting some human figures, getting the effect in Figure 3-31.

Figure 3-31. *The living room with imported furniture, humans, and raw materials*

In Figure 3-31, we see the objects with elementary materials, the lights, and the shading of the 3D Viewport set to Rendered with the Cycles render engine.

After furnishing and populating the scene, we begin to model one of the objects we have designed to insert into the environment.

Exercise 5: Modeling a Chair

We are now beginning to create a customized object for interior design: an artist's chair by Albertini and Moioli. This exercise will show how inorganic and organic modeling techniques work. We will learn to model a chair composed from a geometric structure and one organic pillow, experimenting with two different kinds of modeling.

Again, you can model a chair with other modeling methodology if you like. However, the final model should look the same as we intended, and it may be helpful in future exercises in upcoming chapters.

You can find an example of the chair in the RedChair.blend file that comes with the book.

Modeling the Chair Structure

Let's begin to shape the chair's structure, starting from the base cube, extruding it, and dividing it until obtaining the final result.

1. Prepare the scene as in the previous exercises and save the file as RedChair.

2. Choose Metric as the unit system and Meters as the length in the Units box of the Scene Properties window.

3. Select the camera and light, press M and select New Collection, create a new collection, and rename it **Scene**. You have just located these objects on this collection.

4. Create a plane, scale it five times (S ➤ 5), create a cube, and give it the dimensions of 7 x 3 x 0.2 meters. Align the lower base of the cube with the plane. Then, put them in the Scene collection. You just created a simple environment with the floor and the back wall.

5. Hide this collection with the button Hide in Viewport in the Outliner Editor.

6. Rename the other collection **Chair** and keep the default cube on this collection.

7. Import the reference image for the chair into the front view using the same method as the previous exercises. Create a collection, name it **ChairReference**, and put the picture on it.

8. Select the default cube and set its size to 36 x 36 x 36 centimeters. Then press Ctrl+A and select Scale to apply the transformation.

    Change the name of the cube to **Structure** in the Outliner Editor. Then, adapt the reference picture to the cube measurements from the front view by scaling it until it coincides with the Structure object.

9. Go to Edit mode, select the cube, and subdivide it by right-clicking. Then, in the bottom-left window, choose 5 as the value for Number of Cuts to divide each cube's face into six faces of 6 x 6 centimeters.

10. Then start creating the left leg of the chair. In Edit mode, select the bottom two faces on the cube's left side and extrude them 6 centimeters on the x-axis (E ➤ X ➤ -0.06).

11. Select the lower face of the newly extruded part, extrude it down 12 centimeters on the z-axis (E ➤ Z ➤ -0.12), and then divide it in two (LMB ➤ Subdivide).

12. Extrude the two elements of the backrest by 60 centimeters. So, select the right and left faces and extrude them (E ➤ Z ➤ 0.6).

13. Divide them into 10 squares to maintain a periodic structure (LMB ➤ Subdivide ➤ 9).

14. Then extrude the two internal horizontal structures of the backrest, as shown in Figure 3-32, by pressing E ➤ X ➤ 0.12 to extrude and then Ctrl+R to divide.

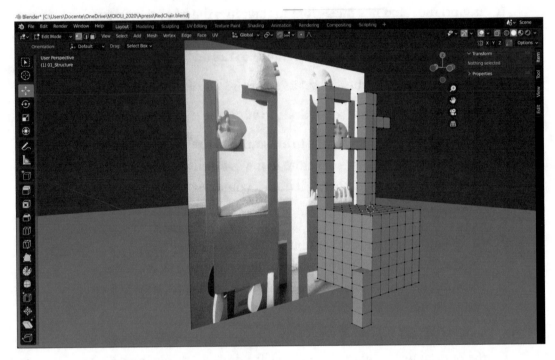

Figure 3-32. *The structure of the chair*

15. Finally, add a Bevel modifier to the newly created structure and change from Offset to Percent, setting Width Percent to 10%, Segments Values to 3, and Profile 0.5. In this way, the corners of the structure become smoother.

We have just built the main structure of the chair. Now we see how to shape the black and yellow feet that hold it up at the base.

Modeling of the Chair Feet

To shape the chair feet, we follow the shapes of the reference image we imported.

1. Select the chair structure; enter Edit mode.

2. Select three vertices at the bottom right and duplicate them (Shift+D ➤ Esc); then separate them from the original object (P ➤ Selection).

3. In the Outliner, rename this new object **Foot**.

4. Go to Object mode, and select the Foot object. Then press Tab to enter Edit mode for the Foot object. Next, go to vertex select and extrude the vertices in the front orthographic view, as shown in Figure 3-33.

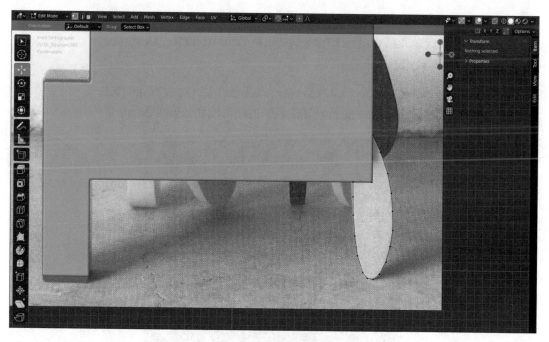

Figure 3-33. *The vertices of the contour of the chair foot*

Draw the entire foot profile by extruding the vertices, following the shape in Figure 3-33. Finally, select the last 2 Vertices and click F to close the curve.

5. Select the profile and extrude it on the y-axis. Then subdivide it in two in thickness with Ctrl+R.

6. Then, with Alt+LMB, select the frontal loop cut and press F to create the frontal surface; repeat the same operation to make the foot's back face.

7. Edit the Bevel modifier using Offset 0.1, Segments 3, and Profile 0.5. right-click the object and select Shade Smooth.

8. From the Object item in the 3D view Header menu, click Set Origin ➤ Origin to Geometry. Then give it a material and change only the color in yellow from the Properties Editor ➤ Material ➤ Base Color.

9. Now model all other feet in the same way. You can also copy the one you created and edit its vertices in Edit mode following the different profiles.

10. Finally, select all the chair components, create a new collection, call it **CHAIR**, and rename all the elements in Figure 3-34.

Figure 3-34. *The collections*

This operation is essential to efficiently managing the chair as a single object to display, modify, import, and export it easily. For example, when we create the pillow, we add it to the list, merely selecting it, pressing M and then clicking the name of the CHAIR collection to add it.

Now, let's model the chair cushion.

Modeling the Pillow

To create the pillow, we add a circle (press Shift+A and select Mesh ➤ Circle) and modify it in Edit mode; finally, refine the shape with the sculpting tools.

1. Import the reference images in the front and top views, align them, and make them coincide with the size of the model of the chair's seating so that the cushion can fit inside the chair's surface. With the two imported images selected, create a new collection, and call it **PillowReference**.

2. Then create a circle with 32 vertices, press M in the window that opens, click New Collection, and call it **Pillow**.

3. Go to Object mode and add to Pillow a Subdivision Surface modifier with values of 2 for Render and Viewport and 3 for Quality to smooth the shape's edges.

4. Start modifying the circle in Edit mode by scaling it in the proportions of the top image. Then move the vertices and adapt them to the pillow, as shown from the top in Figure 3-35.

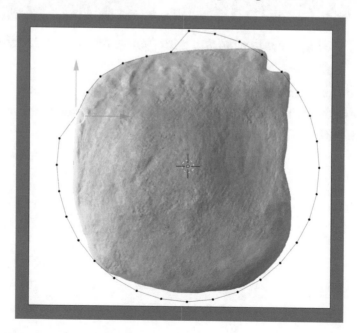

Figure 3-35. *Creating the basic pillow contour*

5. Extrude the profile twice by selecting the loop cut and pressing
    E ➤ Esc and then scaling with S the extruded loop as shown in
    Figure 3-36.

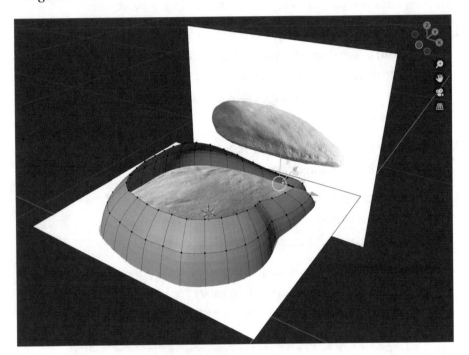

Figure 3-36. *Creating the pillow shape with loop extrusion and scaling*

6. Extrude two more times above and two below, and close the
    shape by selecting the loop cuts and clicking F. You get the form in
    Figure 3-37.

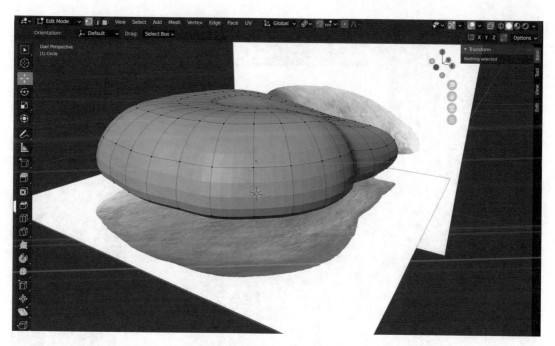

Figure 3-37. *The closed shape of the pillow*

7. Apply the Subdivision Surface modifier.

8. Go to Sculpt mode, set Voxel Size to 0.1 meters, and click the Remesh button at the top right of the 3D window to create a uniform cushion geometry, as in Figure 3-38.

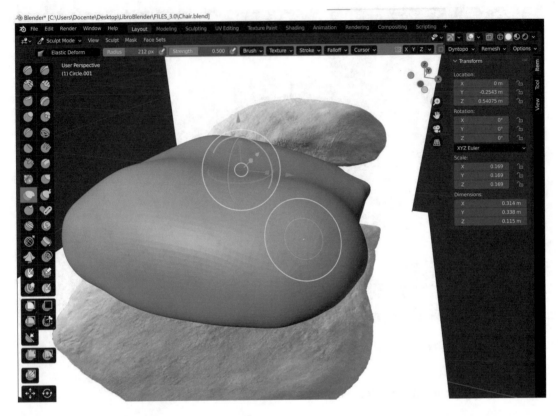

Figure 3-38. *The pillow remeshed shape*

9. Start to model with the Inflate tool with a Radius of 280 and a Strength of 0.6, inflating with the brush and deflating with Ctrl+LMB.

10. Use a Smooth brush to smooth out overly accentuated shapes and Flatten to flatten them.

11. Redo the remesh to redefine a tidier geometry with a lower Voxel Size resolution. Then, set Shade Smooth in Object mode, and apply another Subdivision Surface modifier to get a more defined surface.

12. Give the last touches with Pinch, Inflate, and Smooth. Finally, the cushion is ready; you can see the finished chair in Figure 3-39.

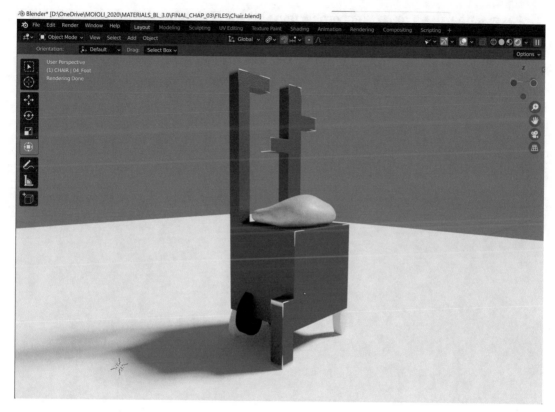

Figure 3-39. *The red chair*

We have created a virtual copy of the real chair, and we can create several different duplicates. Thus, this method allows us to make endless versions of our objects.

Summary

In this chapter, we learned about architectural modeling. The first section taught precision drawing, importing CAD and 3DS format into Blender, and installing exciting add-ons. Then we dealt with procedural and parametrical modeling and character modeling.

All this helped us set up an architectural scene in Exercise 3, populate it with some characters in Exercise 4, and create a custom object to insert in Exercise 5.

It is essential to set the correct proportions in virtual architecture to give maximum authenticity to our scenes.

The next chapter will explain how to give more realism to our scenes by creating nodal materials, setting lighting, and developing realistic environments for our designed objects.

CHAPTER 4

Understanding Materials, Lighting, and World Settings

This chapter will explain how to make materials and textures, assign them to objects, and adequately illuminate the scene to create the environment.

First, we will build a node material; second, we will assign the textures, setting the color and other physical characteristics such as reflection, specularity, and roughness. To get a correct distribution of the textures on the objects, we must perform UV unwrapping and choose the mapping based on the object's shape. So we will add the lights, adjust the shadows, and adapt the world settings. Finally, we will position the cameras to take shots.

In this chapter, we're going to cover the following main topics:

- Nodes and material nodes

- Textures

- UV mapping and unwrapping

- Lights and shadows

- Cameras

- The world settings: Sky Texture and Environment Texture

We will create materials and develop realistic scenes and environments for our objects in the exercises.

© Gianpiero Moioli 2022
G. Moioli, *Introduction to Blender 3.0*, https://doi.org/10.1007/978-1-4842-7954-0_4

Learning Nodes and Material Nodes

We studied Blender's interface and modeling techniques in the previous chapters. Now we will delve into how to set up materials, lights, and environment.

The nodal system is fundamental because it allows maximum flexibility and results. Eevee and Cycles use nodal materials.

Since the 2.8 version launch, the Blender Foundation has abandoned the Blender render engine because it was not compatible with materials created with the node-based system.

As we have seen in the previous chapter, in Blender, there is also a nodal creation system for textures, objects, animations, and much more. In addition, the Blender Foundation has big plans to extend the Blender node system.

As we just explained in Chapter 3, each node applies certain transformations to the material within a nodal system. So, we can obtain sophisticated, complex, and adaptable effects by creating a substance with different nodes.

Each node represents a chain link from left to right, transforming the final result without breaking the general system's structure. Each subsequent node acts on the result affected by the previous one, creating a chain that we can change or extend.

This section shows the Blender tools to work on nodes. In this way, we can obtain more complex and easily controllable materials. In particular, PBR Materials compose the new photorealistic substances and are spreading more and more in computer graphics.

PBR Materials

PBR stands for "physically-based rendering," a shading and rendering methodology that considers how light interacts with surfaces and tries to reproduce reality as accurately as possible with a physical simulation.

PBR materials use realistic shading and lighting models to represent real-world materials as accurately as possible.

In the exercises of this chapter, we will practically realize both kinds of materials: the traditional ones in Exercise 6, the new PBR materials in Exercises 7, and 8.

Also, Blender contains a system to paint textures directly on the object: the Texture Paint Mode, which we will learn about in Chapter 5.

First, however, there are some theoretical concepts that we need to understand to use these materials more efficiently.

We will start with the Light Ray model.

The Light Ray Model

The interaction between light and matter creates the appearance of the objects around us. But the concept is more complicated than it might seem. Many variables influence the path of the light rays, from diffusion to reflection and from transparency to subsurface scattering.

Mathematical models can easily define the interaction of light and material.

We consider the light ray model.

This model involves two different behaviors for metallic and nonconductive materials.

Diffusion and Reflection

These two different types of materials result in opposite reactions when light meets the surface of an object. Diffusion and Reflection are the two main components of the Light Ray model.

In computer graphics, in software like Blender, the Diffuse node represents the diffusion, and the Glossy node embodies the reflection; they are the diffuse and specular light, respectively.

A ray of light in a homogeneous transparent medium like the air has a straight trajectory. Still, when it hits the object's surface, a part of the light is reflected in the opposite direction. However, the thing doesn't reflect all the light; a part penetrates it and spreads internally. As a result, the material absorbs the light and partially diffuses it, creating widespread object illumination.

So it is clear that Diffusion and Reflection are mutually exclusive because materials that do not reflect the light let it penetrate the object's surface and partially diffuse it internally.

Metallic materials reflect light, while nonconductors allow light to penetrate the surface, diffusing it.

Highly reflective materials diffuse little light, and, on the other hand, objects cannot be very reflective if they have high light diffusion.

This concept is the basis of PBR materials and physically based rendering.

A part of the scattered light, in some materials, bounces back to the viewer and becomes visible again. This light becomes Diffuse Light and gives rise to phenomena such as diffusion or subsurface scattering.

Let's give a closer look at another element to consider for a realistic effect with some materials: the Fresnel effect.

Fresnel

The balance between the diffuse and reflected light components in an object varies the surface's appearance. It is inversely proportional to the angle of incidence of light itself. From the physicist's name who first studied it, this effect is called the Fresnel effect.

The objects rendered using the Fresnel effect will better reflect at the edges. We regulate this effect with the Index of Refraction (IOR), which is different in each material. The IOR adjusts the specularity with the incidence of light.

Microsurface

The quality of the surface represents another essential element to understanding the behavior of the interaction between light and matter. Many areas have minor imperfections, often invisible but influence the appearance of materials. In particular, they alter the reflection and diffusion of the light.

The rougher the surface, the more it will reflect the light in a blurred and irregular way.

The Gloss, Roughness, or Smoothness mapping has a fundamental role in physically based shading because of the microsurface details.

Microsurface gloss affects the brightness of reflections, so we can add directly to the Gloss texture details that the PBR system will read.

In this way, in PBR materials, one texture contains reflectivity and microsurface details, so we no longer need a specular map.

PBR Textures

The previous short theoretical introduction will help us to understand the functions of Blender's node materials. Standard node materials and PBR materials work differently.

To create nodal PBR materials, we must first create textures. Textures give different characteristics to the materials and are applied to various channels, as we can see in Figure 4-1.

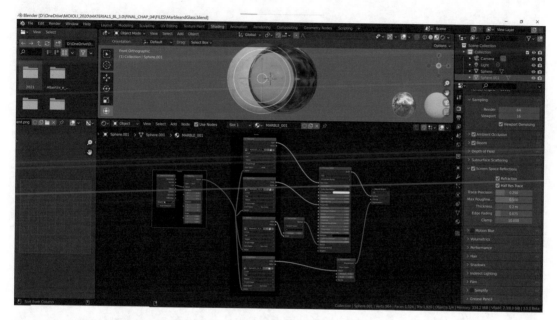

Figure 4-1. *A PBR Marble material node chain*

In Figure 4-1, we can see a Marble material made with four textures applied to four channels: Base Color, Roughness, Normal, and Displacement. These textures make the material look realistic. We can modify photographs with external software like Texturize or directly within Blender or by applying procedural textures.

There are examples of Marble and Glass node materials in the `MarbleandGlass.blend` file that accompanies this book.

Now let's see the most common textures in standard and PBR materials.

Standard Textures

Let's first look at the textures that apply to traditional materials; we mainly use three textures.

- The Diffuse texture determines the primary color.

- The Normal texture controls the relief of the surface.

- The Specular texture determines the specular effect of the material.

We can obtain many physical appearances by creating materials through the Diffuse and Glossy nodes with these three textures quickly, as we will see later in this chapter in Exercise 6.

PBR Textures

As we learned in the theoretical description for PBR materials, some textures are different and applied to other channels.

The following are the main types of textures that we use in PBR materials:

- The Diffuse, Color, or Albedo textures define the color or pattern of the substance. In Blender, we apply it to the Base Color channel of the Principled BSDF node or the color of the Diffuse node.

- The Normal texture simulates the geometry and the surface details; we can use it to add scratches or reproduce the irregularity of the surface of a substance. We use it to simulate model details for which we do not want to add geometry. It is an RGB map in which the three primary colors correspond to the spatial coordinates X, Y, and Z.

- In Blender, we apply it to the normal channel via a Normal Map node.

- We use the Metallic texture to define which parts of the material's surface have a metallic appearance. It works like a grayscale mask and tells the shader how to change the appearance of the base color.

- Roughness establishes the relationship between rough/matte and glossy/shiny characteristics through brightness.

- The Height texture creates displacement and adds depth to the object through the material.

- The Ambient Occlusion reproduces the relationship between objects and light and simulates natural shading.

There are no fixed rules for PBR materials but only the guiding principles we have just explained; for this reason, we can apply the previous textures in different ways from time to time. So, for example, we can use the textures we saw earlier in other workflows, and their names can change, but the general principle is the same.

There are mainly two methods of applying textures for PBR materials: metal/roughness and specular/glossiness. Let's look at their characteristics.

Metal/Roughness vs. Specular/Glossiness

The two most essential workflows for PBR materials are metal/roughness and specular/glossiness.

To perform the procedure with the Metalness-based shader system, we have to use certain textures in particular:

- The Metalness map controls the variables of dielectric surfaces and metals.

- The Roughness texture regulates the effects of the reflection's sharpness.

To apply the Specular-based shader system instead, we need different textures:

- The Specular map controls the impact of reflection color.

- The Glossiness texture allows us to modify the reflection sharpness. For example, in Cycles, we use Roughness, the inverse of glossiness.

There are other methods in addition to these. However, these two are the most functional and interchangeable.

These two methods are represented in Blender by the Principled BSDF and Specular BSDF nodes, respectively.

As mentioned, we will see the practical applications of this theory in the exercises in the second part of this chapter. In Exercise 7, we will create textures for our surfaces, applying the principles studied in this section. By doing this, we will expand our research on materials and textures using image editing and digital painting with open source software. One of the objectives of this book is to try to use mostly free and open source tools.

In this first section, we learned about the theory behind the Light Ray model. In the next section, we will study nodal materials.

Understanding Material Nodes

There are many material nodes and several add-ons that can help us manage them.

Blender developers have grouped material nodes into ten categories according to functions. We will look at all of these nodes later in this section.

First, let's look at the node sets for rendering and compositing. There are three groups of nodes:

- The Material nodes are for the visualization of objects and three-dimensional environments. We can use them to create sophisticated photorealistic materials.

- Texture nodes allow us to build and edit the textures for our materials.

- Finally, Compositing nodes allow us to put two or more photographs or videos together and edit the whole sequence altogether.

These three groups of nodes enable us to create materials and textures in post-production by modifying rendered images flexibly and effectively through node chains.

Each of these nodal systems has its own interface: Shader Editor, Texture Node Editor, and Compositor. We will learn about all three in the following sections and throughout the book.

Material Nodes

We can assign nodal materials and allocate many different substances to one object, applying them at a subobject level.

The materials manage the appearance of the objects and define the elements that characterize their look by controlling the way they react to light and the different physical characteristics, from color to transparency, etc.

We can straightforwardly produce a great variety of different materials, from metal to plastic, glass, and leather, with these tools.

In Blender 3.0, materials are now exclusively nodal. Also, there are nodes expressly dedicated to creating PBR materials as the Principled BSDF, Principled Hair, Principled Volume shaders, etc.

With a few exceptions, most material nodes work similarly with Eevee and Cycles.

Nodes are interfaces containing parts of code in the node editor. We can connect them via sockets, as we can see in the main bottom window in Figure 4-2.

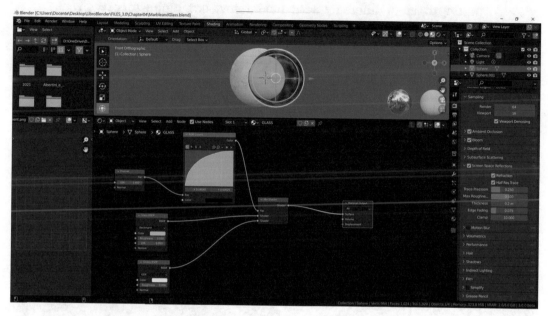

Figure 4-2. *A PBR glass material*

Figure 4-2 shows a glass nodal material made with some of the nodes that we will study in a moment.

However, to effectively create materials, we must use UV editing to properly apply the textures to objects. We will see how to proceed with this operation in the next section of this chapter. In the meantime, let's see how to use nodal materials.

Introducing the Editors

In Blender 3.0, all elements, from geometry to materials, lights, etc., can be defined by nodal systems. The material nodal system is one of them.

This system has nearly the same settings in Eevee and Cycles.

There was only one node editor in the software versions before 2.8 to manage nodes of any kind; now, there are different editor types for creating substances: the shader, texture, and compositor.

- We use the Shader Editor to create and modify materials. However, as we have said, the current internal renderers of Blender, Eevee, and Cycles use nodal materials only.

- With the Texture Editor, we can realize procedural textures; it is a node-based texture generation system that creates new textures by putting together different nodes that interact, combining them with colors and patterns.

- With the Compositor Editor, we edit images and movies and improve them in post-production.

We have seen how to use the editors; now, let's study the material characteristics and the material Properties Editor, starting from the shading workspace.

Introducing the Shading Workspace

To create node materials, we can use the Shading workspace.

We can control and modify the materials from the Shader Editor and the Material Properties of the Properties Editor, both present in the Shading workspace, as shown in Figure 4-3.

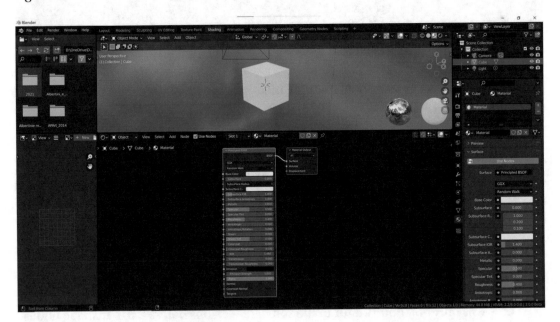

Figure 4-3. *The Shading workspace*

In Figure 4-3, we see the Shading workspace. It contains two main horizontal windows: the top 3D Viewport and the bottom Shader Editor.

Then, there are two vertical windows on the right, the Outliner and the Properties Editor, and two on the left: a file browser at the top and an image editor at the bottom.

The 3D Viewport is in material preview shading mode to show the materials' final aspect interactively; the Shader Editor at the bottom has the default Principled BSDF node that allows us to create many different materials and the Output node to visualize the final result.

Understanding the Material Properties Editor

We find the Material Properties in the Properties Editor.

Here we can add a substance to an object by clicking the New button or clicking the arrow on its left to assign an existing material to the selected entity.

To import materials from another Blender file, we must first click the Topbar and select File ➤ Append and load the file from the material file folder that opens.

In Blender 3.0, we can also do it with the Asset Browser, as shown in the Asset Libraries as covered in Chapter 3.

After importing the material, we drag and drop it from the Asset Browser or select it in the Material Properties box framed in white in Figure 4-4.

Figure 4-4. *The Material Properties button for materials*

Clicking New will activate all the windows to modify the material. Then we go to the Shader Editor to adjust it directly with nodes or to the material Properties Editor, as shown in Figure 4-5.

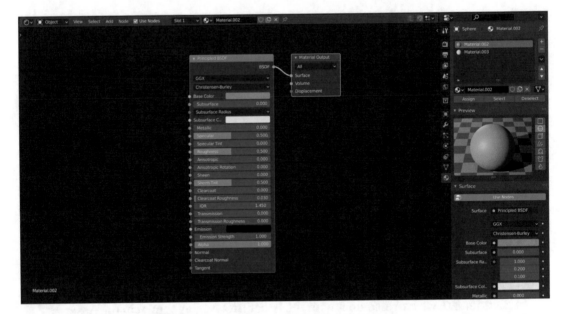

Figure 4-5. *The Shader Editor and the Material Properties*

In Figure 4-5, we can see the Principled BDSF and Material Output nodes with some basic parameters already assigned when creating new materials.

We find many of the same Material Properties buttons inside the Shader Editor nodes and Material Properties: base color, subsurface, etc.

In the Material Properties, on the right of the window, we can find many tools to create and edit nodal materials:

- There is a Material slot. We need more than one slot to add more materials to the same object. We add and remove them with the + or – buttons on the right of the window.

- A button on the right of the name of the current material allow us to choose it for the selected object.

- There is a Preview window that shows the final appearance of the material.

- The Surface window, the most crucial panel, contains many buttons with the same functions in the Shader Editor, including the same features.

- The Volume panel controls the volumetric effects.

- The Settings panel contains essential functions to activate the Refraction and Translucency options in the material.

- The Viewport Display controls display the material in 3D view.

- Finally, use Custom Properties to add and modify customization.

In the Material Properties, we can also add different materials to different parts of a single object by proceeding as follows:

- We select the object and create a new slot in the Material Properties panel by clicking the Add Material Slot button, the + button at the top right of the window.

- Then we click the New button, and we rename the material too.

- We create a new slot and a new material.

- We go to Edit mode's Face Select and select the faces to which we want to assign the first material. Click Assign.

- We choose the part of the object we want to give the second material, select the new material, and click Assign again.

- To assign other substances, we repeat the same process.

Now let's see the Shader Editor, the central window for editing nodal materials.

The Shader Editor and the Material Nodes

In the Shader Editor, we create the materials, compose and edit them through the nodes, and apply the effects and textures.

It contains all the Material Properties functions represented in the nodal system.

We can add different nodes to our material from the Add item of the main menu or the Shift+A shortcut.

We can navigate the Shader Editor by rotating the mouse's central wheel to zoom and by clicking and moving the wheel to grab the nodes in pan mode.

Here we join the nodes through links to create a nodal chain. All of them have input and output sockets, and we connect them by clicking the socket of the first node with the left mouse button and dragging until the socket of the second node.

On the left side, there are the input sockets; on the right, the output sockets. We can distinguish them by the different colors according to the list:

- Violets connect vector-type data.

- Yellows link color data.

- Grays connect numerical data.

- Greens combine the shaders.

It is generally better to connect only the sockets of the same color. Of course, we can make some exceptions, but, in any case, we can connect the input sockets only to the output sockets.

There are ten categories of material nodes, as shown in Figure 4-6, and we can add them to the Shader Editor with the Shift+A shortcut.

Figure 4-6. The material node categories of Blender 3.0

In Figure 4-6, we see the different categories of Blender 3.0 nodes.

- The Input nodes act as a login for the other ones; they generate information for the other nodes. They can be colors, values, images, etc., and they only have output connectors.

- The Output nodes collect the final result of the nodal chain; the final stage in any chain of material nodes is an output node.

- The Shader nodes are the most critical ones for materials because they determine the characteristics of the material.

- We use Texture nodes to input textures into the nodal system: procedurals and images.

- The Color nodes allow us to manipulate colors and change the color parameters: brightness, contrast, etc.

- Vector nodes introduce and modify the vectors that we can use for bump and normal mapping, displacement, etc.

- Converter nodes change through mathematical functions or algorithms the parameters of the other nodes.

- Script nodes allow us to create custom nodes or download public-domain scripts with the Open Scripting Language (OSL).

- The Group nodes allow us to group the other nodes.

- Layout nodes are helpful to organize nodes.

Now let's take a closer look at the essential nodes for each group.

Input Nodes

They serve as input for the other nodes; they do not have an input socket but only an output. They can be simple tools like the Value or the RGB node, which provide a value or color input. There are also more complex nodes like Geometry or Texture Coordinate.

The most critical nodes in this category are as follows:

- *Ambient Occlusion*: This allows us to control the amount of light attenuation of materials. The Ambient Occlusion shading method increases the realism of the scenes by simulating global illumination and imitating reflection with light attenuation near occluded volumes.

  It acts on a single material at a time; to see its effects on all materials simultaneously, we can select the Ambient Occlusion box in the Render Properties panel of the Properties Editor.

Fresnel: The Fresnel node allows us to apply the Fresnel effect discussed earlier. It controls reflections by modifying them according to the viewing angle; the surfaces have little reflection when viewed frontally and are more considerable from an angular view.

- *RGB*: We use this node to introduce the color in the following chain node.

- *Layer Weight*: This controls reflections. It is similar to the Fresnel node but easier to use.

- *Texture Coordinate*: We control the texture coordinates with this node and use them as inputs to control the texture position. Thus, it allows us to change how we apply a texture to a surface. The essential outputs, which determine the mapping, are UV, Object, and Generated.

Output Nodes

While input nodes are the first nodes of the blockchain, the output nodes are the last ones and show us the result of the node chain, the final aspect of the material.

In any case, by deleting the output node, we cannot see the material. They are as follows:

- *Material output*: We use it to display the resulting material of the node chain we created for objects. It is the last node of a material chain.

- *World output*: We use the world node to create the world material, a chain of nodes that make a substance for the world and illuminate the scene.

Now let's see the shader nodes. This is the most crucial group of nodes; this category contains all the shaders that define the characteristics of the physical substance.

Shader Nodes

The term *shade*, or *shading*, is used in drawing and painting to describe the contrasts between light and dark, or light and shade, for a representation closer to our reality.

Starting from this assumption, in 3D graphics, the shader is a node, or rather a script, defining the material shading.

By referring to the theoretical principles discussed so far, we see the two most basic shader nodes: Diffuse and Glossy.

- *Diffuse BSDF*: We use this to add the material diffusion. We can change the color of the surface by clicking the Color button or connect a texture node to the Color input to use a bitmap or procedural texture. We can also modify the roughness of the surface, changing the respective value.

- *Glossy BSDF*: We use it to add reflection to materials. This node helps us simulate metals or mirror materials and is the opposite of the Diffuse BSDF node.

  First, there is a drop-down menu to change the distribution algorithm for blurry reflections; we have five different algorithms available.

  - Sharp is ideal for a perfectly sharp reflection; it doesn't consider Roughness values.

  - Beckmann is ideal for metal materials and provides Beckmann microfacet distribution.

  - GGX is particularly suitable for plastics and provides a GGX microfacet distribution.

  - Ashikhmin-Shirley provides an Ashikhmin-Shirley microfacet distribution.

  - Multiple-scattering GGX provides more significant energy conservation, transformed into a more considerable darkening of the rendered material.

  We can change the surface's color by clicking the Color button. This operation only gives reflection color, so the nonreflective parts will not be affected. We can also modify the material's reflection by changing the roughness. Finally, we can use the Normal input to alter the objects' surface normal.

Diffuse and Glossy are the two historical Blender nodes used to create many materials.

In version 3.0 of Blender, we can use them effectively, but the trend is to utilize more recent nodes such as the Principled BSDF that we will see in a moment.

Otherwise, we can quickly create simple but effective materials by joining them through the Mix and Add shader nodes.

- *Mix Shader*: We use this node to join two shaders together.

  First, we need to insert the shader nodes we merge into the two Shaders input. Then, we can adjust the numerical value of the input Factor to fit the percentage of influence of the two nodes. We can also connect an Input node in the Fac input socket—for example, a Fresnel or a Layer Weight node—to control the influence of the two nodes.

  Add Shader: The Add Shader node is similar to the mix node, and we can use it if we want to add a third shader node to introduce other features in our material. This node is simple and has only three sockets, two in and one out.

We will see an example of simple material combining the Diffuse and Reflection shaders at the end of this subsection in the short exercise "A Node Material."

Now let's continue to analyze the shader nodes and see a recently introduced one that put together the characteristics of different nodes: Specular BSDF.

- Blender developers introduced the *Specular BSDF* node in Blender 2.79 together with Shader To RGB and Principled BSDF.

- We use Specular BSDF and Principled BSDF for PBR Materials.

  Principled BSDF utilizes the Metallic workflow. Instead, Specular BSDF uses the Specular method. In this chapter's metal/roughness versus specular/glossiness discussion, we just talked about that.

  This node is still in development and isn't complete yet, but it already contains several controls, as shown in Figure 4-7.

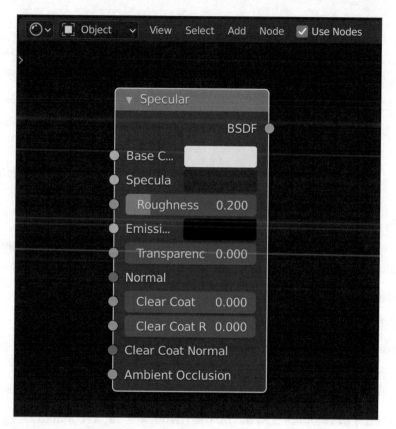

Figure 4-7. *The Specular BSDF node*

The inputs, as in Figure 4-7, are as follows:

- The Base Color regulates the diffuse color. For the metal, it should be black.

- Specular governs the specular reflection and the normal facing reflectivity.

- Roughness determines the microfacet roughness of the surface for diffuse and specular reflection.

- The Emissive box controls the color of the light emission.

- Transparency is the inverse of the Alpha channel of an image. It controls the opacity that affects the substance only if we set blend mode, other than opaque, in the Settings window of the Material Menu of the Properties Editor.

- The Normal box controls the normals of the base layers.

- Clearcoat, Clearcoat Roughness, and Clearcoat Normal create a layer of helpful paint for car paint and control a transparent layer that protects and illuminates the color.

- Ambient occlusion controls the environmental occlusion of the material.

  The only Output is BSDF, which we must connect to the Material Output node.

Now let's see Principled BSDF, the default Blender 3.0 shader.

Also, this node is a recent one that put together several characteristics and allows us to create PBR materials.

- With the *Principled BSDF* node, we can create any material, from glass to iron, marble, concrete, etc.

  It uses physically based formulae and dramatically simplifies the work of nodes composition. It puts together some previously separated nodes such as Diffuse, Glossy, Refraction, and Subsurface Scattering.

  Blender developers based it on the Disney Principled Shader designed for other renderers like Pixar's Renderman and Unreal Engine.

  This node, however, does not replace or contribute to dismantling other nodes that are still useful.

  It groups together Anisotropic BSDF, Diffuse BSDF, Glass BSDF (with Input Value Transmission), Glossy BSDF (called with Input Value Specular), and Subsurface Scattering.

  These nodes are more complicated to use individually but allow more fine-tuned results. Unfortunately, Principled BSDF doesn't support several functions such as Volumetric shaders, Ambient Occlusion, Hair, Velvet, Toon.

The Principled BSDF shader makes the interactivity between Cycles, Renderman, Unreal Engine, and Substance Painter possible. For example, we can connect textures painted with Substance Painter or similar software with the input sockets.

Let's continue the list with the other shader nodes.

- We can simulate metallic materials with the *Anisotropic BSDF* node by adding controls over the U and V direction roughness to the glossy reflection.

  Only Cycles supports this shader. At the top, it has a drop-down menu similar to that of the Glossy node. Here, we can choose the algorithm to use from Beckmann, GGX, Multiscatter CGX, and Ashikmin-Shirley.

  Its Input sockets are Color, Roughness, Anisotropy, Rotation, Normal, and Tangent.

  Its Output is BSDF, which allows us to directly connect it with the Material Output node or a Mix node to join it to another shader.

- *Emission*: We use this node to create a material that illuminates the scene without lights. This way, we can flexibly modify the light by adding other nodes to the nodal chain; for example, we can combine a Light Falloff node from one of the outputs sockets to create a softer light.

- *Glass BSDF*: We use this node to create a glass-like mixing refraction and reflection material that must refract light passing through it and reflect light at certain angles.

  For completely transparent materials or to simulate a full transparency effect, we can use the Transparency BSDF node; instead, for a pure reflection, without transparency, that is, without refraction, we can use the Glossy BSDF node.

- *Principled Volume*: This node is used to render fire and smoke and combines the characteristics of different nodes such as Emission, Volume Absorption, and Volume Scatter.

- *Refraction BSDF*: It is a node to make transparent materials with refraction but no reflection.

- *Subsurface Scattering*: This node adds a simple multiple subsurface scattering to the surface. It simulates partial transparency in certain materials where light is not reflected directly from the surface but penetrates and bounces it internally before being absorbed or refracted.

  This node is helpful for human skin, gelatin, wax, and similar materials.

- *Toon BSDF*: The Toon BSDF shader is used for a cartoon-like effect and to edit Diffuse and Glossy materials. It has a very defined type of shading, and to accentuate this effect, we can use strong and direct lighting. Currently, it is available only for Cycles.

- *Translucent BSDF.* We can use translucent BSDF, for example, for fabrics that partially allow light to shine through. It has only two input nodes: Color and Normal and a BSDF output node.

- *Transparent BSDF*: This simulates transparency without refraction. It adds to Glass and Refraction, which we have already seen. It affects opacity by allowing light to pass directly through the surface as if there were no geometry. We must use it with alpha maps.

- *Velvet BSDF*: This node simulates fabrics and clothes, particularly for the simulation of velvet combined with other shaders, usually with Diffuse. Currently, this node works only with Cycles.

- *Volume Scatter*: We use Volume Scatter to simulate volume effects such as smoke and steam. We must connect it to the input volume of the Material Output node to work correctly and develop a volumetric effect.

  We must couple it with the Volume Absorption node to create a smoke effect.

  It has three inputs:

  - Color simulates the color of the volume.

- Density replicates the thickness of the scattering effect.

- Anisotropy controls the look of the scatter's impact of light.

- *Volume Absorption* is associated with the previous one to create volumetric effects.

    We can use it also to create stained glass or water together with other nodes such as Glass or Transparency bonded to the volume input of the Material Output node to create light absorption effects.

A Node Material

We have covered the Input, Output, and Shader nodes. However, before continuing with the other categories of nodes, let's create a simple material with some of the shaders introduced so far, as shown in Figure 4-8.

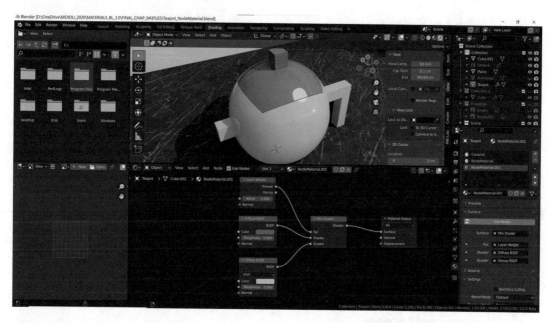

Figure 4-8. *Creating the first material with the Diffuse and Glossy nodes*

Figure 4-8 shows a first nodal material built with the Diffuse and Glossy shaders joined by a Mix node and regulated by a Layer node. Next, we visualize the result with the Material Output node. It is a simple but flexible material that we can quickly modify to obtain different effects that are more or less shiny.

We can use this node chain also with a Fresnel node as an input Fac (standing for input factor)of the Mixer node instead of the Layer node to add more realism to the reflections and control the material's index of refraction.

Now let's learn about texture nodes.

Texture Nodes

We use these nodes to insert textures into nodal systems.

We deal first with the Image Texture node, which is the only one that is not procedural but controlled by a raster image and not by an algorithm.

- *Image Texture node*: We use this node to insert pictures into nodal materials. We have seen that we can use an image for the Color channel. But, still, we can use it for the Normal channel and simulate the surface relief.

  With this node we can simulate the Metallic effect in PBR Materials, Roughness, Ambient Occlusion, and so on.

  So, this is a central node for creating traditional and PBR nodal materials.

  Of course, each channel needs the right image, as we will see in the exercises later in this chapter.

After that, we treat all the central procedural texture nodes.

While we obtain the bitmaps from images, the procedural ones are created directly by Blender algorithms.

- *Brick texture*: This is the first procedural node that we encounter.

  We use it to simulate quadrilateral elements such as bricks, but it contains numerous parameters to adapt it to create grids and other procedural textures.

  It uses three color buttons to give primary color to the bricks and mortar distributed on the x- and y-axes. To control the arrangement of this node on the surface of the object, we must use it together with the Mapping and Texture Coordinate nodes.

- *Checker texture*: This node is valid for creating grids; it establishes a chessboard initially in white and gray, and we can then control the colors and dimensions through the Color and Scale buttons.

  It's similar to Brick but more straightforward, with fewer variables for editing.

  We can use it for the Diffuse channel and other channels such as displacement.

  Also, we must use the Mapping and Texture Coordinate nodes to control the arrangement on the object's surface.

- *Environment texture*: We use this node to illuminate the scene through an environment map image file in a World material. We must combine it with a Background node to achieve the desired effect. Usually, it is an HDRI image. It illuminates the environment and creates mirror reflections. We will see its use in "The World Settings: Sky and Environment Texture" section of this chapter.

- *The Gradient Texture node*: This is quite simple; it creates a gradient for various linear, diagonal, and radial shading effects. This Texture node creates interpolated color and intensity values effects. The input socket helps change the intensity gradient's orientation, shape, and size.

- *The Magic Texture node*: This creates psychedelic color patterns. We can also use it for luminescent effects through a strange design repeated endlessly. With the Depth value, we can control the number of iterations.

  We then have three input sockets:

  - Vector controls the mapping coordinates.

  - The Scales node varies the texture size.

  - Distortion contains the amount of distortion.

  The Magic Texture requires some experience because it's pretty unpredictable.

The Noise Texture node can simulate the effects of shadows, smoke, and clouds.

There is a drop-down menu to find the size of the effect application space and five inputs:

- Vector to set the texture coordinates to evaluate the noise at

- Scale to size the effect

- Detail Number to increase the detail of the Noise effect

- Roughness to establish the definition of the surface bumpiness

- Distortion to develop the amount of the pattern distortion

We can use it as a mask or as a texture. For example, we create a mask by connecting the node from the output factor to the shader's input factor. Instead, we obtain a texture from the output color to a shader's input color.

- *Musgrave Texture node*: It creates effects like noise but allows us more control over the results.

There are two drop-down menus; the first, like in the Noise node, allows us to identify the application space of the effect.

The second one allows us to choose the algorithm to create textures from five possibilities: Multifractal, Ridged Multifractal, Hybrid Multifractal, fBM, and Hetero Terrain. The inputs Vector, Scale, and Detail also have the same functions as the Noise node, but instead of the Distortion menu, we have two menus.

- Dimension changes the difference between the magnitude of each two consecutive octaves.

- Lacunarity adjusts the difference between the scale of each two successive octaves.

The different algorithms and the numerous modification parameters lead to many other solutions.

- *Sky Texture node*: We assign this type of texture to the world via the Background or Environment Texture node. The Sky Texture node creates physically correct lights and colors from the sun's direction.

  It allows us to choose between three algorithms that generate the light and color from the Sky Type drop-down menu.

  - Nishita is the most accurate and sophisticated of the three and allows us to adjust several parameters such as the Size, Intensity, Elevation, and Rotation of the sun. It also allows us to control our light model's Altitude, Air, Dust, and Ozone. Currently, this algorithm works only with Cycles.

  - Hosek/Wilkie is valid for Earth-like and extra-solar worlds.

  - Preetham is a brighter and less accurate algorithm than the other two.

  In the last two models, we can control the sun direction by clicking and dragging on the sphere in the node's window with the left mouse button.

- *The Voronoi Texture node*: This creates Voronoi procedural texture patterns. Also, this node presents the possibility to choose between various algorithms that modify the shape and size of the geometries produced by this procedural texture.

- *Wave Texture node*: We use this type of node to simulate the effects of specific materials such as marble or wood and those of waves and similar elements. It creates a wave-like pattern of black-and-white concentric rings that are more useful when introducing distortions and details.

Color Nodes

Color nodes allow us to change colors, brightness, contrast, saturation, etc. First, let's see the central nodes.

- The Bright/Contrast node allows us to modify the color, brightness, and contrast of the material. There are two parameters.

  - Bright, which modifies the brightness of the material to which it is applied

  - Contrast, which adjusts the contrast

- The *Hue Saturation Value node* changes the material color's Hue, Saturation, and Value.

- The *Mix RGB node* combines two colors or two images, such as the Mix node shader, which combines the results of two shaders.

- *RGB Curves node* allows us to edit colors through RGB curves similar to those found in any image editor and provides editing for each of the three color channels.

Vector Nodes

We can use them for mapping and transmitting a vector to the next node.
The following are the most critical nodes in this category:

- *Mapping node*: We use this node to apply a translation, rotation, or scaling of the texture and modify its coordinates. Thus, we can change the texture's rotation, position, and size applied to the object or the world. It works with both bitmaps and procedural textures.

- *The Normal Map node*: This generates vectors from a bitmap for normal mapping. So, in the input socket, we connect an image texture, and in the output, we get a vector, which we link to the Normal input of a Shader node. So it works using normal maps.

Converter Nodes

These nodes convert one value to another using different options such as mathematical functions.

These are some nodes in this category:

- *Math* performs mathematical operations on two input values and returns the output value results.

- The *Shader to RGB node* works only with Eevee and is used for nonphotorealistic rendering to apply post-production effects to BSDF nodes.

  It has only one input socket that supports BSDF shaders or emission nodes. It has two output sockets:

  - Color for BSDF nodes and lighting surface color

  - Alpha for transparency, from a transparent BSDF input

After the Converter nodes, let's look at the Script, Group, and Layout nodes.

Script Node

It is a single node, and we use it to create our custom nodes in Cycles. This node takes advantage of the Open Shading Language (OSL). This programming language, supported by Cycles in CPU rendering, allows everyone to develop their nodes. Unfortunately, Eevee doesn't support the Open Shading Language.

Group Nodes

We simplify the node tree by using these nodes because they allow us to group and hide a set of nodes.

Grouping the different nodes also allows us to treat them as one, copy and paste them into other materials, and reuse them more easily.

- *Make Group*: Select all the nodes to include in the group; you cannot insert Input or Output nodes.

  Press Ctrl+G and then Tab to display the whole group as a single node.

  By pressing Tab, you open and close the node group.

- *Edit Group*: Press Tab to open the group; then, move and modify the nodes inside the group. Finally, press Tab again to close the group.

- *Ungroup*: Press Ctrl+Alt+G to delete the group and separate the nodes again.

Layout Nodes

These nodes simplify the reading of the interconnections and are helpful when controlling many nodes.

There are two types of these nodes:

- The *Frame node* creates a framework to insert nodes to group them visually.

  Make the frame, select the nodes to add, press Ctrl+P, or drag the nodes inside the frame.

- *Reroute* is helpful to insert a node between the connected nodes.

We learned about the Shading workspace and the different editors to create and edit nodal materials. Then we studied the central nodes to make materials.

After seeing some of the nodes Blender provides us, we can install an essential add-on that gives us several tools to speed up the workflow with the nodal system: the Node Wrangler.

The Node Wrangler Add-on

In this section, we will see how to simplify the creation of nodal materials using Node Wrangler, an interesting Blender add-on.

This tool gives us several essential elements that help to speed up the creation and modification of nodes, making the work more fluid.

In addition, it is helpful in the Shader Editor and the Compositor.

We activate it from the Preferences ➤ Add-ons tab by searching for and selecting Node Wrangler to enable the script.

To use it, we open the Node Wrangler window from the Shader Editor or compositor sidebar or with the shortcut Shift+W.

Figure 4-9 shows the menu that opens.

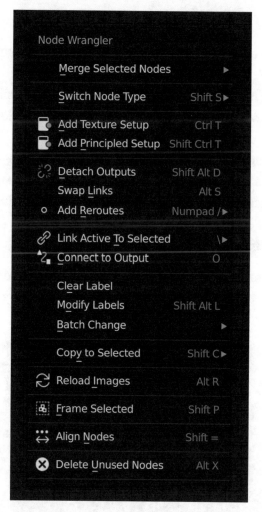

Figure 4-9. *The Node Wrangler add-on interface*

Figure 4-9 shows that this add-on provides many valuable node creations and editing tools.

Let's discuss its three most interesting tools: Merge Selected Nodes, Add Texture Setup, and Add Principled Setup.

Merge Selected Nodes

This tool merges the selected nodes by adding a Shader node as Mix, Add, Math, or using various other nodes for the materials.

In the Compositor, with this function, we can make post-production and modify images and videos and join the selected nodes using the Z-combine or Alpha-over nodes.

Like all the other functions, this add-on speeds up the work of node composition.

Add Texture Setup

We use this function to add a texture setup to a node. This node can be a Shader or a Texture node.

We can select any Shader node and press Ctrl+T, and, magically, we will add an Image texture with the other two nodes controlling the coordinates: Mapping and Texture Coordinate.

With one click, we add three nodes if we select a Shader: Image Texture, Mapping, and Texture Coordinate. However, if we choose an Image Texture node, then we press Ctrl+T, and we add only two nodes: Mapping and Texture Coordinates.

Add Principled Setup

This feature is critical and allows us to load a set of PBR textures directly into the chosen principled node by merely selecting the node itself and importing them with a click, as in Figure 4-10.

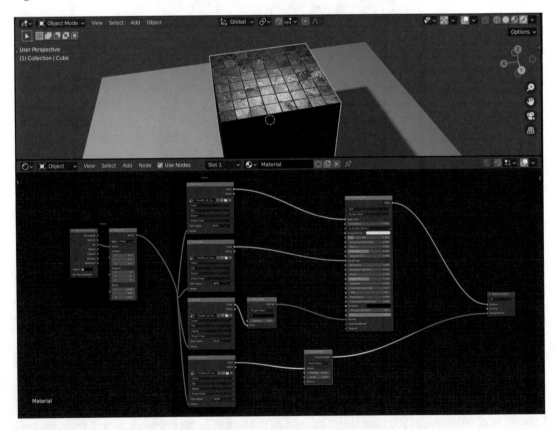

Figure 4-10. *The application of the Add Principled Setup tool*

In Figure 4-10, we can see the creation of a PBR material. We obtained this result by applying to the Principled BSDS node some textures that we have downloaded for free from https://ambientcg.com/.

As we can see in Figure 4-10, the result is excellent, and the process is simple, and we can explain it in a few steps:

1. First, select the BSDF Principled node.

2. Then, with Ctrl+Shift+T, open the textures folder.

3. Select the textures and, on the bottom right, click Principled Texture Setup and import them.

4. The tool automatically builds the nodal system for you.

Of course, we must first have downloaded the textures from the Internet or created them. In the next section and the exercises of this chapter, we will see how to do this.

This ends the node material analysis conducted in this section.

We learned about the PBR materials first and then the Blender's nodal system and some of its material nodes that help us to give more realism to our scenes.

Now we will begin to create and apply textures, another fundamental element for the quality of our materials.

Learning More About Textures

Textures are a fundamental element to obtain life-like materials, and they have a dedicated editor since Blender 2.8: the Texture Node Editor, shown in Figure 4-11.

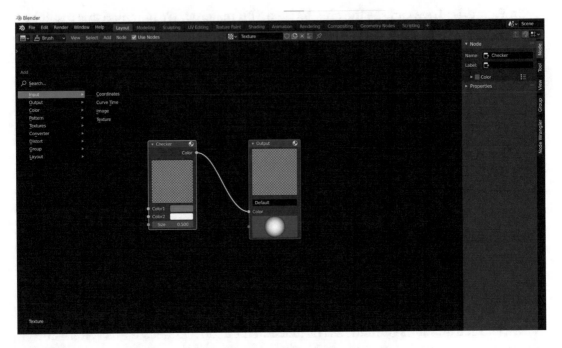

Figure 4-11. *The Texture Node Editor in Blender 3.0*

Figure 4-11 shows the specific Texture Node Editor where only the nodes that we can use for textures appear.

As shown in the previous section, there are different types of textures to control various effects; the Diffuse texture contains only the material's color.

We can control other channels and other effects with different textures.

In the Texture Node Editor, we can create procedural textures with the Blender nodal system, and we have specific nodes for each type of texture; we can divide these into categories like the other nodes: Input, Output, Color, Pattern, Textures, Converter, Distort, Group, Layout.

Otherwise, we can also use image textures.

There are many sites where we can download quality textures and materials, but if we want a particular effect, we must also learn to make it ourselves from a photograph.

So, it is crucial to learn how to make our personalized textures from photographs. In fact, for some specific projects, we will undoubtedly need custom textures that we cannot find in online libraries.

But let's start from the beginning. There are two types of textures: procedural and bitmap. We can create procedural and image textures inside or outside Blender. For procedural textures, we can use software such as the Substance tools by Adobe or the Quixel suite; instead, we can use software like Materialize, Photoshop, or Gimp for bitmaps. But, first, let's see the difference between the two texture types.

Bitmap and Procedural Textures

We create procedural textures parametrically with algorithms while generating bitmap textures from images. Both methods have positive and negative aspects.

Algorithms that generate procedural textures are mathematical functions created directly inside Blender or other software. These textures are more challenging to create and manage because they depend entirely on mathematics, the equation that makes them, and the nodal system of the software we are currently using.

Procedural textures are three-dimensional, infinite, and directly controlled by mathematics. But instead, using a bitmap texture, we can simulate a material realistically, applying different images to the various material channels. We get the maps for the multiple channels from a single photograph in most cases.

The fundamental elements of raster images are pixels, small squares containing the image's color and brightness information.

In this case, we have to use images of a suitable resolution; for example, a size of 2048 x 2048 pixels is usually sufficient in most cases to obtain good-quality textures for our Blender node materials.

Also, we need to eliminate lateral join points: image textures are repeated several times in a material. Finally, we must avoid too apparent repetitions. If an image is repeated too many times on the material's surface, the result does not appear realistic.

We can create all kinds of textures, both for traditional and for new PBR materials, starting from photographs and modifying them with software such as Materialize, Photoshop, Gimp, and Krita.

These software programs allow us to edit materials or create textures by painting them with digital brushes.

Open Source Image Editors: Gimp and Krita

We must mainly use software external to Blender to create textures from photographs.

Gimp and Krita are two free and open source software applications, and we use them for editing images, drawings, paintings, etc.

Gimp is the software we will use in the exercises of this chapter for our textures. It is an image editor and digital painting tool for professional drawing and photo retouching, with many features. This software is open source; we can access its source code and freely create extensions or download the many online plug-ins.

Gimp is cross-platform and available for GNU/Linux, Windows, and Apple's macOS.

It has some characteristics that allow us to work professionally on images, including the following:

- Layers and channels for overlapped image control

- Curves and levels to change the attributes of pictures

- Full Alpha channel support for working with transparency

- Selection tools to select image parts and apply transformations and effects to images in a controlled way

- Image and layer transformation tools, including rotate, scale, shear, and flip

- Well-equipped painting tools including pencils, brushes, airbrushes, cloning tools, etc.

- Support for importing and exporting many file formats, including BMP, PNG, TIFF, TGA, GIF, JPEG, PDF, PSD, and many others

- Possibility to install numerous plug-ins to extend the opportunities of this software

Another handy tool like Gimp is Krita, which is a digital painting and drawing software for designers, artists, and architects. Gimp has more tools for image manipulation tasks. Still, Krita's tools, interface setup, and numerous digital painting options make it unique for texturing, illustration, and concept art.

We will go deeper into using this software in this chapter and the next. Also, in the exercises of this chapter, we will practice creating textures with different methods with Gimp.

In the meantime, let's see how to develop and apply textures, which are two-dimensional elements, to three-dimensional objects in Blender.

UV Mapping and Unwrapping

This section will deal with the texture development method to properly apply them to 3D objects.

We can precisely apply 2D textures to 3D objects using Blender's unwrapping system. We can create the proper UV mapping and unwrapping for our entities.

Before applying a texture to the surface of an object, we must develop the three-dimensional shape of the object on a two-dimensional surface while keeping the dimensions and proportions of the areas as intact as possible.

In short, we must project a three-dimensional shape on a flat surface. It is essential to avoid stretching the shape when we do UV mapping. To perform this operation, Blender has several algorithms that allow us to develop the three-dimensional shape bidimensionally and apply it in the best possible way to our three-dimensional object.

UV Editing Workspace and UV Editor

To unwrap a 3D object, we can use the UV Editing workspace with a UV Editor on the left, a 3D view in the middle, and the Outliner and Properties Editors on the right, as shown in Figure 4-12.

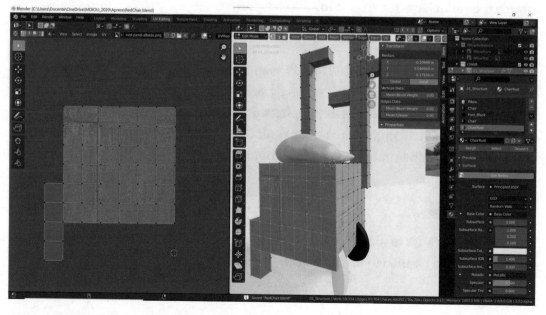

Figure 4-12. *The UV Editing workspace*

We can easily activate the UV Editing workspace from the Topbar by clicking UV Editing.

We see the tridimensional object in the 3D viewport and the two-dimensional development of its shape in the UV editor on the left. With the UV Unwrapping techniques, we can unwrap our objects and apply textures without deforming them or creating artifacts.

In Figure 4-12, we have applied a Rust texture to the chair, downloaded from the site `https://freepbr.com/`.

We have done the unwrapping of the chair with the easiest method for polygonal objects: Smart UV Project. We will see how it works in the "UV Mapping" section of this paragraph.

To unwrap a mesh, we select the object, go to Edit mode, select all the subobjects by pressing A, and press U to Unwrap. Then we choose one of the available options from the UV Mapping window that opens, the most suitable for the shape we have to develop.

In this case, we clicked Smart UV Project; Blender automatically performs the shape development for the texture application.

In the UV Editor, on the left of the interface, we can see the development of the object's faces, and we can change its position, rotation, and size concerning the background texture. We can also modify the shape of the UV Map by selecting and moving the subobjects as we do in the 3D viewport.

The changes will affect the application of the texture on the three-dimensional object.

In this example, we have scaled the UV Map to match the texture's size to the object's dimensions. This way, we can apply correctly sized textures practically to everything.

In this case, it was a matter of developing the shape of a relatively simple geometric object to apply this technique with few operations. Naturally, we will have to use more time and sophisticated strategies for more complex things.

UV Mapping

Let's see the best ways to unwrap a UV shape to apply a texture without deforming or stretching it when applied to the 3D object.

There are several ways to do the UV mapping of an object; in Figure 4-13, on the left, we see the menu to open them all.

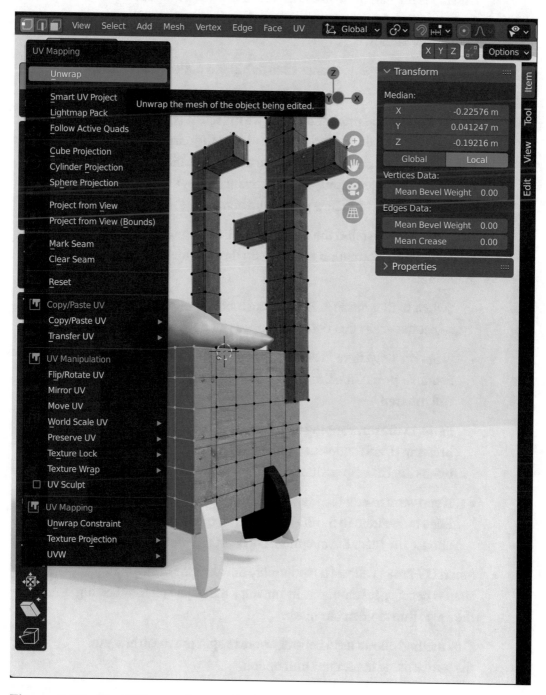

Figure 4-13. *The UV mapping methods of Blender 3.0*

Every shape has a better way to be developed, and Blender presents several of them:

- Unwrap is the first item on the list and allows us a manual development of the form. It develops the mesh surface following the seams' indications.

  It is helpful for organic shapes such as human body parts, natural elements, etc.

  To use this method most effectively, we must first create areas to be carried out, delimiting the boundaries to guarantee the minimum deformation of the surface during flattening. Then, we can divide the object using the Mark Seam option that tells the unwrapping algorithm how to split the item.

  To do this, we must find the demarcation line by looking for the least possible deformation of the mesh; then we must do the following:

  - Switch to Edit mode in Edge Select mode by clicking button 2 and select the edges that define the areas you need to separate.

  - From the Edge item in 3D view's header menu, choose Mark Seam, or press Ctrl+E and select Mark Seam; the marked Edges will turn red.

  - Perform the unwrapping by selecting all the mesh with A, pressing U, and choosing from the UV Mapping window that opens the Unwrap option.

  - If you want to edit the Marked Edges, select Clear Seam from the Edge menu item in the 3D View Header menu or press Ctrl+E, choose the Clear Seam option, and start the process again.

- Smart UV Project allows us to simplify the work for orthogonal shapes because it automatically unwraps the object after indicating the angle threshold in our mesh.

  This method allows us to control where to split the mesh and put the seams using the Angle Limit option.

It is a valuable tool for simple and complex geometric shapes such as architectures, orthogonal or mechanical objects, etc.

However, this method becomes less effective with organic shapes, especially when they become more complex.

- Lightmap Pack can be used effectively only for regular and straightforward meshes, especially for creating video game objects and taking advantage of all the available UV Map space. It maintains face development within texture size.

- Follow Active Quads arranges the faces according to a loop of straight faces. However, it does not respect the image's size so that a resizing action may be necessary.

- Cube Projection is good to develop shapes close to the cube or parallelepiped. It unwraps the mesh onto the faces of a cube.

- Cylinder Projection is suitable for developing cylindrical shapes. However, with this option, to obtain a satisfactory result, we must unwrap the curved surface of the cylinder viewed from the front and then separate the circular faces viewed from above with the Project from View option.

- Sphere Projection develops UV maps for spherical shapes. First, we place the sphere with the poles up and down. After we unwrap with this method, in this way, we will obtain an equirectangular projection. Finally, we will have a correct mapping result by applying an equirectangular projection map of a planet.

- Project from View develops the mapping by flattening the mesh as it appears in 3D View.

- Project from View (Bounds) develops mapping like the previous method taking up all the available space of the texture.

Finally, at the bottom of the same menu, we find Mark Seam and Clear Seam to create and delete surfaces' divisions. The last button, Reset, returns the UV Map to its most exact geometric shape.

These are Blender's default techniques.

With these basic methods, we can already get outstanding results. In addition, some add-ons can come to our aid and help us develop UV maps quickly and better.

For example, magic UV comes to our assistance with many new tools when we need to create maps for more complex objects and help create UV Maps.

Let's see now how it works.

Magic UV Add-on

Magic UV is an add-on that puts together different options for the development of UV maps and speeds up the textures' unwrapping for our objects.

It is a handy tool that we can activate from the User Preferences like the other pre-installed add-ons. We can click Magic UV to enable the script from the main menu Edit ➤ Preferences ➤ Add-ons ➤ Magic UV.

We find these tools below the standard UV Mapping tools by pressing U.

We get them also in Object and Edit modes in the 3D view's Sidebar on the right, as shown in Figure 4-14 in the part of the interface framed in white.

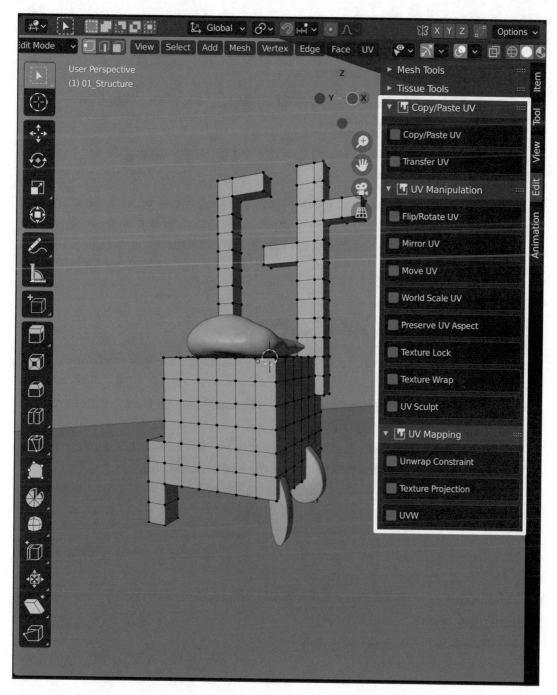

Figure 4-14. *The UV Magic add-on interface*

The add-on developers subdivided these devices into three windows:

- Copy and Paste UV contains collected tools to copy and paste UV Maps from one object to another.

- UV Manipulation contains tools for editing UV Maps, for example, to flip or rotate or mirror them.

- UV Mapping performs other types of automatic unwrapping other than the default ones.

We close this section dedicated to UV mapping and unwrapping with these tools. But, of course, we will also apply these concepts in the exercises later in this chapter.

Now let's see which lights and cameras Blender uses to light and photograph or film our environments.

Lights, Shadows, and Cameras

Lights and shadows are essential tools for creating the right atmosphere in our virtual spaces.

Blender has several lights and many control options to create different kinds of lighting, both natural and artificial.

In addition, there are several add-ons, both free and paid, to simulate different types of light, such as extra lights, that we will see at the end of this section.

It is time to learn how to position lights to illuminate the scene. Eevee and Cycles have the same lights, but they behave slightly differently in lighting and shadow projection.

Eevee has a lighting system that is still under development; for example, at the moment, Eevee's lights don't support nodes yet.

The nodes are usable for lights still only for Cycles and allow us many variations not yet possible in Eevee.

But let's see the main types of light in Blender 3.0.

Light Types

There are different types of light inside Blender, useful for other occasions and various types of lighting.

We must take into account that in Blender, we have two sources of illumination that act simultaneously.

- The *direct light* that the illumination sources produce inside the 3D view. We will see it briefly in this section.

- The *indirect light* that the world produces and that we can turn on, off, and modify in the World Properties panel of the Properties Editor. The following section will study the world settings called the Sky and Environment texture.

We have various tools to simulate both natural and artificial light.

We can simulate, for example, the light of the sun or the artificial light of the spotlights.

To insert the lights in the scene, we select Add and then Lights in the 3D View header menu or we click Shift+A ➤ Add ➤ Light. Then, in the window that opens, we can choose our light.

Let's see next the possibilities of direct lighting offered by Blender's lighting sources. The first and most simple is the Point Light.

Point Light

The point light is the most direct light and illuminates the scene in every direction. We can move the point light in 3D view with G or the Transformation gizmo like with other Blender objects.

We can modify some parameters by selecting the light in 3D view and then clicking the Object Data Properties button in the Properties Editor. For example, we can change some settings such as the color and the power of the light in watts. However, these watts do not correspond to the actual lighting sources.

We can see the main parameters in Figure 4-15.

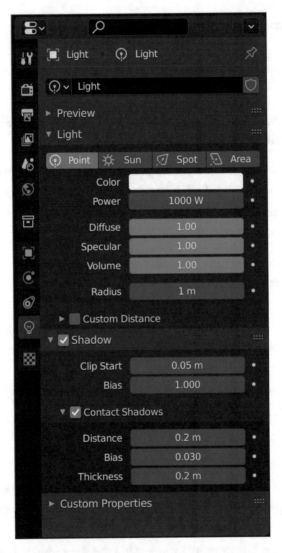

Figure 4-15. *The Point Light commands*

In addition to the Color and Power parameters, as we see in Figure 4-15, we can also change the Diffuse, Specular, and Volume values and the light's radius. We can then control shadows and contact shadows.

The distance of the objects from the point light influences the intensity of the light itself, and the further-away elements will be illuminated less and will be rendered darker.

In Cycles, we get a spherical light that emits softer shading and shadows by increasing the size value.

Moreover, in this render engine, we can use nodes to modify this light source by clicking the Use Nodes button and adding the nodes from the Shader Editor or the Object Data Properties panel of the Properties Editor.

Sun Light

This is a directional light that simulates sunlight and produces a constant intensity, which is excellent for simulating daylight situations.

It works excellently as a direct light source coordinated with the indirect lighting of the world using, for example, the Sun Position add-on, as we will see in the "Sun Position" section of this chapter.

The location of the lighting point is not essential and does not create any distance falloff.

We can move this light with G and rotate it with R, or the transformation gizmos move and rotate. We can change the direction of the light by rotating the sun light in 3D view by improving lighting and shadow.

We have more or less the same parameters as the point light. But the sun light, unlike the point light, projects constant directional lighting from a source placed at infinity.

The Strength value determines the light intensity in watts per square meter, while the Angle value controls the ratio between the size of the light and its angular diameter as seen from Earth.

Spot Light

The spot light illuminates the scene by emitting a directional light projected inside a light cone cast by the light icon, which widens more and more according to the data we establish, as shown in Figure 4-16.

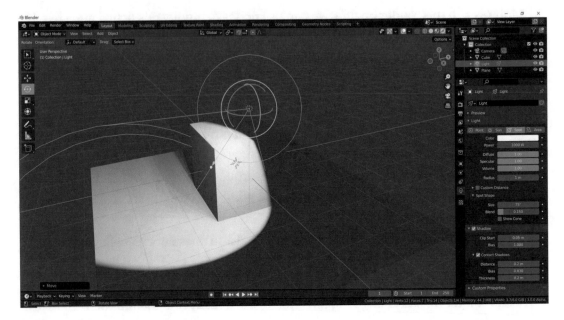

Figure 4-16. *The Spot Light*

Figure 4-16 shows that the basic parameters are almost the same as the previous lights. Also, here the power of the light is in watts.

The Beam Shape window controls the values of the emitted light cone. When the Spot Size value is more significant than zero, the shape of the emitted light becomes spherical. So, we can control the softness of the edge from the Blend value and the light size from the Radius box; lights with larger sizes cast softer shadows and specular highlights.

Area Light

Area light illuminates from an area such as a rectangular or elliptical surface or another flat shape. Parameters are, more or less, the same as the other lights. This tool can correctly simulate the light emitted from a window, screen, or neon light. We can control the area shape and size by modifying the values in the respective boxes.

In addition, it produces shadows with soft borders differently from point or sun light, which provides them with very defined edges.

These lights are available directly inside Blender; now, we see an external add-on that adds a fair number of lights to our software.

Add Extra Lights Add-on

This add-on joins new physically based and photometric lighting tools to the Light menu, which we can open by pressing Shift+A and selecting Add ➤ Light.

There are four lights sectors: natural, incandescent, LED, and fluorescent.

These lights are from the Illuminating Engineering Society (IES), created to transfer photometric data over the Web electronically and used by many lighting manufacturers.

These lights use IES textures to create a realistic simulation, elements currently only supported by Cycles and not Eevee.

We can download this add-on from GitHub at `https://github.com/jlampel/extra_lights`.

To install it, we must use the usual method: click Clone or Download and then click Download ZIP and save the file on the computer's hard disk; then install it in Blender from the main menu by selecting Edit ➤ Preferences ➤ Add-ons ➤ Install.

To insert the lights in the scene, we click from the 3D View header menu on Add and then on Lights or press Shift+A and select Add ➤ Light. Then, in the window that opens after the four default lights, we find the Extra Lights, click that choice, and add it.

To conclude the section dedicated to lights and cameras, let's quickly see how to use cameras in Blender.

Cameras

A camera is an object that allows us to capture our scenes and render the framed part of our 3D environment.

We add a camera by clicking the 3D view header menu on Add and Camera. We can also use the shortcut Shift+A and select Add ➤ Camera.

We can move the camera like any other object, and by moving it, we shift the framing of our rendering. So, by pressing 0 on the numeric keypad, we can transform the 3D view window in the Camera window and see the window on the right of Figure 4-17.

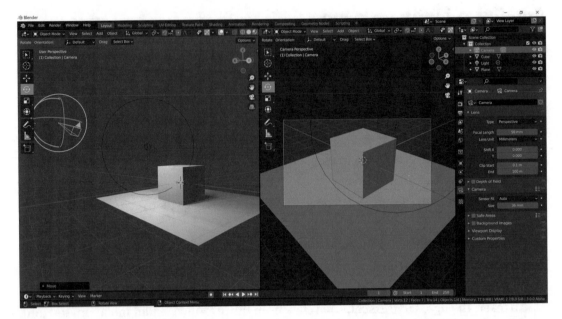

Figure 4-17. *The camera in the 3D view and the Camera viewpoint on the right*

On the right of the figure, we can see the Object Data Properties panel, where we can modify the parameters of our camera.

Here we can modify the view from Perspective to Orthographic to Panoramic.

The first type of view reproduces a real prospect or perspective. The second one produces flat objects as in an orthogonal projection and is helpful to create a basis for the technical architectural drawing. Finally, the third provides a broad view of framed spaces.

We can also modify some settings, such as Focal Length, which reproduces photographic lenses, or the depth of field representing the area where objects still appear sharp.

Instead, from the Output window of the Properties Editor, we can modify the frame size, the proportions, and the file format to create the image or video and choose the folder where to save the file.

In Blender, in addition to the direct lighting of the lights that we have just seen, we have the indirect lighting of the surrounding environment, which, as we have mentioned, we can control in the World Properties panel of the Properties Editor.

Let's see how it works.

The World Settings: Sky and Environment Texture

The world environment can emit light with different modalities in Eevee and Cycles.

We can modify some of the world illumination parameters from the World Properties panel of the Properties Editor. For example, we can alter the color and strength of the world's light.

But if we want to customize the scene's lighting more, we must use the nodal system and the Shader Editor.

With the nodal system, we can change many parameters of the world such as as the light's strength, color, and mapping in the Cycles and Eevee render engines.

Also, we can use other nodes that allow us great flexibility.

In this way, we define the environment illumination of our scene, and we can control the background and lighting environment through the Background shader.

So we can modify the light intensity and the color and apply a texture to illuminate our scenes.

For this purpose, we can use two different nodes that we have already seen in the section "The Shader Editor and the Material Nodes."

- The Environment texture node, which usually uses HDRI image maps.

- The Sky texture node contains three algorithms that simulate a physically correct illumination.

We can also create a mist or other volumetric effects in our world through a Volume shader node.

Let's first see how the environment texture node with HDRI maps works.

Deepening HDRI Environment Maps

HDRI textures are High Dynamic Range Images maps, which have a more comprehensive dynamic range than other images; i.e., the interval between the brightest and darkest visible areas is more defined.

They are ideal for representing the environment's natural lighting conditions and transmitting them to the scene as lighting and reflection. Therefore, they should be used as image textures to illuminate our environments.

Linked to the input color of the Background node, through an Environment Texture node, they significantly improve the realistic lighting quality of the scene.

Lighting our Blender 3.0 scenes with physically accurate HDRI environment maps is straightforward and supported by both renderers.

To access the environment's materials, in the Shader Editor, we must go from the Object to the World shaders in the box on the left of the header of the Shader Editor, as highlighted in Figure 4-18 on the left.

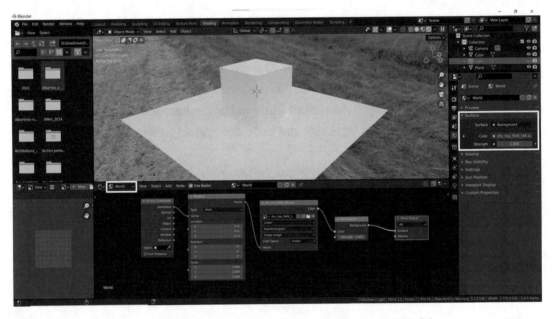

Figure 4-18. *The Shading workspace with the Shader and World Properties editors*

In Figure 4-18, we can also see on the right the World Properties panel of the Properties Editor with the lighting adjustment parameters Color and Strength.

We see the Shader Editor with the nodal system in the lower center of the picture.

The figure reproduces a scene in Cycles with only ambient lighting and no direct light source.

Instead of using the color of the world, we have illuminated the scene with an HDRI lighting map by connecting the input socket of the Background node with an Environment Texture node and loading the HDRI Image as shown in the figure.

We can, however, modify the Strength value of the scene's lighting with the same box.

Note   We downloaded the HDRI lighting map from the site `https://polyhaven.com/`. Another excellent site is `https://hdrmaps.com/`.

Finally, we added the Mapping and Texture Coordinate nodes to control the mapping.

The section "The Node Wrangler Add-on" explains how we can add the two nodes with a single click.

By illuminating our environments with the HDRI map, we create colored lights and shadows and very realistic reflections for glossy materials, significantly improving the quality of our renderings.

Every texture pixel becomes a light source that enriches the scene with light and reflections.

The following are the two most common formats for this type of texture:

- OpenEXR (`.exr`)

- Radiance HDR (`.hdr`)

The first one is the most effective to use in Blender. It makes post-processing easier because it allows us to store renders with multiple layers and passes and allows us to get better results in rendering.

A second system to illuminate the environment indirectly is the Sky Texture node. Let's look at how it works.

The Sky Texture Node

A second node that allows us to control the indirect lighting of our scenes is the Sky Texture node. We already analyzed it theoretically earlier in this chapter when we reviewed the texture nodes.

It creates physically correct lights and colors using a procedural texture.

It allows us to choose between three algorithms: Nishita, Hosek/Wilkie, and Preetham. Currently, Nishita does not work with Eevee.

Now let's experiment with a simple, practical application of this node's functionality.

1. Open Blender and create a simple scene. Start with Eevee, the default renderer. Move to the Shading workspace and activate the Rendered button in the Viewport Shading Display with the button on the right of the 3D view header of the 3D Viewport editor.

2. Select the default point light, turn it into a sun light, and adjust its intensity by selecting it and modifying the Strength value in the Object Data Properties.

3. Go from the Object to World shaders' type in the box by changing from the Object to the World option on the left of the Shader Editor header.

    Then press Shift+A, add a Sky Texture node, and connect it with the Color key of the existing Background node.

    In the Render Properties panel of the Properties Editor, activate Ambient Occlusion, Screen Space Reflections, and Refraction.

4. Then change the Nishita algorithm to Hosek / Wikie.

    You will see that the illumination will change by rotating the sphere in the Sky Texture node window and modifying the Turbidity values.

5. Then try changing the algorithm to Preetham and again rotate the sphere and change the Turbidity values.

    If you want to control the scene's colors more accurately, you can add an RGB Curves node between Sky Texture and Background.

6. Now try to change the render engine: in the Render Properties panel of the Properties Editor, change from Eevee to Cycles and activate the Denoise button from the path: Properties Editor ➤ Render Properties ➤ Sampling, to decrease the noise of the viewport and change the Denoiser to OpenImageDenoise.

    Try the two algorithms Nishita and Hosek / Wikie in Cycles, especially Nishita. Edit the RGB Curves node, the Strength value of the Background node, and the Nishita algorithm's values in the Sky Texture node window.

If then you want to obtain more sophisticated light effects, you can use the add-on Physical Starlight Atmosphere by downloading it for a fee from `https://blendermarket.com/products/physical-starlight-and-atmosphere`.

This outdoor lighting system allows excellent customization. It is not free, but it has a meager cost and helps us create refined lighting effects with just a few clicks.

To conclude this section, we will learn about Sun Position: an interesting pre-installed Blender add-on that allows us to create realistic lighting and quickly link a sun light with an HDRI texture and the Sky Texture node.

Sun Position

This interesting Blender add-on makes it easy to place the environment's brightness to illuminate our objects diffusely.

It uses physical characteristics such as geographic location, time, and date to position the sun in Blender in a realistic way. In addition, we can connect it with the Earth System Research Laboratory's online calculator, which we can find at `https://gml.noaa.gov/grad/solcalc/`, to position and animate the sun in our environment.

Like all the other internal Blender add-ons, we must activate it from the User Preferences window.

Then we find this tool in the Properties panel's World Properties tab. We can adjust the solar lighting settings in this window, giving the Latitude and Longitude values.

With this add-on, we can easily adjust the sun's orientation to a precise time and calendar date, change the sun position's latitude and longitude, and simulate real-world natural lighting.

Once we have set the latitude and longitude, we can adjust the time and the GMT zone offset. We can even animate the time, day, and month to create lighting effects in our videos.

But let's see how to connect direct and indirect light using this tool.

Synchronize Sun Light with an HDRI Texture

We can synchronize the sunlight with the HDRI texture effortlessly with this add-on.

1. Open Blender, keep the default cube and add a plane (press Shift+A and select Mesh ➤ Plane), and scale it four times (S ➤ 4). Select the cube and raise it one unit (G ➤ Z ➤ 1).

2. Activate Node Wrangler from the main menu by selecting Edit ➤ Preferences, select the World's Background node in the Shader Editor, and press Ctrl+T to create all the necessary nodes with a single click.

   Upload an HDRI image with the Open button of the Environment texture.

3. Adjust the indirect lighting with the Strength value of the Background node.

4. Select the default point light, turn it into a sun light, and adjust its intensity by selecting it and modifying the Strength value in the Object Data Properties.

5. Activate the Sun position add-on through the main menu by selecting Edit ➤ Preferences.

6. Open the Sun Position panel in the World Properties of the Properties Editor and select Sun + HDR Texture in Usage Mode.

    Select the light in the box Sun Object.

7. Then, lower down, click the button Sync Sun to Texture.

    In the 3D View in Rendered Viewport Shading, click the crossing point of the two perpendicular lines in the HDRI map at the spot of maximum illumination, where the sun should be.

8. Now that the two lighting sources are connected, you can change the scene's lighting with the Distance and Rotation buttons of the Sun Position panel.

    You can also change the color and strength of the sun light with the boxes of the same name in the Object Data Properties panel.

Let's now see how to synchronize our direct light source with the Sky Texture node instead.

Synchronize Sun Light with a Sky Texture

We can connect the sun light with the Sky texture with these simple steps:

1. Repeat step 1 of the previous exercise and create a scene or open the environment you want to light.

2. Activate the Sun position and the Node Wrangler add-ons in the User Preferences if they are not already active. Then, enable the Rendered button in the Viewport Shading of the 3D view header.

3. Keep Eevee as the render engine. Then, turn on Ambient Occlusion, Screen Space Reflections, and Refraction in the Properties Editor's Render Properties panel.

4. In the Shading workspace, in the Shader Editor, go to the World material type, add a Sky Texture node, and link it with the Color key of the existing Background node.

5. Select the default point light, turn it into sun light, and adjust its intensity by selecting it and modifying the Strength value in the Object Data Properties. For example, a Strength value from 3 to 7 should be correct.

6. Then, change the Nishita algorithm to Hosek / Wikie.

7. Open the Sun Position panel in the Properties Editor's World Properties and select the Sun Light in the Sun Object box.

    Then in the Sky Texture box, select Sky Texture.

8. Enter the coordinates of the place whose lighting you want to reproduce in the box Enter Coordinates and adjust the UTC zone in the same box. For example, for Milan, you can type **45°28′01″N 9°11′24″E** and **UTC+2** hours.

9. If you want to change the lighting, you must adjust the Time, Day, Month, and Year boxes.

This way, we have created natural lighting related to where we want to set our scenes.

This section on ambient lighting concludes the theoretical part of the chapter dedicated to materials, lighting, and world settings.

Before moving on to Chapter 5 dedicated to digital painting, let's practice the ideas learned in this chapter through some targeted exercises.

Exercises: Creating Materials

In the following exercises, we will apply the concepts learned in the previous sections of this chapter.

We will create and assign materials to objects; we will give the proper lighting to our scene and build a world environment.

Let's start creating a traditional material node.

Exercise 6: Creating Standard Material Nodes

Now let's create customized material for the living room floor built in the previous chapters.

We can download many images available online for free.

Several sites excellent materials and textures make available. Here are some of the most interesting in our opinion:

- https://www.textures.com/

- https://ambientcg.com/

- https://store.chocofur.com/

- https://freepbr.com/

- https://texturebox.com/

- https://gumroad.com/l/ekRhc

- https://www.poliigon.com/

We can undoubtedly achieve professional-level results with these materials, but if we want a particular effect, we must create the textures personally with a little bit of work.

So, first, we take a picture of the material we want to reproduce. This image, suitably modified with an image editor, will become the Diffuse or Color or Albedo map of our material, and then from this texture, we will create those for the other channels.

Creating Standard Textures with Gimp

So, let's start by creating the Diffuse texture from a photograph. This texture determines the material's color; then, we will build the Normal and Specular maps.

Diffuse Map

Let's create the Diffuse texture of the material for our scene from the photograph of some marble tiles.

Follow these steps:

1. First, take some pictures of the floor you want to reproduce
    and choose the best one. We have chosen the one shown in
    Figure 4-19.

Figure 4-19. *The photograph of the floor*

2. Download the installer for the last stable version of the Gimp
    software from `https://www.gimp.org/downloads/`
    and then install it.

3. Open the photograph with Gimp (in the main menu, select
    File ➤ Open).

4. With the Perspective tool, with Shift+P, eliminate the perspective
    of the photography by straightening and making the floor tiles
    orthogonal. You can help yourself with the software's rulers that
    you can create by left-clicking and dragging the mouse on the
    profile's window with the measurements delimiting the working
    space of the photograph.

    You can zoom the image with Ctrl+MMB.

5.   Use the Crop tool with Shift+C to crop the image by selecting the nine central tiles shown in Figure 4-20.

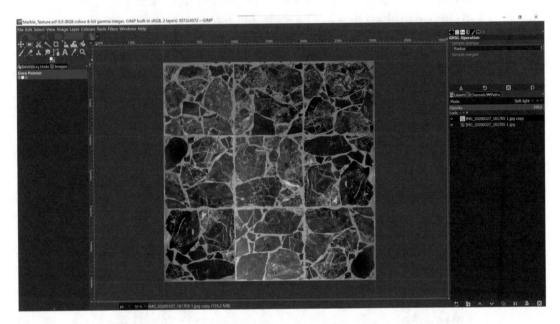

Figure 4-20.   *Editing the image in GIMP*

Resize the picture by typing 2048 x 2048 in the Width and Height fields of the window Canvas Size (in the main menu, select Image ➤ Canvas Size). Then click Resize.

6.   You can adjust the tiles' proportions to the image size with the Scale tool with Shift+S.

You can edit the Curves to change the image contrast (in the main menu, select Color ➤ Curves).

Now change the light distribution of the picture to make it uniform and remove the reflection.

1.   First, duplicate the layer, rename it **Gaussian**, and select it. Now apply the Gaussian Blur Filter (in the main menu, select Filters ➤ Blur ➤ Gaussian Blur).

2.   In the window that opens, ensure that the box "Clip to the input extent" is checked and then type **10** in the Size X and Size Y values. Then click OK. The photograph will be blurred.

3. Duplicate the layer a second time, rename it **High Pass**, put it
    at the top of the list by dragging it with the left mouse button
    pressed, and select it. Next, you have to apply the Gimp High Pass
    Filter from the main menu, select Filters ➤ Enhance ➤ High Pass.
    In the Std. Dev. box type **130** and change the contrast to 1,75,
    which helps restore details and colors. Click OK.

4. Right-click the Layers window and choose New from Visible to
    create a new layer that contains the result of your work. In this
    way, we have two layers: the one below is more opaque and less
    colored, and the one above is glossier and more colored.

5. Change the blending mode of the Visible layer from Normal
    to Luminance or Soft Light in the window on the right under
    Opacity, as shown in Figure 4-21.

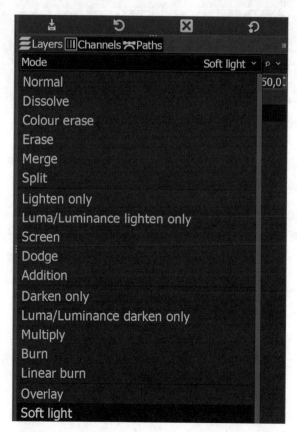

Figure 4-21. *From Normal to Soft Light Blending mode*

6. You can hide the Basic layer and the Gaussian layer and adjust the Opacity of Visible to control the transparency effect with the underlying texture. We used a 60% Opacity, as you can see in Figure 4-22.

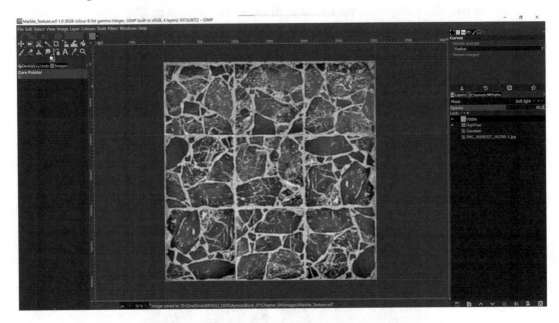

Figure 4-22. *Creating the diffuse map in GIMP*

The image has lost its reflections and has an opaque appearance, just what we need for a correct diffuse or color map.

7. Save the image as Marble_Texture.xcf. Then export it as a .png file (File ➤ Export ➤ Marble_Texture.png). This way, you have created the Diffuse or Color or Albedo texture for your material.

Now let's go ahead and prepare the normal texture.

Normal Map

We create the map for the Normal channel using a Gimp plug-in dedicated to this purpose.

This channel simulates the details of the surface without adding geometry; in our case, it reproduces the irregularities of the marble floor as scratches or cracks.

1. Install the GIMP Normal Map plug-in from link `https://code.`
    `google.com/archive/p/gimp-normalmap/downloads`. Drag and
    drop the `normalmap.exe` file to the GIMP plugins directory, usually
    `C:\Program Files\GIMP 2\lib\gimp\2.0\plug-ins`. Then drag
    and drop the three DLL files to the GIMP bin directory, usually
    `C:\Program Files\GIMP 2\bin`.

    Unfortunately, this plug-in works only with Windows.

    For other operating systems, we can instead use Adobe
    Substance 3D.

    This is a complete Adobe package for creating textures, but
    unfortunately, there is no free version, currently not even the
    educational one.

    It collects Substance 3D Painter, Designer, and Sampler. The
    first is to paint the textures on our materials, the second is to
    make seamless materials, and the third is to create photorealistic
    surfaces or HDRI environments from photographs.

2. Open the Marble _Texture image in Gimp created in the last part
    of this exercise.

3. From the main menu, select Filters ➤ Map, click Normalmap, and
    open the Normalmap window, as shown in Figure 4-23.

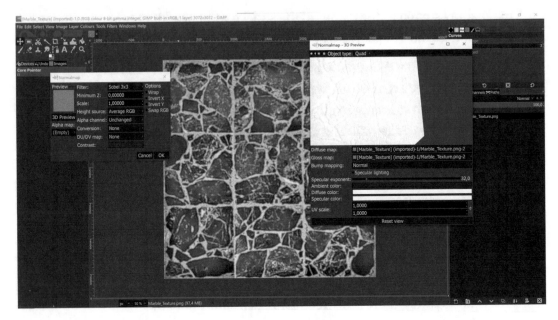

Figure 4-23. *Creating the normal map in GIMP*

4. Click the 3D preview button of the Normalmap window and open the Normalmap - 3D preview, enlarge it, and click with the right mouse button to bring it closer and rotate with the left mouse button the white plane of the preview to see the Normal effect, as shown in Figure 4-22.

5. Select Sobel 3 x 3 filter from Filter and click OK.

You have now created the normal texture for your material. You just have to export the file as `Marble_Texture_Normal.png`. Do not save the `.xcf` file.

We will create the Specular Map for our material in a few clicks, and then we will be ready to import them into Blender to generate the material.

Specular Map

We will create the Specular map for our material in a few clicks. The Specular map controls the specular effect of the material. Finally, we will import all the created textures into Blender to generate the material.

1. Open the Marble _Texture image in Gimp.

2. From the main menu, click Colors ➤ Desaturate ➤ Desaturate, choose Lightness (HSL) from the options, and click OK. Also, click Colors ➤ Levels from the main menu and adjust the input levels toward the middle, creating a contrasting black-and-white texture as shown in Figure 4-24.

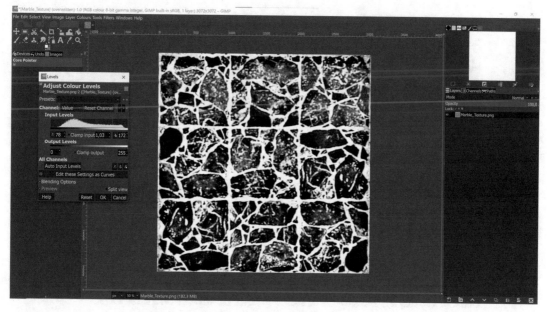

Figure 4-24. *Creating the Specular map in GIMP*

3. Export the texture with the name `Marble_Texture_Specular.png`.

We have just created the three main textures for our standard material.

Creating the Material

Now let's apply the textures we just made to a material composed of Diffuse and Glossy Shader nodes to practice using Blender's nodal system. To use the textures, follow these steps:

1. Open Blender, open the `LivingRoom` file, and save it as `LivingRoom_Material` (File ➤ Save as ➤ LivingRoom_Material ➤ Save as) to keep a spare copy of the `LivingRoom` file.

    The file `LivingRoom.blend` is in the code download for this book.

2. In the Topbar, click the Shading button to enter the Shading workspace.

3. Then left-click in 3D view on the Walls object and momentarily hide it by pressing H or clicking the eye to the right of the Walls object in the Outliner; perform the same operation on Roof.

4. Select the floor object and rename it to **Floor** in the Outliner.

5. Then move to the Properties Editor and click the Material Properties button to open the Material Properties window that allows you to edit the material. Next, click the New button, add a New Material, and rename it **Marble_Floor**. The Marble_ Floor material already has the Principled BSDF and Material Output nodes.

6. Delete the Principled BSDF Shader node.

7. Add a Diffuse Shader (press Shift+A and select Shader ➤ Diffuse) and connect the Diffuse BSDF Output with the Input Surface of the Material Output.

8. Create an Image texture (press Shift+A and select Texture ➤ Image texture), import the `Diffuse Marble_Texture.png` file with the button Open, and connect the Color output socket with the Color input socket of the Diffuse Shader.

9. Then add a Mix shader and drag it between the Diffuse BSDF and the Material Output.

10. Add a Glossy shader and connect its BSDF Output with the other Input of the Mix node.

11. Connect the Output color of the texture with the Input Color of the Glossy shader, as shown in Figure 4-25.

Figure 4-25. *The Marble_Texture Image node with Diffuse and Glossy shaders*

12. Duplicate the Image Texture node; select the Specular Map
     Marble_Specular Texture and change the Color Space to
     Non-color.

13. Add an RGB Mix node and change the Mix mode to Multiply by
     clicking Mix.

14. Put the texture in the upper socket called Color 1, set the lower
     plug to black, and then insert it into the Factor input of the
     Mix shader.

15. Now select the Specular texture node and the RGB Mix
     node, duplicate them, and put them in the material Output
     Displacement socket.

16.   Add the normal map with an Image Texture node, connect the
       output Color with the input Color of a Normal Map node, and
       connect the Normal Map node output with both the normal
       inputs of the two shaders, as shown in Figure 4-26.

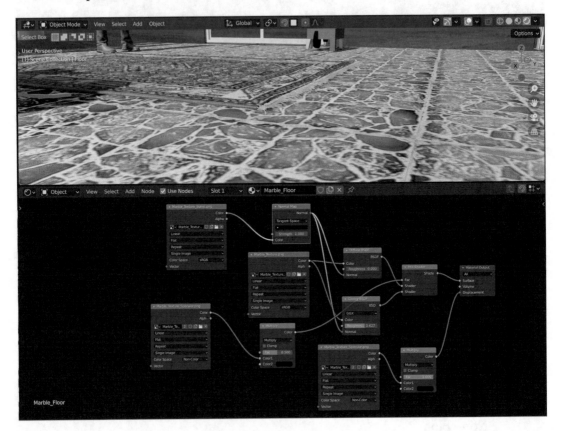

Figure 4-26. *The Marble material*

We experimented with traditional materials and textures, familiarizing ourselves
with Blender's standard materials. In the next exercise, let's create a PBR material that is
a physically correct substance.

Exercise 7: Creating a PBR Material

This section will create a PBR material for the living room floor using Blender's
Principled BSDF shader and some PBR textures downloaded from the Internet.

We can use this method to create other materials such as wood, marble, and
ceramics.

A great site to download free PBR textures from is `https://freepbr.com/`. From here, download the set of textures named oakfloor_fb1-bl.

1. Open the `LivingRoom` file.

2. In the Topbar, click the Shading button to enter the Shading workspace.

3. Select the Floor object in the Outliner.

4. Then in the Properties Editor, open the Material Properties window. First, click the +, and then on the New button, add a new material, and rename it as **Oak_Floor** material.

5. The floor has material assigned to the Principled BSDF and Material Output nodes.

6. Start to decrease the Roughness value to 0.12 and make the substance a bit darker by reducing the Lightness value of the Base Color to increase the specularity and to see the reflections of the HDRI map set by default in 3D view, which has the Viewport Shading set on Material Preview.

7. Select the Principled BSDF Node material and press Ctrl+Shift+T, and open the folder where you downloaded the textures.

8. Then on the right, click Principled Texture Setup and import the pictures; the tool automatically builds all the nodal systems for you. Of course, you must have installed the Node Wrangler add-on first; if you haven't, go to "The Node Wrangler add-on" section of this chapter and follow the installation instructions. Also you may need to modify some input connection towards the Principled BSDF node, because the textures are not always placed correctly by Blender. This inconvenience may depend on the names of the pictures being unrecognizable to the Node Wrangle algorithm.

9. Then, if you haven't done it before, unwrap the floor. Select the Floor object, go to Edit mode, press the A button to select everything, click U ➤ Unwrap, and in the window that opens, click Smart UV Project. Then, without changing any parameters, click OK. In this way, you have unwrapped the Floor object.

10. Connect the Albedo (or Diffuse or Color) texture to the Base Color
     socket of Principled BSDF. Then, to control the color even better,
     you can add a Hue/Saturation node between the Diffuse Texture
     Node and the Base Color socket to change the colors as you prefer.

11. We can see the final result of the rendered material and the
     completed nodal chain in Figure 4-27 or in file LivingRoom_Oak_
     Floor available with this book.

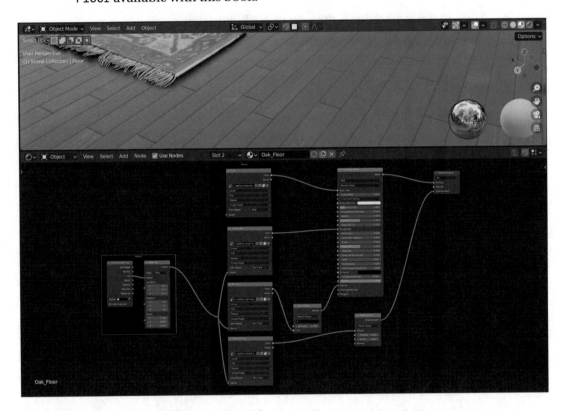

Figure 4-27. *The Oak_Floor material*

All the nodes have been inserted automatically in a click with the Add Principled
Setup option of the Node Wrangler with PBR textures.

If we replace the textures of this material with different textures and modify the
parameters Specular and Roughness, we can create different substances. For example,
by changing the wood textures to different woods, we can create parquet; or by using
Marble textures, we can make other types of marble.

In the following exercise, we will see how to create these textures from a single
material photograph.

Exercise 8: Creating Textures for PBR Materials

In this exercise, we will create textures for the channels of a PBR material.

In Exercise 6, we saw how to create textures for standard materials; now, we will learn how to make PBR material textures.

We will use Materialize, which is simple open source software that will allow us to create all the maps from a photograph.

Materialize

We begin our work by realizing the Diffuse texture from a photograph.

We will use Materialize, a free software dedicated to creating textures of this type. This tool is easy to use and very useful.

We can download it from `https://boundingboxsoftware.com/materialize/downloads.php`, and we can find information at `http://boundingboxsoftware.com/materialize/`.

This software works only on the Windows operating system. The source code is released as open source and downloadable from GitHub at `https://github.com/BoundingBoxSoftware/Materialize`, but you need a programmer to create an executable for another operating system.

Currently, the alternative is to use one of the versions of Materialize for Unity or Unreal Engine when already using one of those applications.

However, to create our materials and textures, we can use Substance 3D, the complete Adobe package we spoke about in Exercise 6.

The operations to create the desired textures with Materialize are straightforward: we need a picture of the material we want to make. Then, we create the Diffuse texture and the maps for the other material channels.

We can create textures for Blender, Unity, and Unreal Engine materials.

After downloading the zipped file of the software, let's extract it and set a folder to contain the textures we will create.

To launch Materialize, we must click inside the folder on the executable file Materialize. Then we can create many textures for different channels and control them precisely.

Let's open the software that presents a straightforward interface, as shown in Figure 4-28.

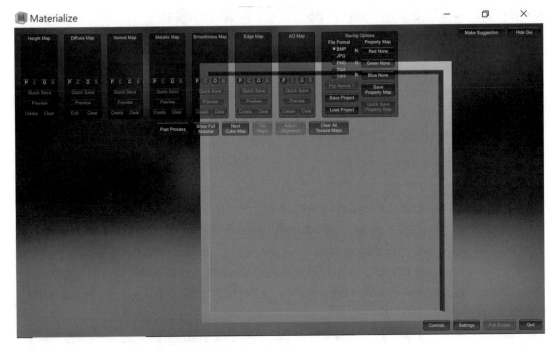

Figure 4-28. *The Materialize interface*

The interface has a frame that shows the textures we are creating. In addition, some panels contain the editing tools for the maps.

We can grab the panel containing the texture with the mouse buttons: we move the frame by clicking, holding down, and moving the middle mouse wheel; we zoom in or out by rotating the middle mouse wheel; and we turn the frame by clicking, holding down, and moving the left mouse button.

But let's get started on the images.

We have downloaded from `https://www.textures.com/` a basic image to create a PBR material for the wall of the building we modeled in the previous chapter. Let's see how to make the different textures.

First, we have to adapt the available image to the texture format. As explained in the subsection Bitmap and procedural textures, the 2048 x 2048 pixels format is usually sufficient to create well-defined materials. However, the picture we have downloaded is 1600 x 1200 pixels.

We will create a plaster material for our walls.

1. Open the photograph of the material serving to create the Diffuse texture in Gimp. From this texture, you will obtain the maps for the different channels.

We have downloaded the one in Figure 4-29.

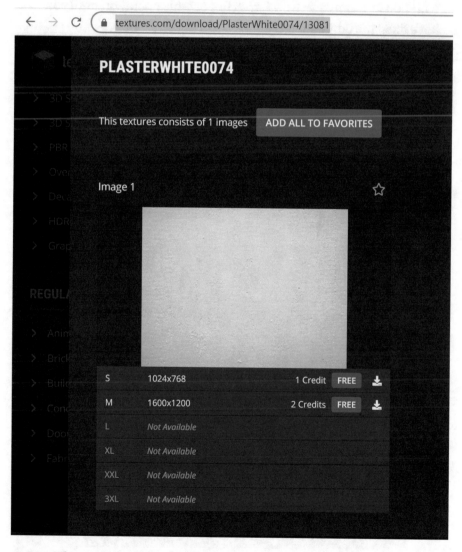

Figure 4-29. *The texture of the Wall material on the site Textures.com*

2. From the main menu, select Image ➤ Canvas Size, change the image size to 2048 x 2048, and click Resize.

3. You need to adapt your image to the final texture format of 2048 x 2048 and make it square and seamless.

    Copy it from the in the main menu, select Edit ➤ Copy and paste it with Edit ➤ Paste as ➤ New Layer. Repeat this operation until you have filled the entire image.

4. On the right side of the interface, right-click one of the layers and choose Flatten Image from the Layers window.

5. Then with the Clone brush, eliminate the junction line between the pasted parts.

6. To make the Texture seamless, you must do another operation in Gimp: from the main menu, select Filters ➤ Map, choose Tile Seamless, and click OK in the window that opens. We can see the result in Figure 4-30.

Figure 4-30. *The Diffuse Texture modified in Gimp*

7. Save the texture from Gimp main menu, choose File ➤ Overwrite, and overwrite the original picture.

    Now let's start creating the various maps for the other channels with Materialize.

8. First, import in Materialize the Diffuse texture you have just created.

    In the Diffuse window, click O (which stands for Open) and open the texture, which must be square and seamless.

9. Now start adding a Height texture to the PBR Material Wall to create the displacement.

    On the left side of the Diffuse panel, we have the Height Map window; click Create inside this window, and we will have a result like the one in Figure 4-31.

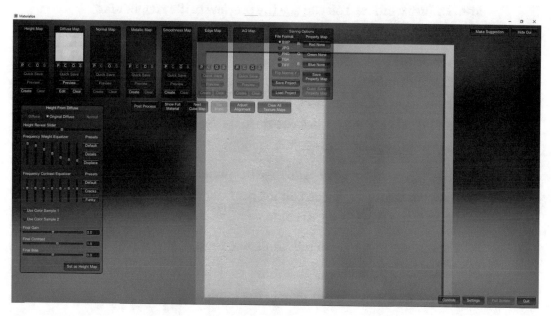

Figure 4-31. *The creation of the Height Map in Materialize*

The picture shows the left half of the material frame with the Diffuse texture and the right half with the Height texture.

As you can see in the figure, there are several control possibilities for realizing exact textures. The ones to use now are only Final Gain, Final Contrast, and Final Bias. A Height texture works with tonal variations between black and white. The darker colors create lower parts of the texture and the lighter stakes higher, giving the impression of a three-dimensional surface.

10. Work on the map until you get a soft but satisfying contrast. The Final Contrast tool is the one that can provide the best results. The experience will help you understand the most effective tonal values according to the type of materials you need to create. If you need, for example, a texture for tiles or bricks, the joints must be dark because the darker they are, the deeper and thicker the material.

11. When satisfied, click the Set as Height Map button in the Height from Diffuse window. You can see the preview of the Height Map in the interface at the top left of the Diffuse.

12. Now create the normal map to the right of Diffuse. Normal maps calculate the object's reaction to sunlight and simulate surface details such as bumps, grooves, and scratches as if they are present in real geometry. Click Create in the Normal Map window so the texture appears in the frame.

In general, you do not have to change the parameters of the window. For example, you can adjust the intensity of the surface details with the Final Contrast value.

When you are satisfied with the result, you must click Set as Normal Map.

13. Finally, create a Smoothness map in the same way.

14. You can see your material in the frame by clicking Show Full Material, as shown in Figure 4-32. The material is three-dimensional and has an outstanding graphic representation.

Figure 4-32. *The final material in the interface of Materialize*

15. Now you can export the textures from the Saving Options window highlighted in white in Figure 4-32. First, select the PNG format, click Save Project, and in the interface that opens, choose the path, click New Folder, and create a new folder called Wall. Then name the file **WallTexture** and click Select.

16. In this way, in the Wall folder, you will find the .mtz file for any subsequent changes and all the textures created in PNG format to apply to the material.

Finally, we apply the textures to the material in Blender.

Apply Textures to the Material

Now we must apply the textures to the material. To speed up the process, we use the Node Wrangler add-on again.

Let's create a new Wall material for our living room walls in the LivingRoom_ Material.blend file, apply the texture in the channels of the Wall material, and apply the same material to the Roof object.

1. Open the LivingRoom file.

2. In the Topbar, click the Shading button to enter the Shading workspace.

3. Select the object Walls in the Outliner. Then, from the Properties Editor, click the Material Properties button to open the Material Properties window and click the + button, add a New Material, and rename it **Plaster**.

   This material already contains two nodes: Principled BSDF and Material Output.

4. Select the Principled BSDF node of the Plaster material, press Ctrl+Shift+T, and open the folder where you created the textures.

5. Then on the right, click Principled Texture Setup and import the maps; even this time, the tool automatically builds all the nodal systems for you. Of course, you must have installed the Node Wrangler add-on first; if you haven't, go to the this chapter's section "The Node Wrangler add-on" and follow the installation instructions.

6. Then, if you haven't done it before, unwrap the Walls. Select the Walls object, go to Edit mode, press the A button to select everything, and click U ➤ Live Unwrap. In the window that opens, click Smart UV Project. Finally, without changing any parameters, click OK.

7. Repeat the Unwrapping operation for the Ceiling object and apply the Walls material to the Ceiling object too.

8. We can see the final result of the rendered material and the completed nodal chain in Figure 4-33.

Figure 4-33. *The applied material with the nodal chain*

In this exercise, we learned how to create the textures for PBR material channels, the physically based materials supported by Blender's PrincipledBSDF and SpecularBSDF shader nodes.

Finally, let's learn how to produce a procedural substance.

Exercise 9: Creating a Procedural Material

We will now proceed with the creation of a procedural material. This exercise will help us understand the difference between bitmap and procedural substances.

As we have already explained in the section "Bitmap and Procedural Textures," we make some materials with images and others with procedural textures.

The latter is composed of maps created by algorithms. In this example, we use the Noise procedural Texture. Still, we can easily alternate this with the Musgrave Texture.

There is a procedural materials' example in the `ProceduralMaterial.blend` file attached to the book.

Let's see how to create this material by following these steps:

1. Turn on Screen Space Reflection, Refraction, and Ambient Occlusion in the Render Properties window of the Properties Editor.

2. Set the world in the World window of the Properties Editor to illuminate the scene, using an HDRI map to ensure a realistic reflection, and change the viewport shading to Rendered.

3. Create a new plane, scale it four times, and move it down one unit. Finally, select the default cube and rename its material to **Metal**.

    Next, in the Shader Editor, decrease the lightness of the Base Color of the Principled BSDF shader to make the material a little darker and to see the reflection better.

4. Increase the Metallic value of the Principled BSDF node from 0 to 1 to increase the reflection of the material surface.

5. Add a Noise Texture node. For the parameter values, refer to Figure 4-34. Then, connect it with the Base Color and Normal Inputs of the Principled Node.

6. Add a Bump node and insert it between Normal and Principled BSDS; connect its Normal output socket with the Normal input socket of the Principled BSDS and its Input Height with the Output Color of Noise Image. This way, you get a total surface bumpiness effect.

7. Then use the Add Texture Setup tool of the Node Wrangler add-on to add mapping and texture coordinates. So, select the Noise Texture Node and, by pressing Ctrl+T, add two nodes: Mapping and Texture Coordinates.

8. Change Generated to UV in the Texture Coordinate Node and unwrap the cube with one of the methods studied in the "UV Mapping" section of this chapter. For example, you can use U ➤ Smart UV Project. Then you can scale the UV Map to size the material to the object.

9. Now add a Color Ramp node with the colors set as shown in
    Figure 4-34 and insert it between Noise Texture and Principled
    BSDF Nodes. Next, add a second Color Ramp node, entering it
    between Noise Texture and Bump.

You can refer to Figure 4-34 or the ProceduralMaterial file available with this book
to check if all the connections and values of the different nodes are correct and see the
values assigned to the various parameters.

Figure 4-34. *The Procedural Metal material*

The figure shows that we have created a simple procedural material with a
few nodes.

We can modify the parameters of the nodes and realize the great editing possibilities
offered by this material.

We can, for example, add Color Stops in the Color Ramp node connected to the Base
Color of the Principled BSDS to add colors and shades to create rust, etc.

We can also try different types of nodes to see what happens and better understand
the nodal materials.

Here also ends the part dedicated to the exercises of this chapter.

The thorough but straightforward studies we have conducted in this chapter on materials, textures, and lighting systems will also be helpful in the following chapters on numerous occasions. In addition, creating more personal and accurate scenes with the proper lighting, materials, and textures will also be beneficial in the professional future.

Summary

In this chapter, we learned what a node chain is, and we studied nodal materials and how to create them in Blender 3.0. Then, we saw how to create and apply the textures to the different materials to simulate surfaces. We also learned how to perform the UV mapping and unwrapping of the object.

Moreover, we became familiar with direct lighting and how to create indirect lighting through world settings. We can achieve photorealistic results with objects, materials, and lighting with this information.

The next chapter will investigate Blender's painting modes: Texture, Vertex, and Weight Paint. These features will allow us to paint textures as two-dimensional images and apply them to objects or directly paint on 3D objects.

CHAPTER 5

Painting

You already saw how to use some brushes in Sculpt mode to change the mesh's topology in Chapter 2. You can use similar tools to achieve different effects in Texture Paint, Vertex Paint, and Weight Paint. In Blender, we can paint or modify a texture in Texture Paint mode, both in the UV Image Editor as a two-dimensional image or in the 3D Viewport applied to the object.

Vertex Paint assigns a color to the vertices to create particular effects. In Weight Paint, we give weight to the vertices to control the intensity of the impact of something, for example, particles. In addition, we can create textures for our PBR materials by painting them within Blender, or we can make them with external software such as Gimp, Krita, and Materialize, and then apply them to our materials. This chapter will teach us how to use Blender's internal digital painting tools and devices available in other software like Krita, with or without using a graphics tablet. These tools will be helpful to get better and more customized textures and materials.

In this chapter, we are going to cover the following main topics:

- Introduction to color theory
- Digital painting
- Texture Paint: paint or modify a texture
- Vertex Paint: assign a color to the vertices to obtain particular effects
- Weight Paint: assign a weight to the vertices to control the intensity of some effects

Painting in Blender 3.0

This chapter will show us how to use Blender 3.0 for digital painting on two- or three-dimensional surfaces.

© Gianpiero Moioli 2022
G. Moioli, *Introduction to Blender 3.0*, https://doi.org/10.1007/978-1-4842-7954-0_5

Doing digital painting and drawing with 3D software allows interaction between the second and third dimensions. We have acquired a good mastery of our software in the previous chapters, and now we will begin to see some new features.

In Blender, as we have seen before, we can sculpt the topology with Sculp mode. This chapter will deepen the exciting union between the second and third dimensions. First, we will cover the basics of color theory, including primary colors and all the theoretical tools needed to understand the color's language.

Then, we will learn about Blender and Krita's painting tools and see how to use and customize them for a graphics tablet.

But let's start with a brief introduction to theory.

Introducing Color Theory

Let's begin to consider the importance of color. It influences the atmosphere of the scene and the observer's mood.

To achieve quality effects for photorealistic renderings and paintings or drawings, we need to understand the basics of color theory. This section will deepen our knowledge of color theory using the available Blender tools. We also begin to become familiar with Blender's devices for color modification.

In Ancient Greece, Aristotle studied the theory of color, then came Sir Isaac Newton, and later Goethe.

Several elements determine the color of an object. These characteristics remain constant in traditional painting, digital painting, and 3D graphics renderings.

Let's see what they are:

- The color of the object

- The color of the surrounding environment that the object reflects

- The intensity and color of the light

- The atmosphere of the environment

We must consider all of these elements when creating our 3D scenes. In addition, we must understand the basis of color theory that scientists and philosophers have developed over the years.

In these studies, the researchers have created several types of color wheels to help understand the relationship between one color and another.

The most used is the 12-color wheel, developed on Newton's color circle, which allows us to figure out the basic structure of color.

Understanding Color Relationships

Color theory teaches us about relationships through colors using the wheel. It helps us understand the language structure of colors and supports us when we need to use them.

First, let's understand what primary, secondary, and tertiary colors are and their relationships. Primary colors differ according to the model we are considering.

There are two different color models:

- The *additive method* (RGB) is where the light makes the colors. That's the digital method. The primary colors are Red, Green, and Blue, and, if combined with the same intensity, they give white as a result. Instead, the absence of light creates black.

- Instead, the *subtractive method* (CMYK) is composed of matter. That's the analog method. In this model, adding pigment subtracts the light. The model refers to the four ink colors: cyan, magenta, yellow, and black.

Newton was the first researcher who composed a color wheel to understand the relationships between colors, explaining his theories in the treatise "Opticks, or, a Treatise of the Reflections, Refractions, Inflections, and Colours of Light."[1]

We create secondary colors by mixing primaries, and we make tertiary colors by combining a primary with a secondary color. We have 12 colors, of which three are primary, three secondary, and six tertiary.

In addition, there are analogous colors, which are harmonious and close to each other in the wheel. There are also complementary colors, which are contrasting and opposite to each other on the color wheel.

Betty Edwards studies color theory theoretically and develops it from a practical point of view in some books.

---

[1] Isaac Newton, "Opticks or, a Treatise of the Reflections, Refractions, Inflections and Colours of Light." Printed for Sam. Smith, and Benj. Walford, London, 1704.

For a deeper understanding of the concepts developed in this section about theory and its practical application in painting, it is interesting to read her book *Color: A Course in Mastering the Art of Mixing Colors.*[2]

From color theory comes the terms *hue, saturation,* and *value,* of extreme importance in defining the properties of a color.

Let's learn their definitions and main concepts.

Value, Saturation, and Hue

Continuing with the discussion on color theory, we can say that each color has three main properties: value, saturation, and hue.

Blender allows us to control and modify them through the Blender color picker window shown in Figure 5-1.

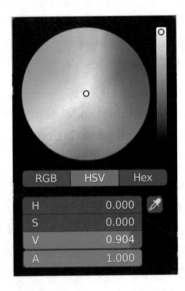

Figure 5-1. *The Blender color picker*

[2] Betty Edwards, *Color: A Course in Mastering the Art of Mixing Colors.* Jeremy P. Tarcher/Penguin, New York 2004.

Let's see first how the color picker works. In this window, we can modify the colors according to three different spaces:

- RGB is the additive model that uses Red, Green, and Blue as primaries colors.

- HSV (or HSB) measures color intensity through brightness.

- Hex (or Hexagesimal) allows us to define colors in code like HTML, CSS, etc.

The HSV panel will enable us to determine the material color's hue, saturation, and value in Blender. We have the eyedropper and the Alpha value in addition to these tools in the color picker.

We can copy any desired color from the Blender window with the eyedropper. With the Alpha value, we set the transparency. Finally, we can see the effect of the trasparency applied to the object in 3D view only after setting the blend mode to Alpha Blend, Alpha Clip, or Alpha Hashed in the Settings window of the Material panel in the Properties panel.

HSV is the default method in Blender; it is an additive color composition method that considers the perception of hue, saturation, and value.

Let's see the meaning of these three components and how we can use them in Blender by modifying the Blender color picker.

Let's move to the Shader Editor and edit the base color of the Principled BSDF shader of the object's material with the color picker highlighted in Figure 5-2.

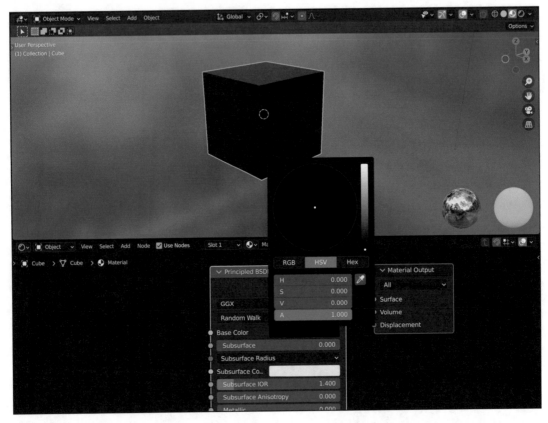

Figure 5-2. *Hue, saturation, and value at zero in the Blender color picker*

The figure shows that we obtain pure black by setting the Hue, Saturation, and Value values to zero. First, let's describe these three color components.

The value modifies the ratio, or percentage, of black and white.

The value can also be defined as lightness and specifies the amount of white or black in the perceived color, as shown in Figure 5-3. In fact, in the image, we can see that we get the white color by keeping the hue and saturation at 0 and bringing the value to 1.

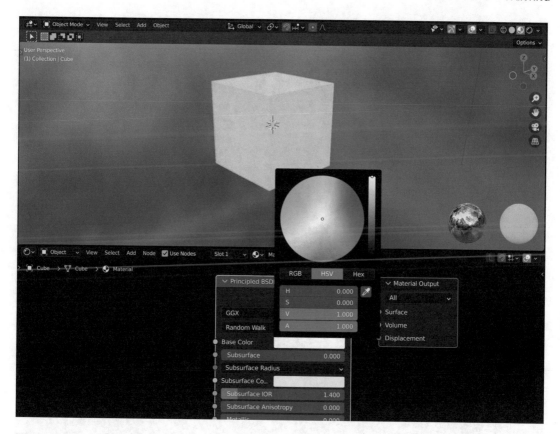

Figure 5-3. *The effect of value in a standard Blender 3.0 material*

So, the value is the degree of lightness, or darkness, of the color. In the Blender color picker, if this intensity is 0, no light will be added to the tone, while if this intensity is 1, the color will be visible in all its brightness.

Instead, the Saturation measures the color intensity, as shown in Figure 5-4.

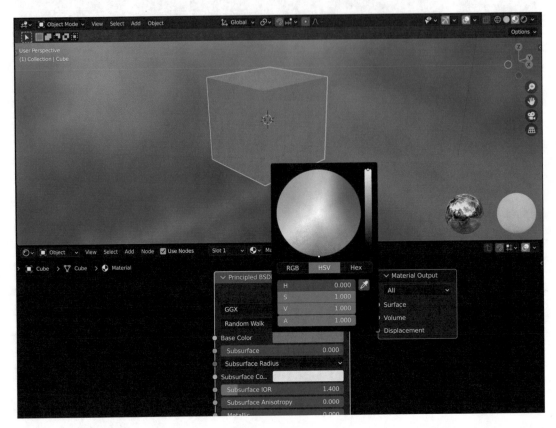

Figure 5-4.   *The effect of value and saturation*

If the saturation value is equal to zero, the color is achromatic.

When bringing the value to one, the color reaches the maximum intensity, as shown in Figure 5-4. Finally, the hue is the pure color. If we set the value and saturation to 1, we can select the colors at their maximum purity by modifying only the hue values rotating in a circle.

These concepts are more easily understood if we look at the simple scheme in Figure 5-5.

Figure 5-5. *The changing movements of value, saturation, and hue*

Changing the values of the Blender color picker boxes, we see the sliders move according to the white lines highlighted in the figure. So, the value cursor moves on the black-and-white diagram on the right, while saturation and hue go around in the color wheel.

This simple operation allows us to understand the influence of every single component.

Now that we have faced the main concepts of color theory, let's go on with digital painting and drawing.

Introducing Digital Painting

Digital painting brings many advantages over traditional art, and we can talk about *augmented painting* because of the additional techniques available.

- We can import drawing or painting works, 3D models, textures, etc., into a digital workspace through digital scanning or photography.

- We can work with masking techniques and virtually reproducing the paper masks used when painting with the airbrush, hiding parts of the drawing that we don't want to paint.

- We can use grids and composition aids that are displayed on the screen but not shown in the final image.

- We can work on different layers and create multiple copies of the same drawing while maintaining a base layer and painting on the others.

- We can add effects made available by various software.

- We can apply our drawings or paintings to the objects and make them interact in multiple ways with the three-dimensional space in Blender.

Blender has sophisticated tools for digital painting, as we will see in later sections.

We can use various software such as Photoshop and Gimp to do digital painting. In addition, some software is created specifically for artwork. We can integrate these products into three-dimensional modeling and graphics workflow.

The first one we'll discuss is Krita.

Krita

Krita gives us critical help to extend the features of digital painting. We mentioned it in Chapter 4, when we talked about Gimp.

As we already said, the difference between the two pieces of software is that while Gimp is more suitable for image editing, Krita is better for drawing and digital painting.

It's worth dwelling for a moment on its painting tools that we can use to create textures, painting and sculpting devices, masks, etc.

As we will see in the exercises of this chapter, Blender painting tools, joined to those of Krita, offer us infinite creative possibilities and extend our pictorial possibilities.

Krita allows us to realize painted textures for Blender materials with its numerous brushes. We can implement cartoon, pictorial, or even realistic textures.

As far as digital painting is concerned, Krita is probably the best open source alternative to Photoshop and Gimp, with a wide range of customizable brushes, layering, blending modes, etc.

Moreover, Krita's interface is more attractive, friendly, and intuitive for digital painting than Gimp's. In Figure 5-6, we can see the default interface.

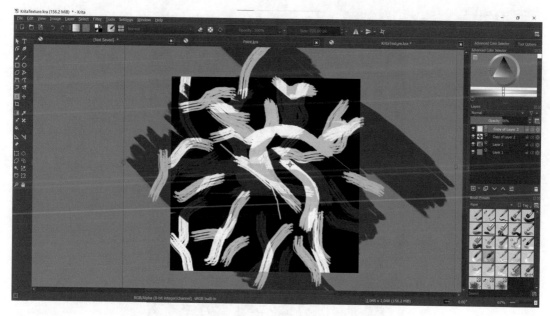

Figure 5-6. *Krita default interface*

As we can see in the image, all the tools for digital painting are in an intuitive interface. If we want to change the interface layout and the tools, we can change the workspace, as in Blender. We click the icon "Choose workspace" in the upper-right corner and choose the favorite workspace in the opening window.

On the other hand, if we want to add some panels or re-add one that we closed by mistake, we click its name in the window that opens from the main menu by selecting Settings ➤ Dockers.

Let's see some of the tools Krita gives us.

Krita's Tools, Palettes, and Color Selectors

Brushes are the most exciting tools for us, but before learning about them, let's briefly mention the devices that help us modify the image data.

In Figure 5-7 we see one above the other; the most important Krita panels are the toolbar, the default palette, the Advanced Color Selector panel, and the Brush Presets panel.

Figure 5-7. *Krita's tools, palettes and color selectors, and brush presets*

The Krita toolbar contains all the main tools for creating, selecting, and editing graphic objects.

We have five different types of devices.

- The Selection tools allow the selection of parts of the drawing in different ways.

- The Paint tools create various strokes, which we define with a shape, a size, a kind of opacity, and other elements. They depend on the definition of the image.

- The Vector tools do not depend on image definition, but we can modify them using control points like the Bézier curve or freehand path tool.

- The Guide tools are drawing aid tools, such as a grid, perspective, or assistant tool.

- The Transform tools transform objects or layers on the canvas.

Then we have customizable palettes, which allow us to choose the right colors to get the visual impact of the final project. Krita provides some predefined ones and enables us to create customizable ones. A range of colors is grouped according to different logic and the result we want to achieve.

On the other hand, the color selectors are the tools that allow us to choose the color model, depth, and profile. They allow us to select an additive or subtractive color model; a depth of 8, 16, or 32 bits; and different color profiles.

In this chapter's "Introducing Color Theory" section, we already saw some of these concepts.

The Brush Presets panel contains all the brush tools divided into categories such as Paint, Sketch, Ink, Texture, etc.

The range of tools is comprehensive and customizable in endless ways.

Now let's see how to use Krita for digital painting.

Krita's Brush System

Krita contains a palette of predefined brushes, the Brush Presets panel. These brushes are ready to use and were built to demonstrate the different creative possibilities of this software.

They are divided into several categories and are helpful for other modes of use, ranging from digital painting to 3D texturing, pixel art, etc.

We can paint with the brushes by clicking and dragging the left mouse button or, as we will see shortly, with a graphic tablet.

We can modify the size of the brush by pressing Shift+LMB; we can decrease the opacity by pressing I and increase it by pressing O.

We can modify the brush type in the Brush Presets window.

This system of integrated brushes is quite extensive, as we can see in Figure 5-8.

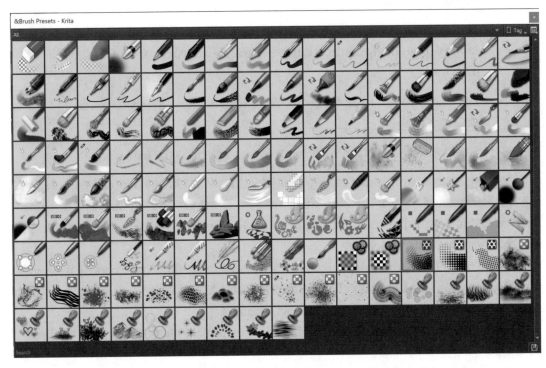

Figure 5-8. *Krita's Brush Presets panel with all the available brushes*

It is just like actual painting or drawing, where we can use many tools: pencils, charcoals, chalks, watercolors, oil painting, etc.

With its numerous tools, Krita imitates the effects of real painting very effectively.

The available tools give us many editing possibilities because each is customizable in the Edit Brush Settings window, which allows us to edit options and create a virtually infinite number of Drawing and Painting tools.

We can open this panel in the toolbar under the main menu with the top-left Edit Brush Settings button, which is framed in white in Figure 5-9.

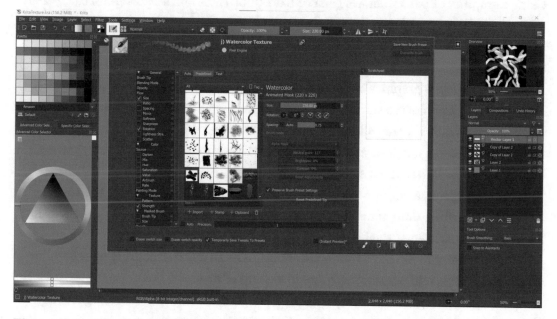

Figure 5-9. *The Edit Brush Settings button in Krita*

Many parameters allow us to vary presets in this window, including Size, Rotation, Opacity, etc.

As in the case of Blender brushes, also in Krita, we start from standard models that we can then modify and save for later use. We find the saved tools together with the others in the Brush Presets panel.

As we saw in Chapter 2, in Blender we must distinguish between tools and brushes. The tools are on the toolbar and have general settings; brushes are our tools saved with the customized settings, and we can save them directly in the Edit Brush Settings panel.

Also in Krita, we have the brush tips and the brush presets: the former are the basis for the latter. We can choose and modify primary forms from time to time with all the parameters provided by the Edit Brush Settings window.

It is essential to use a graphic tablet to make the best use of these tools and extend the pictorial or sculptural functions beyond the use of the mouse.

Let's see how to choose the graphics tablet and set up our work.

Graphics Tablets with and Without Screens

Using a graphics or pen tablet, we can control our brushes and strokes more easily than with a mouse.

For example, we can modify the pressure sensitivity to alter the radius and the strength of the brushes in every painting or sculpting mode.

We can choose a graphics tablet or a drawing tablet with or without a screen.

The graphics tablet is a sensitive surface connected to a computer. In contrast, the drawing tablet with a screen allows us to draw directly on the display. In some ways, a tablet or PC with a touch screen is easier to use than a pen because we can draw by looking simultaneously at the screens.

In other aspects, a graphic tablet without display is more comfortable because it shows the view freely and allows us to work at a certain distance from the screen, as in traditional painting and drawing.

Also, a graphic tablet has a much lower cost. We can use it effectively with Blender and image editing and painting software like Gimp or Krita.

There are many good-quality graphics tablets such as Wacom, Huion, Ugee, etc. They work well and have many functions, including the following:

- Availability of a large work area with a surface that simulates the tactile experience of paper

- Possibility of tilting up if we think it necessary

- High-level pen pressure sensitivity

- Hotkeys that we can customize with our keyboard shortcuts

- Easy to install and easy to use for left and right hands

- Possibility of connection with mobile phone and support of the Android operating system

- Support for multiple operating systems and compatibility with numerous software including Adobe Photoshop, Pixologic ZBrush, and of course Blender

A graphics tablet is also great to use with the Grease Pencil, the recent Blender painting and animating tool that we, unfortunately, don't cover in this book.

We prefer the graphics tablet without a screen. We can comfortably use it in Blender Sculpt and Edit mode. Also, it is perfect for experimenting with painting and sculpting in Blender and Krita.

The Graphics Tablet with Blender

First, we prepare the graphics tablet to use with Blender by setting the pen keys and tablet hotkeys for optimal use of our software.

We will give Blender settings for sculpting and painting.

First, we install the software provided with the tablet, open it, and perform the simple operations by setting the interface as shown in Figure 5-10.

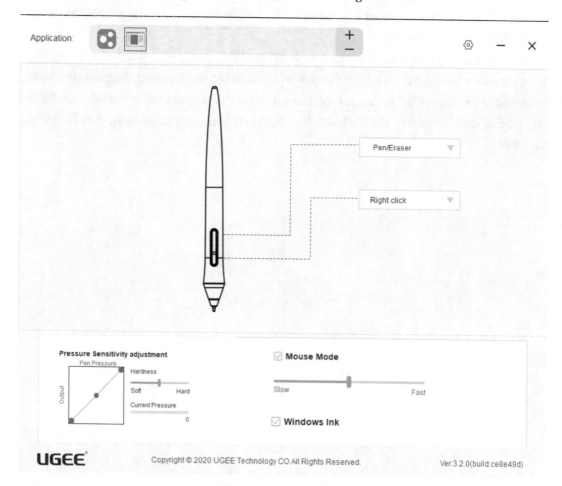

Figure 5-10. *Setting the pen functions and sensitivity*

Let's define the functions of the pen's buttons with the same functionalities as the mouse's buttons and middle wheel.

In Blender, as we have already seen, we navigate in 3D view with the middle mouse wheel.

- By rotating it in one direction, we zoom in, and by turning it the other way, we zoom out.

- By pressing the wheel and moving the mouse, we rotate the 3D view.

- Pressing it and simultaneously moving the mouse while holding down the Shift key, we move horizontally in 3D view in pan mode.

So, it is crucial to be able to use the same functions when using the graphic tablet to work efficiently and quickly.

We set the single button of the pen with the middle mouse wheel function to rotate 3D view easily. We can then adjust the pen's pressure sensitivity according to our needs in the same window. Our graphics tablet has 8,192 levels of pressure sensitivity available, and we can adjust them in the Pressure Sensitivity Adjustment window to match the way we draw.

Instead, in the next window, we can adjust the screen area to the sensor size of the graphics tablet, as shown in Figure 5-11.

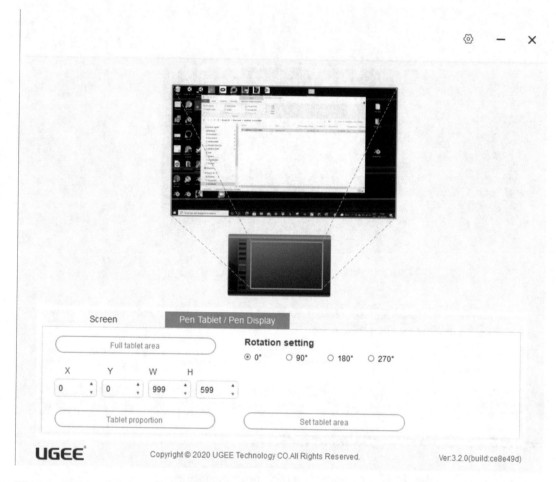

Figure 5-11. *Setting the working area*

Finally, we can customize the Express Keys setting. We define eight hotkeys in the case of our tablet, as shown in Figure 5-12.

Figure 5-12. *Customizing the tablet hotkeys*

Let's associate the first four keys of the tablet to navigation:

1. We use the first button to open the tablet interface, so we can change all settings at any time during our work session if necessary.

2. We set the second button as Scroll Up to zoom in on the view.

3. Let's set the third button as Scroll Down to zoom out the view.

4. Associate the fourth button on the tablet with the Shift shortcut so that we can quickly pan 3D view by clicking it simultaneously with the pen button.

The other four keys are for the drawing, painting, and sculpting tools.

1. Use the fifth button for the Ctrl key to reverse the brush/chisel function from positive to negative.

2. Associate the sixth key to the shortcut F to change the brush size.

3. Associate the seventh command to the shortcut Shift+F to modify the brush strength.

4. Use the eighth and final key on this tablet for the Ctrl+Z shortcut to the Undo function.

Now let's see the Blender brushes and how we can use them.

Blender's Painting Brushes

Blender provides us with brushes and chisels and digital tools for sculpting and painting. We have already met Blender's chisels in Chapter 2. Also, there are other tools for painting in the Texture, Vertex, and Weight Paint modes. Moreover, we have various exciting painting tools in the Draw mode of the Grease Pencil object.

Blender's tools change in the different object modes. We find the necessary tools in the toolbar on the left of the interface: in Sculpt mode, we have at our disposal instruments to sculpt; in Texture, Vertex, and Weight Paint mode, we have devices to paint.

Instead, the keyboard shortcuts to perform operations usually do not change in the different modes and ways of painting and sculpting. This characteristic of Blender is attractive. If we learn to use one editor's interface, we also know how to use the others.

This method makes our work much more manageable. Of course, the sculpting brushes will be a bit different from the painting brushes, but the adjustment tools, the keyboard shortcuts, and the graphic tablet settings will be almost always the same.

Brush Controls

As we already saw in Chapter 2, working with shortcuts in Sculpt mode is faster; for this reason, we have set the most important of them in the side buttons of the graphics tablet: Shift, Ctrl, F, Shift+F, Ctrl+Z.

Here are reminders of some of the functions of these shortcuts for brushes:

- F adjusts the brush size.

- Shift+F modifies the strength of the brush.

- Ctrl+F changes the brush rotation.

- Ctrl reverses the brush action from positive to negative.

- S samples the color from a sample identified by the cursor.

After typing these shortcuts, we must move the mouse or type the value we want to apply and then press Enter or click the left mouse button (LMB) to confirm the operation. Instead, if we press Esc or the right mouse button (RMB), we abandon the change. For example, by pressing F ➤ 50 ➤ LMB, we obtain the brush size of 50 pixels; by pressing Shift+F ➤ 0.5 ➤ LMB, we apply 50 percent of the force.

The fact that we have set some keyboard shortcuts on the graphics tablet does not prevent us from using them on the computer keyboard.

Now let's see how to paint in Blender in the various painting modes.

Painting in Blender

We deal first with Texture Paint, then with Vertex Paint, and finally with Weight Paint.

Each of these systems has a dedicated Object mode.

We can set them in the Object Interaction mode of the 3D view header, as shown in Figure 5-13.

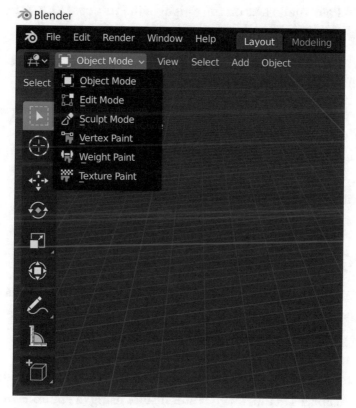

Figure 5-13. *The Select Object Interaction Mode button*

We've already looked at modes in Chapter 1. So now, let's quickly review them, distinguishing between those for three-dimensional modeling and those for painting. The first three object modes in the list are for modeling.

- Object mode, to work at the object level

- Edit mode, to make changes on subobjects such as vertices, edges, and faces

- Sculpt mode, which modifies the topology of the object with modeling tools

The following are used for painting:

- Texture Paint mode changes the texture directly by modifying the pixels.

- Vertex Paint mode changes the color of the mesh vertices in the active vertex color layer.

- Weight Paint mode acts on the weight of the vertices in the active vertex group.

- Draw mode appears in the window only after creating a Grease Pencil object.

In this first section, we talked about color theory and digital painting with Blender and Krita; then, we presented the painting modes in Blender.

We will study the various creative possibilities and tools available in these different modes.

Let's start with the Texture Paint mode.

Practicing Texture Paint

As we have already said, textures are fundamental to obtain the materials we want, from photorealistic to cartoon ones. The aspect of our materials and objects, the render quality, and the mood of our 3D environments all depend on textures.

The texture is the thing's "skin," and we project it onto the object.

Through texture painting, we can also paint our textures directly inside Blender. We can load or create images in the Image Editor header using the buttons highlighted in Figure 5-14.

Figure 5-14. *The header of the Image Editor*

We have three ways to use an image as a UV texture in our software:

- The first is to create the image inside a graphic editor like Gimp or Krita and then load it in Blender from the Image Editor header menu by clicking the Open button.

- Also, we can create a new texture by clicking New from the Image Editor header menu and then paint it with the tools that Blender gives us.

- Finally, we can paint a new texture or modify the existing one by painting directly on the object in 3D view of Blender.

The first step to easily paint a texture is to access the Texture Paint workspace that allows us to paint surfaces in Blender both bidimensionally on the images and directly on three-dimensional objects.

Texture Paint Workspace

So, the quickest way to start painting a texture in Blender is to go to the Texture Paint workspace, as shown in Figure 5-15.

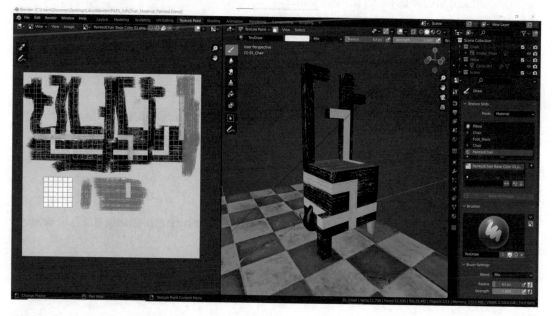

Figure 5-15. *The Texture Paint workspace*

We have an Image Editor in Paint mode on the interface's left in this workspace.

In the center, there is 3D view in Texture Paint mode.

When we move in the Texture Paint workspace, the mouse cursor turns into a brush, and we can draw with the painting tools available in the toolbar on the left of the two mentioned windows.

Then, on the right of the interface, we find the Outliner at the top and the Properties Editor's Active Tool and Workspace Settings window at the bottom.

This workspace gives us all the tools we need to paint an image or an object. These devices are as follows:

- The Image Editor has a two-dimensional painting space to create an image to paint, or import a texture.

- 3D view in Texture Paint mode allows us to paint directly on the object.

- From the column on the right, in the Outliner at the top, we can select the objects to paint. Then, at the bottom, in the Active Tool and Workspace Settings of the Properties Editor, we can change the characteristics of all the brushes:

  - The size with the Radius button

  - The intensity with the Strength button

  - The color with the color picker

To understand how this process works, let's see how to paint a texture on our chair or another object.

Painting on an Object

Before starting to paint, we have to prepare the workspace by performing the following operations:

1. Select the object you want to paint. In 3D view, switch to Edit mode by pressing the Tab button.

2. Then select all the subobjects by pressing A, and with U, open the UV Mapping window and click an Unwrapping method to create the UV map of the object, as shown in Chapter 4.

After choosing to make our texture in Blender or import one, we click the New or Open button on the header menu of the Image Editor and create the new image with the following steps:

1. In the Image Editor, create a new image by clicking the New button. Then, when the window opens, type the resolution you want, for example, 2048 x 2048.

Give a name to the image, choose Color Grid as Generated Type, and click OK.

Then save it in the desired path from the menu Image ➤ Save.

2. Now, to create a material, click New in the Material window of the Properties Editor on the right side of the screen.

    Then, in the Base Color box, select Image Texture with the button highlighted in Figure 5-16. Next, click the down arrow in the box and choose the texture from the opening window.

    This way, the texture is now part of the material.

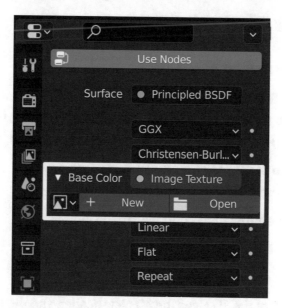

Figure 5-16. *The Base Color box and the buttons to create or upload textures*

3. Press Z and click Rendered in the 3D Viewport. The texture appears.

4. In the 3D view header's Viewport Shading panel select Lighting
    Method and set the lighting to Flat, as shown in Figure 5-17.

Figure 5-17.   Setting lighting to Flat

Now we can finally start painting.

5. Go back to Texture Paint mode in 3D view and start painting the
    texture with the toolbar devices. Create and adjust the brushes in
    the Properties Editor's Active Tool and Workspace Settings panel.

    You can also use F and move the mouse to change the brush
    radius and press Shift+F to modify the strength.

Now let's see the painting tools contained in the toolbar.

The Toolbar

The toolbar, on the left of the 3D view, the 3D view header, and the Properties Editor's
Active Tool and Workspace Settings panel contains the essential tools to paint.

These devices are more or less the same in Texture Paint, Vertex Paint, and
Weight Paint.

In the toolbar, we have the main painting tools; let's take a closer look at them in
Figure 5-18.

Figure 5-18. *Painting with the toolbar*

We see Blender's main painting tools in the Figure's 3D view in Texture Paint mode. Let's list them with their main functions:

- Draw is the essential brush and paints a strip of color. This instrument allows us to paint on the texture or directly on the object. We can use it to paint whole textures or to modify existing images.

- Soften is the second instrument in the toolbar. According to our needs, this tool applies a blur effect to modify the image to make it more nuanced in some places.

- Then we find Smear. This instrument distorts the image achieving an effect similar to a gradient or a smudge brush" in the traditional drawing. For example, if we click a point in the texture, it checks the color below and blurs it in the direction we move the mouse.

- Clone copies the texture color from one point to another in the image.

- In the 3D Viewport, we can use Ctrl+LMB to copy the texture from one part of the object. Then we click with the left mouse button to paint the clone.

- Fill fills large areas of the image with the chosen color.

- We use masks to hide the image's parts that we do not want to paint with the active brush. Unfortunately, at the moment, it works only when we paint directly on the object in 3D view. But there are other masking methods that we will see shortly in the section "Practicing Masking."

- The selection tools are visible only when activating the Paint Mask button in the editor header. This button activates selection, as we will see shortly in "The Paint Mask and Face Selection Masking" section.

- There are four tools: Tweak, Select Box, Select Circle, and Select Lasso.

- We use these devices to choose the vertices we want to paint.

- Below these instruments, we find the Annotate tools.

As in Sculpt mode, in the toolbar, we can create our custom brushes, setting them as we prefer and saving them for later use when needed.

We can change the brushes' characteristics by right-clicking in the window or by using the window's header or keyboard shortcuts.

Brush Settings

In the second line of the 3D view header, the Tool Settings, we find the details of the Texture Paint tools, as shown framed in white in Figure 5-19. Here we can create our custom brushes and reuse them when needed.

Figure 5-19. *The brush settings in the header of 3D view*

In the first box in the figure, we find the name of the original tool, in this case, Draw.

In the second, we can name our custom brush and save it for subsequent sessions; by default, it is called TexDraw.

To create a new brush, we must click the number of users next to the brush's name in the Active Tool and Workspace Settings window of the Properties Editor, as shown in Figure 5-20 framed in white. This operation makes the tool unique.

Figure 5-20. *The Active Tool and Workspace Settings window in Texture Paint mode*

We can rename the brush with the desired name in the white framed box of the figure. Then we start editing it with the different tools settings available.

Here, or in 3D view's Tool Settings, we change the brush settings:

1. In the first box, we change the various blending modes of painting.

2. In the second, we change the Radius value of the brush.

3. In the third, we change the brush's Strength value.

Then we find the color picker for color adjustment. In the same window, we can also create a gradient. Afterward, we can customize our brushes using the Falloff section of the Active Tool and Workspace Settings window.

With this window, we can control, for example, the sharpness or softness of our brush.

To get a tool with very defined edges, we proceed as follows:

1. Open the Falloff window.

2. Click the inverted white triangle highlighted in Figure 5-21 and change the handle to Vector.

3. Add a control point by left-clicking in the center of the diagonal straight line of the graph. Then, drag the curve as in Figure 5-21.

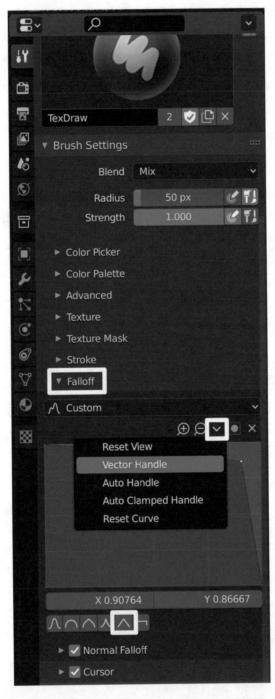

Figure 5-21. *The Active Tool and Workspace Settings window in Texture Paint mode*

From now on, our brush will create very defined strokes.

Instead, to get a very blurred brush, we need to change the handle to Vector as in the previous example and flatten the curve by lowering the control point to the left, as in Figure 5-22.

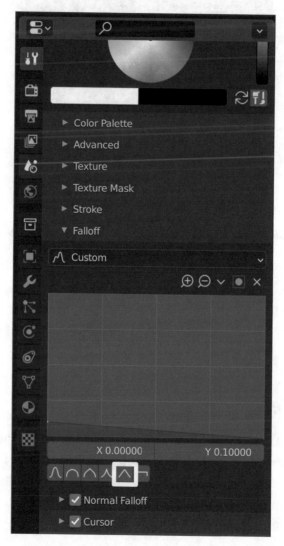

Figure 5-22. *The Active Tool and Workspace Settings window in Texture Paint mode*

This brush has very fuzzy outlines.

We can customize the brushes in many ways by editing the control chart, as in Figure 5-23.

Figure 5-23. *The Active Tool and Workspace Settings window in Texture Paint mode*

For example, by setting up a curve like Figure 5-23, we get a line with many blurred points similar to LED lights.

After exploring the tools, let's now see the blending modes, which can significantly modify the action of our brushes.

Blending Modes

We use mixing modes in computer graphics to determine how to merge two layers.

Image editing software, such as Adobe Photoshop and GIMP, allows users to choose between blending modes. For example, the Multiply blending mode multiplies the RGB channel values of each pixel in the two layers.

In Blender's Texture Paint mode, blending modes apply the brush color with the color underneath.

These modes change the image's appearance and are almost the same as any layered 2D graphics software, like Gimp, Krita, or Photoshop.

In Figure 5-24, we can see the blending modes that Blender provides us within the Texture Paint mode in the Brush Settings window of the Active Tool and Workspace Settings panel.

Figure 5-24. *Blend modes of Texture Paint*

In this case Blender works like some image editors.

These are the main modes:

- Mix simply combines the color added by the brush with the color of the underlying texture.

- Darken uses the darker value between the color added by the brush and the existing image.

- Multiply multiplies the color of the brush by the RGB value of the base.

- Lighten increases the RGB value of the base color by the color of the brush.

- Add joins the brush color to the RGB value of the existing image; the result is the sum of the two RGB colors.

- Subtract deducts the brush color from the current base.

- Erase Alpha makes transparent the parts of the image on which we paint with the brush.

- Add Alpha has the opposite effect of Erase Alpha. That is where we brush the image if it has a percentage of transparency; it becomes more opaque.

As we can see, the blend modes directly affect the way we paint in Blender by changing the color overlay modes.

After analyzing how Blender mixes the brush colors, let's practice with another valuable tool for Texture Painting: masks.

Practicing Masking

We can improve the results and speed up the realization time in Texture Painting mode using masks. When we do not want to apply the brush modification to a part of the object, we can mask the portion we want to maintain unchanged, just as we do in software like Gimp or Photoshop.

When we apply a mask, the brush will affect only the unmasked parts or, vice versa, only the hidden region. This option is similar to the sculpting masks in Chapter 2, with some brushes able to mask part of the mesh.

Now let's see how to use the different types of masks. The first one is Paint Mask.

The Paint Mask and Face Selection Masking

This device is the fastest but is less complex than the ones we will see next. It is available in the 3D view header in Texture Paint, Vertex Paint, and Weight Paint modes.

It allows us to draw only the portions we want to modify and mask where we don't want to paint.

We select the object to paint, go to Edit mode, and select the faces to paint on.

Let's go to Texture Paint mode and choose the Paint Mask button in the 3D view header. We can see the button highlighted in white in Figure 5-25.

Figure 5-25. *The paint mask*

From now on, we can paint only on the parts we have previously selected in Edit mode.

We can paint with a brush or use the Fill tool from the toolbar to evenly fill all the selected parts.

Afterward, if we want to smooth the line between two colors, we can turn off the paint mask and use the instrument Smear.

Now let's see a different, more sophisticated method to mask the texture with a stencil.

Create a Stencil

Painting with stencils can add intricate details to our textures effortlessly. With this method, we can create any image in our favorite image editor and then use it inside Blender as a mask to paint our surfaces, as practiced in the Teapot_Stencil file attached to this book.

Let's see how to do it in a brief exercise:

1. Select the object to paint, create a material, and add a base texture.

2. Make the UV unwrapping, and then move to the Texture Paint workspace.

3. Create a black-and-white image in Krita or Gimp or another image editor. Keep in mind that when you use the texture in Blender, the white will be transparent and the black will be opaque, so you will paint with the white strokes.

4. In the Texture Properties tab of the Properties Editor, add a New texture by clicking the New button shown in Figure 5-26. Call it **Stencil**.

Figure 5-26. Add a New Texture button

5. Then with the Open button, load the image previously created
    with Krita, as shown in Figure 5-27.

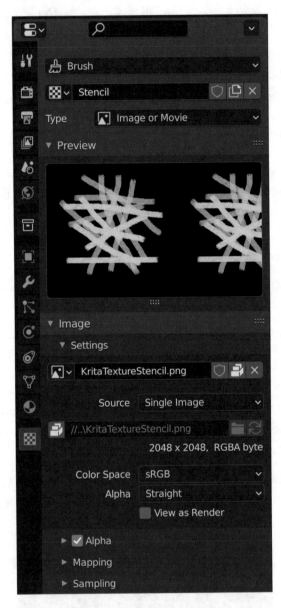

Figure 5-27. Loading the texture

6. You can see the texture loaded in the texture window in the Properties Editor's Active Tool and Workspace Settings panel. In the same window, change the brush mapping from Tiled to Stencil.

When you move with the cursor in 3D view using the Image Editor, you can see the stencil in the window, as shown in Figure 5-28.

Figure 5-28. *Painting with the stencil mask*

7. Now you can move the stencil and start painting on the mask.

To work profitably, we need to know how to use some controls. Let's see them.

We can move the stencil by clicking the right mouse button (RMB) and dragging the mouse. To change the mask size, we click with Shift+RMB and drag. To rotate, we click and drag with Ctrl+RMB. Then we paint with the brush Draw. So, the white parts are transparent, and the black portions mask the brush strokes.

Reset Tiled instead of Stencil in the Properties Editor's Active Tool and Workspace Settings panel to return to normal painting mode.

We have just created a custom mask on which we can paint with different colors, and with the same method, with Krita, we can create an infinite number of patterns.

Now we see another masking system that makes a different result.

Painting with a Mask

This masking system is different from the previous one.

Also, with this method, we can create an image inside or outside Blender and then use it inside Blender to paint our surfaces.

But while the black parts hide the brush in the first example, the white portions paint on the object's surface in this one.

Let's see how to do that with another quick exercise.

1. In Blender, create a material connecting two different materials based on Principled BSDS shaders with a Mix Shader node and call it **Mask**.

   You can use any material; for example, you can use metal and overlay rust or scratches.

2. Then create an Image Texture node and add a new image by clicking the button New, keep the default settings but change the width and height to 4096 x 4096, and rename the image Mask. Then connect the Color output of the Image Texture node with the Fac (that is the factor input) input of the Mix Shader node, as shown in Figure 5-29.

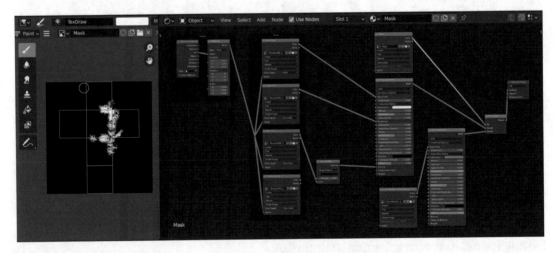

Figure 5-29. *The nodal chain for the mask*

3. Now go to the Texture Paint workspace, change the viewport
    shading to Rendered, and in the Texture Properties tab of the
    Properties Editor, choose Brush Mask on the menu that opens;
    then click New, as in Figure 5-30.

Figure 5-30. *Creating the brush mask*

Choose one of the procedural textures in the Type menu, such as
clouds or marble, etc. Now you can paint directly on the object in
3D view or the texture in the Image Editor. Where you paint, the
underlying material appears.

4. Then, to improve texture distribution in the Texture Mask window
    of the Active Tool and Workspace Settings panel of the Properties
    Editor, change Mask Mapping from Tiled to Random. Next, select
    the option Random and increase Jitter in the Stroke section, as
    shown in Figure 5-31.

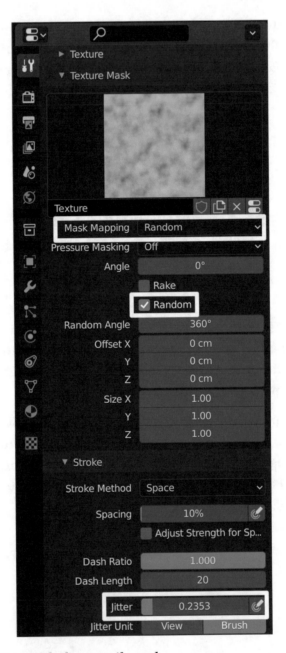

Figure 5-31. *Painting with the stencil mask*

If we want more control over the brush marks, we can create a more defined image in an external editor and add it to the already made brush mask.

Let's see how to do that with a quick exercise. So, let's take another small step and add a custom image.

1. Create an image with Krita or Gimp or another image editor of your choice. So, first, make a black-and-white image for a brush. The white portion of the texture will paint the surface.

2. Then in Texture Properties, change the texture type from Marble to Image or Movie and load the texture created in Krita with the Open button.

3. Now select the Mask texture in the Texture Slots window on top of the Active Tool and Workspace Settings panel and start to paint again.

Now we can paint with an image we created instead of using the procedural textures produced by Blender.

There is an example in the `Teapot_Mask.blend` file that comes with the book.

After this long introduction on Texture Paint, we will learn about two more of Blender's painting modes in the next section. Instead of operating on a texture, we work on vertices and weight in these two modes. So, we don't modify the colors of the image we are painting on. Instead, we will paint the vertices of an object and assign a weight to each vertex. In this way, we control the distribution of many effects of various kinds, as we will see in the following two sections.

Now we study Vertex Paint mode where we can paint the vertices of our objects.

Learning Vertex Paint

Blender doesn't just allow us to paint only on the objects' textures. So besides painting on the things' surface, we can do it on the vertices.

The vertex is the simplest element, equivalent to a point. Thus, we can say that it is the basis of all the objects' geometry and three-dimensional spaces in virtual reality. Two vertices make an edge, and four, joined by four edges, create a face. The whole set of vertices, edges, and faces makes the mesh, which is the structure of the 3D model.

We can create and edit subobjects manually in Edit mode by acting directly on the object's shape; instead, we can paint surfaces in Vertex Paint mode by applying colors to the vertices.

With Vertex Paint, we can act on vertex colors. Vertex Paint and Weight Paint modes give us great freedom to select the chosen vertices quickly.

With this feature, we directly modify the colors of the object's vertices and assign a hue not directly related to the material but connected to the data of the vertices themselves or groups of subobjects. For this reason, before working in Vertex Paint, we must add vertices to the mesh by subdividing the surfaces and adding geometry to have enough elements to modify.

To paint an object, we must add a Vertex Color Index in the Vertex Colors window of the Properties Editor's Object Data Properties panel.

When we paint on a vertex, we also edit the color of the edges and faces assigned to the vertex itself through a gradient.

As in Texture Paint, we can color the object and have the same brushes, but instead of painting the surfaces, we assign the colors directly to the vertices. To activate the Vertex Paint mode, we use the Object Interaction mode button and select Vertex Paint, in the same way as we selected Texture Paint mode.

There is no Vertex Paint workspace, as for Texture Paint, and the toolbar is composed of only four instruments. To access the vertex color information, we can use the Attribute node; we use the Vertex Paint node to render them. We have several tools available to paint the vertices: the Vertex Paint Tools in the toolbar.

Let's see what they are.

The Toolbar

In Vertex Paint mode, we can find the tools in the toolbar on the interface's left. However, the Tool Settings are in the 3D View Header and the Active Tool and Workspace Settings panel.

These panels contain the essential tools for working in this mode.

In the toolbar, as we can see in Figure 5-32, we find tools for painting, tools for selection, and the usual Annotate tools.

Figure 5-32. *The Vertex Paint mode toolbar*

These devices are similar to those in Texture Paint mode but are fewer in number. So let's list them and see what we can do with them.

- The Draw device allows us to paint on the objects.

- Blur shades the color painted with Draw and applies a smoothing effect to change colors fading them.

- Average like Blur allows us to obtain a blurred effect, but with the calculated media of the colors.

- Smear instead distorts colors by mixing them.

- The selection tools are visible only when we activate the Paint Mask or Vertex Selection button in the editor header highlighted in Figure 5-32.

  We will see shortly how to use these tools to choose the vertices we want to paint. There are four different instruments: Tweak, Select Box, Select Circle, and Select Lasso.

Also, in this modality, we can customize our brushes and save them for later use.

We can modify these tools in the 3D view header or the Active Tool and Workspace Settings panel, as we will see in a moment.

The 3D View Header and the Tool Settings

The Tool Settings and the panels in the Active Tool and Workspace Settings of the Properties Editor are interactive and automatically change when selecting another tool in the toolbar.

The Tool Settings is in the 3D view header, and we can see it in Figure 5-33 highlighted in white.

Figure 5-33.   *The Tool Settings in Vertex Paint mode*

In the upper line, highlighted in white, we can see the Paint Mask and Vertex Selection buttons, which allow us to select the vertices we want to paint on.

To use Paint Mask, we must first select the vertices in Edit mode. On the other hand, Vertex Selection activates the vertex selection tools in the toolbar to create masks.

Here we find the same Tool Settings tools of the Paint Texture mode. We can create our custom brushes; then, we find the color picker to select the brush color. Finally, we find the options to choose blending modes and adjust the Radius and Strength values.

As we have seen, blending modes modify colors concerning the background. The Darken mode, for example, mixes the colors darkening the base layer.

Also, in this modality, the Falloff window presents a chart that allows us to change the transparency and definition of the brush edges.

Using Vertex Paint

In this mode, we can act directly on the colors of the vertices. In practice, we directly modify the colors of the mesh's subobjects by changing the vertices' data.

But what happens if we want to render the color assigned to the vertices? In this case, the nodal system comes to our aid with the Vertex Color node. We can paint a model and render the vertex colors as a texture with this node.

Let's do an exercise to see how to do it.

1. Open Blender and select the model to paint. Then, subdivide it in Edit mode to increase the number of vertices with a value of at least 50 Number of Cuts.

2. Add a Vertex Color Index with the + button in the Vertex Colors window of the Object Data Properties panel of the Properties Editor, as shown in Figure 5-34.

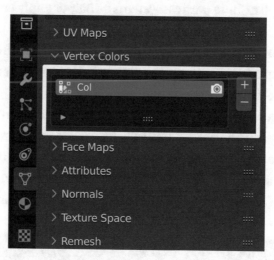

Figure 5-34. *The Vertex Color Index*

3. Click Shading in the Topbar to move to the Shading workspace.

4. In the Shader editor at the bottom, add a new material, and then add a Vertex Color node with the shortcut Shift+A and select Input. Link the output color of this node with the input color of the Principled BSDS node already present in the window.

5. Choose Vertex Paint in the Object Interaction mode. Select a color in the Color Picker in the 3D view header and start painting on the object.

6. You will see the colors painted in Vertex Paint mode in the 3D Viewport Material Preview and Rendered Viewport Shading display mode. Then, if you perform a rendering, you will have the same result.

After learning how to render vertex color, we conclude this section by analyzing the last mode of painting, Weight Paint mode.

Getting Started with Weight Paint

This type of Object mode is not related to painting but involves Blender modeling, animation, physics, etc. For example, we can use the chromatic scales available in Weight Paint mode to distribute particle systems as hair or apply controlled modifiers or rigging.

Weight Paint mode, similar to Vertex Paint, works directly on the vertices, and for this reason, before starting to use it, we must be sure to have enough geometry available to ensure the desired effect.

Weight Paint assigns a weight to each vertex affected by its painting tools. This weight is marked numerically by value and graphically by a color. For example, a blue-colored vertex has a zero value and a weight equal to zero, while a red one has the maximum value and power. In the middle, we have a scale of colors and values that assign proportional shares of influence between zero and one, as shown in Figure 5-35.

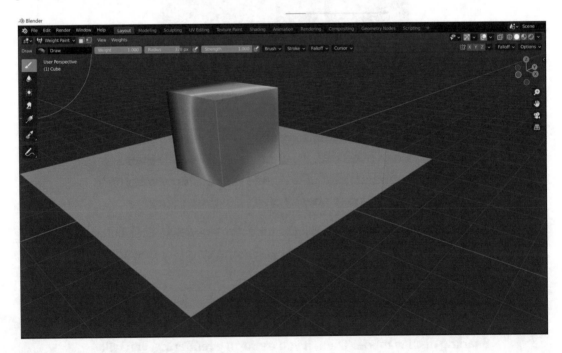

Figure 5-35. *Weight Paint mode*

With these Weight Painting values, we can precisely control different tools like modifiers, particle systems, rigging, and other essential functions of 3D graphics.

As for the Texture Paint and Vertex Paint modes, we can enter Weight Paint from the window that opens by clicking the Object Interaction mode button in the 3D view header.

The Weight Paint tool is helpful in different situations. For example, by using Weight Paint in character rigging, we can precisely determine the part of the mesh influenced by the movement of every single bone.

In physics, we can define which vertices of an object will be affected by the simulation.

In managing particle systems, we can use the Weight Painting tools to determine which parts of the object to place the static particles or which sections of the thing itself will emit dynamic particles.

There are many other cases in which this tool will be helpful.

But let's see with which instruments we can determine the weight of the painted vertices. The first thing to see is the toolbar.

The Toolbar

Also, in this mode, the editing tools are collected in the toolbar on the left of the screen. We can edit them in the Tool Settings in the 3D Viewport header or in the Active Tool and Workspace Setting panel of the Properties editor.

We can also click with the right mouse button in 3D view and modify three values by using the three boxes that appear: Weight, Radius, and Strength.

The devices in the toolbar, as we can see in Figure 5-36, are similar to those in Vertex Paint mode.

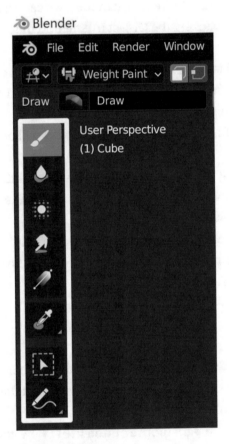

Figure 5-36. *The Weight Paint toolbar*

There are only two more tools compared with Texture Paint: Gradient and Sample. Let's see them all very quickly.

- The Draw brush allows us to paint.

- Blur shades the color painted.

- Average allows us to obtain a blurred effect by calculating the average of the colors. It has a much more pronounced effect than Blur.

- Smear instead distorts colors by grabbing them.

- Gradient creates a gradation effect in color.

- Sample consists of two color-selecting instruments: Sample Weight and Sample Vertex Group.

- The selection tools selects the vertices to paint. It consists of four tools: Tweak, Select Box, Select Circle, and Select Lasso. We can see them only when activating the Paint Mask or Vertex Selection button in the editor header.

- Annotate allows us to make drawings and annotations in the 3D view.

Let's see how to edit these tools in the Tool Settings.

The 3D View Header and the Tool Settings

In this case, the Tool Settings and the Active Tool and Workspace Settings interact with the toolbar, changing when a different tool is selected.

We can see the 3D view's header and the Tool Settings in Weight Paint mode in Figure 5-37, highlighted in white.

Figure 5-37.   *The 3D view header and the Tool Settings in Weight Paint mode*

Here, we find the masking buttons, namely, Paint Mask and Vertex Selection, in the first line of the 3D header. They work in the same way as in Vertex Paint. The other tools are also the same as in Vertex Paint mode.

We can create our brushes.

The color picker is not there because we have the Weight button that determines the color and weight of the painted vertices. We won't find blending modes either.

Then we have the buttons to modify the values of the Radius and Strength brushes.

Also, here we find the Falloff panel to modify the definition of the brush edges.

Now, let's see with a short practical exercise of how to use the Weight Paint tool in Blender 3.0.

Using Weight Paint

When we enter this mode, the mesh turns blue, which signifies it is completely weightless, and we can already start painting it with the toolbar functions.

In this short exercise, we want to apply a relief controlled by the weight distribution of the vertices to our teapot.

1. Open Blender, open the file Teapot, select the model to paint, and subdivide it in Edit mode to have a sufficient number of vertices. You can divide the teapot with two cuts.

2. Select Weight Paint in the Object Interaction mode. The teapot turns blue.

3. You can start painting on the object. In the beginning, the model is blue: all values are zero.

   When we start painting, the model becomes blue, green, yellow, orange, and red. Red represents the maximum value, equal to one.

   These colors are not visible in the other object modes; they represent the values assigned to each vertex. We can use these values to control particle systems, physics, rigging, etc.

4. Now go back to Object mode and add a Displace modifier from the Modifier Properties panel of the Properties Editor to the teapot.

5. On the Object Data Properties tab, add a vertex group to the object in the Vertex Groups window and add it in the Vertex Groups box of the Displace modifier. Lower the strength of the Displace modifier to 0.1.

6. The portions painted in Weight Paint turn into reliefs, as shown in Figure 5-38.

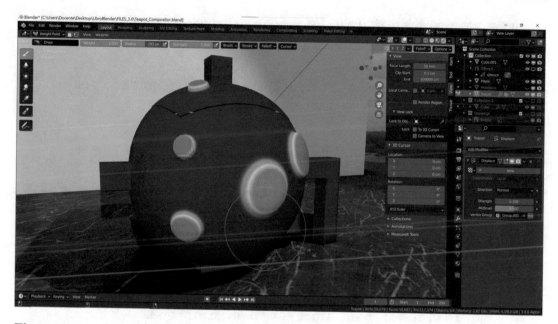

Figure 5-38. *Painting the teapot in Weight Paint mode*

As we have used Weight Paint in this exercise to create relief on the teapot, in the same way, we can use the system of selection and definition of areas of influence of this operating mode, for example, to define the effect of some modifier or particle system, etc.

We have concluded the theoretical part dedicated to digital painting; now, let's deepen our experience by applying what we have learned in some practical exercises.

Exercises: Introducing Digital Painting

The exercises of this chapter will introduce digital painting and new ways of making textures for our objects. Moreover, we will take some of the contents performed in the earlier chapters and develop them creatively using the painting tools provided for 3D modeling.

For example, we will paint a texture directly on the teapot or apply a Krita painted image on the chair in Blender.

In the preceding theoretical part, we have covered some technical topics about painting. Now let's apply them practically. We have applied new textures and materials to the objects modeled until now.

In the first exercise of this chapter, we will paint a diffuse texture directly on the teapot created in Exercise 1 of Chapter 2.

Exercise 10: Painting a Texture

This chapter will create new materials and textures and study techniques to paint the objects created in previous chapters.

Inside Blender, there are two main methods to paint textures.

- We can draw directly on the object.

- We can create textures in an external image editor such as Gimp or Krita and then apply them in Blender through materials.

We will study these methods in the first two exercises of this chapter.

We will start painting directly on the object in the first exercise, particularly on the teapot.

Unwrapping the Mesh

We start doing the UV unwrapping of the mesh. In this way, we obtain the two-dimensional development of the three-dimensional object's form.

Let's do this by following these steps:

1. Open the Teapot file with the teapot modeled in the first exercise of Chapter 2.

2. Move to the UV Editing workspace to create the UV map.

3. In Edit mode, select all the teapot subobjects by pressing A and then clicking U. Unwrap the object and choose Smart UV Project in the UV Mapping window. Leave all the values unchanged and click OK.

Now we can correctly apply the texture to the object.

Creating and Painting the Texture

Now that we have developed the object's shape on a two-dimensional surface, we can quickly paint on the thing or apply the texture through the material. Let's paint first.

1. Select the teapot. Click Texture Paint on the Topbar and go to the Texture Paint workspace.

2. Go to the Properties Editor's Active Tool and Workspace Settings panel. Here, in the Texture Slots panel, create a new texture by clicking the + Add a Texture Paint Slot button in the white highlighted rectangle in Figure 5-39. Next, choose the Base Color channel.

Figure 5-39. *The Texture Slots window and the Add a Texture Paint Slot button*

In the window that opens, name your texture **CeramicBaseColor**, give it a white color, and set the dimensions to 4096 x 4096 pixels. Click OK to confirm.

3. Go to the Shading workspace, and you will see that, in the Shader editor, Blender automatically added an Image Texture node containing the CeramicBaseColor texture.

4. Back in the Texture Paint workspace, you can start painting on the teapot. Select one of the available tools in the toolbar, set the Radius and Strength settings of the Brush to the values you prefer, choose the color, and start painting in 3D view directly on the object.

5. Also, try changing the blending modes to check the different effects.

Note   Blender does not save image changes automatically, so remember to keep the texture from time to time in the Image Editor header menu by clicking Image ➤ Save. If you see an asterisk next to the word *Image*, it means that there are unsaved changes.

---

6. You can paint directly on the three-dimensional object in the 3D View and on the texture in the Image Editor. In the case of the teapot, since the element is spherical, it is easier to paint some parts directly on the image.

To conclude the example, let's see how to paint only some object parts with Paint Masking. We talked about different masks in the "Painting with a Mask" section of this chapter.

In this exercise, we will use the method to paint only on the selected portions. It's quick and easy.

1. To enable face selection masking, move to Edit mode and select the faces you want to paint.

2. Then we go back to Texture Paint mode and click the Paint Mask button in the 3D viewport header between Texture Paint and View, highlighted in Figure 5-40.

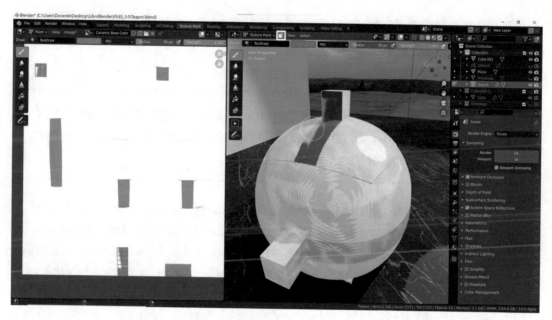

Figure 5-40. *Painting with a mask*

3. The picture shows that we can paint only on the parts previously
    selected in Edit mode.

To activate and deactivate this masking system, click the Face Select button.

The masking doesn't work with the button deactivated, so we can paint the whole
object and not only the parts selected in Edit mode.

In the next exercise, we will apply the second painting method we talked about and
make a UV map of an object in Blender.

Exercise 11: Creating a Painted Texture

The second method involves the creation of the UV layout of the chair in Blender. In the
previous exercise, we painted an image directly in Blender 3.0. We worked on an image
applied to material through a UV map in the Image Editor. Thus, the object in the 3D
view reflected the changes we made on the two-dimensional image, and vice versa.

This second exercise will change the process: we will export the UV layout, paint it
on an external editor, and reimport the image in Blender.

Following this method, we can export the UV layout of our object from the UV Editor header menu UV ➤ Export UV layout. Then we choose the .png format and click the Export UV Layout button.

Note   It's better if the textures for Blender materials are square because the UV layout is square. The most suitable image format to use in Blender, in our opinion, is PNG because it supports transparency.

Then we open the file with Gimp, Krita, or Photoshop; paint our texture in the UV layout; and import it back into Blender to apply it to the object through the UV map.

We can manually paint the texture on the UV map in Krita. So, we can use all Krita's brushes, the filters, the blend modes, and all the other instruments provided by the various image editors.

We will use another object in this second exercise, the red chair.

To do this, follow these steps:

1. Open the file RedChair. It contains the chair modeled in Exercise 5 of Chapter 3.

2. Move to the UV Editing workspace and unwrap the red chair by selecting all the subobjects in Edit mode by pressing A.

   Press U, and in the UV Mapping window, choose SmartUVProject at the bottom of the window and OK.

   In this way, we perform the unwrapping as we learned in Chapter 4.

   This tool works mainly for geometric objects and automatically unwraps our models rapidly. Once done this, it usually takes only a few manual changes to get a practical map.

3. Arrange the developed parts by scaling and rotating them as shown in Figure 5-41 on the UV editor on the left.

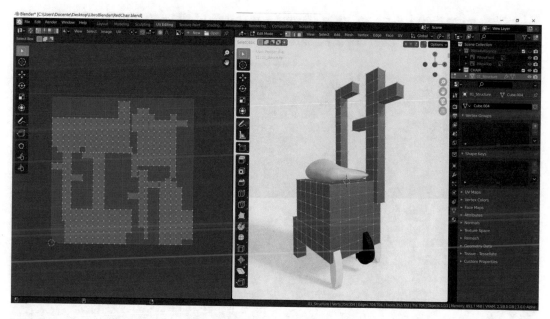

Figure 5-41. *The UV Editing workspace with the chair UV layout*

4. In the UV Editor header menu, from the window that opens when you click the main menu on UV, click Export UV Layout, and select the PNG format and the size 4096 x 4096; choose the path and click Export UV Layout. In this way, you have saved the object's layout in a format that both Blender and Krita can support.

5. Now open the UV layout of the Chair object, the Chair.png file, with Krita, and start painting or pasting images to create a texture for the chair.

With this method, we can work with brushes, paste photographs, etc.; in short, we can create whatever we want.

As shown in Figure 5-42, we have created a texture in Krita with the Dry Bristles brush that simulates the effect of the charcoal drawing.

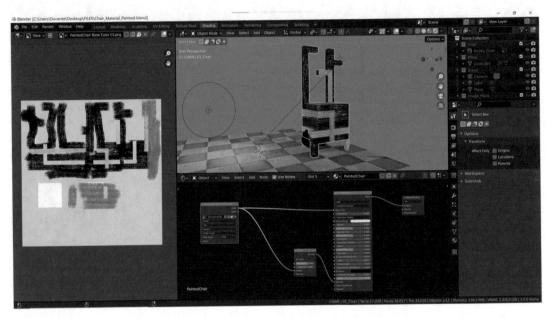

Figure 5-42. *The texture painted with Krita applied to the object*

So, we painted in Krita the parts of the UV layout corresponding to the faces of the chair and imported them into Blender. Then in the Shader editor, we connected this texture with Color Base and Normal inputs through a Bump node of the Principled BSDF shader.

In this way, we applied the texture painted in Krita to the color and the Normal Blender channels. We have used only the Diffuse textures dedicated to the Color channel until now.

But we can also create textures for all other channels directly inside Blender in Texture Paint mode.

In the next exercise, we'll see how to do it.

Exercise 12: Node-Based Texture Painting

In the first exercise of this chapter, we learned how to create color textures internally in Blender, painting them directly on the objects.

Then, in the second exercise, we saw how to make images in other digital painting software, import them into our 3D modeler, and apply them to Blender 3.0 materials.

Now we will see how to create directly inside Blender effects and textures for the other channels such as Metallic, Specular, Normal, etc.

In this exercise, we will also deepen our knowledge of layers and blending modes.

Introducing the Add Texture Paint Slots

In Exercise 10, we have already seen how to make a Base Color texture in the Texture Slots window.

From the Texture Slots window in the Texture Paint workspace of the Properties Editor, we can add the paintable textures for different channels of the Principled BSDF shader directly in Blender, as shown in Figure 5-43.

Figure 5-43. *Adding texture paint slots*

Let's quickly summarize these channels that we have already explored in Chapter 4:

- Base Color defines the color or texture of the substance.

- Specular controls the specular effect of the material.

- Roughness adjusts the balance between rough/matte and glossy/shiny.

- Metallic defines the metallic appearance of a material.

- Normal imitates the geometry and the details of the surface with RGB colors.

- Bump mimics the bumpiness of the substance as normal but with black-and-white textures.

- Displacement simulates depth to the object through the material.

When adding a texture from this box, Blender connects it to the dedicated shader's inputs and automatically adds the nodes needed to join it correctly.

Now let's see how to create layers in the Blender Image Editor.

Understanding Layers in Blender 3.0

The Blender Image Editor still lacks a layer system such as Gimp, Krita, or Photoshop.

This exercise will create three layers to modify light and shadow in Blender, directly manipulating textures without using the 3D view lights.

To do this, we must follow these steps:

1. Open the file Teapot.

2. Assign a material to the teapot.

3. Then go to the Texture Paint workspace in the Texture Slots panel of the Active Tool and Workspace Settings window of the Properties Editor and create a new texture by clicking the Add a Texture Paint Slot (+) button and choosing Base Color. Retain the default settings by changing only the color to gray and then click OK.

4. Click Shading in the Topbar to set the workspace with this name. Notice that Blender automatically added a Material Base Color node with the gray texture to the shader Principled BSDF of the object material.

5. Duplicate the Material Base Color node (Shift+D), create a new image with the node's New image button to the right of the Texture Name, and call it **Lights** while keeping the color black.

6. Add a MixRGB node and change its blending mode from Mix to Add and insert it between the Material Base Color node and the Principled BSDF Node.

7. Connect the Color output of the Lights node with input Color2 of the RGB Mix Node.

8. Duplicate the Lights node and add a new texture as previously, by pressing the node's New image button to the right of the Texture name, but make it white by changing the Color in the Color box and call it **Shadows**.

9. Add another RGB Mix node, and this time use the Multiply blending mode. Insert it between the previous RGB Mix node and the Principled BSDF shader, and then connect the Color output of the Shadows node with input Color 2 of the RGB Mix node.

10. Change the object mode of 3D view from Object to Texture Paint.

11. Open the Active Tool and Workspace Settings window in the Properties Editor.

    In the Texture Slots panel, click the Material Base Color.

    Change the color from white to gray in the brush Color Picker, and paint the 3D Viewport object.

12.   Then select the Lights slot, try to paint over this slot, and repeat
the same operation with Shadows, as shown in Figure 5-44.

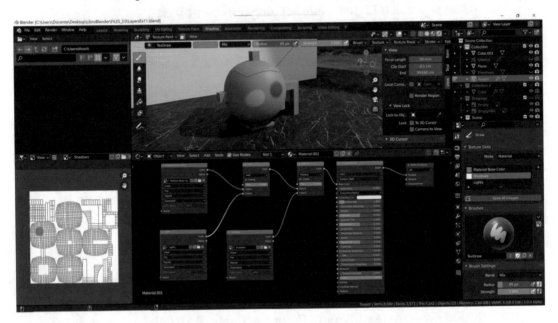

Figure 5-44. *Controlling light and shadows with layers*

With this technique, we can easily paint on three levels, creating black-and-white
spots on our teapot, as shown in the figure.

As we can notice, painting with the gray brush on the Material Base Color layer
doesn't result.

Instead, if we paint on the Lights layer, we get a lighter color, and painting on the
Shadows layer gets darker. So, we have built two layers to control lights and the intensity
of the shadows.

Also, by changing the factor of the two nodes, Add and Multiply, we can modify
the shades of the two slots, Lights and Shadows. Modifying the Factor value of Add, we
change the intensity of the lights. Likewise, while adjusting the Factor value of Multiply,
we influence the power of the shadows. We have the maximum contrast with a value of 1,
while with the value 0, the tones are uniform.

Let's expand this example using another channel we can create in the texture slots: a
Normal map.

Drawing a Bump Map Directly on the Object

We learned how to create textures in the texture slot for the Base Color, i.e., the Diffuse maps.

Now let's add a Bump map to the teapot by following these steps:

1. Go to the Texture Paint workspace and create a new texture from the Texture Slots panel of the Active Tool and Workspace Settings window of the Properties Editor by clicking the Add a Texture Paint Slot (+) button and choosing Bump. Keep the default settings by changing only the color to gray and clicking OK.

    In the Shader editor Blender automatically adds a Bump node connected to the normal input of the Principled BSDF shader. In addition, to simulate the relief, Blender adds an Image node with the texture Material Bump.

2. In the Texture Paint editor paint on the teapot with the black-and-white brush while keeping the Material Bump slot selected.

    Now, if you draw with white, you get a relief effect, and if you paint with black, you get a hollow result. You can see the result in Material Preview or Rendered Viewport Shading display. But, of course, we don't change the geometry this way.

Instead, we get a Bump texture that simulates the relief, with the node chain shown in Figure 5-45.

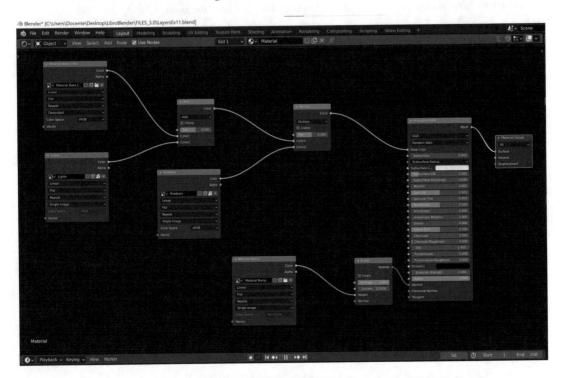

Figure 5-45. *The final node with the Bump map*

We can also add maps for other channels by creating them in the texture slots, editing them in Blender, and eventually exporting them to other software.

So far, we have created textures in different ways inside Blender. We also looked at modifying them directly in the software or externally in Krita or similar programs. This software has many brushes and an almost endless possibility of creating textures.

That concludes this chapter on painting inside and outside Blender.

As we have seen, we can use the painting tools very flexibly, either to paint directly into Blender or to create images or textures for our materials.

Summary

In this chapter, we dealt with digital painting. We have seen various painting tools that allow us to use Blender differently, strictly combining the second and third dimensions. We introduced the use of the graphic tablet both for painting and sculpting in Blender to work more professionally and effectively. After reading this chapter, you will know different painting techniques applicable in Blender: Texture, Vertex, and Weight Paint.

In the next chapter, we will analyze rendering with Blender's two internal renderers: Cycles and Eevee.

Then we'll delve into compositing and video editing techniques learning how to use Blender 3.0 as a Compositor and Video Sequence Editor with a wide range of effects available through the nodal system.

CHAPTER 6

Render, Compositing, and Video Editing

It is time to render our scene and transform it into a two-dimensional image or video. Blender 3.0 supports a wide range of professional file formats for images and videos. There are three internal renderers: Eevee, Cycles, and Workbench. It's also possible to activate Freestyle if we need nonphotorealistic line-based rendering for blueprint and cartoon effects.

We will also talk about compositing and video editing in this chapter. You'll then have intermediate knowledge of these two topics, without having fully delved into all the details, because of the numerous features that can be used with these two tools. Blender can be used for video editing as a compositor, and a video sequence editor, with a wide range of effects available through the nodal system.

In this chapter, we're going to cover the following main topics:

- Cycles and Eevee

- The Eevee rendering engine

- The Cycles rendering engine

- Freestyle

- Post-processing: the Compositor Editor and the Video Sequence Editor

Comparing Cycles and Eevee

To transform 3D scenes and objects into two-dimensional images or videos, we have to render them. Blender provides us with two render engines with different characteristics: Eevee and Cycles. In Blender 3.0, the developers have improved both renderers.

© Gianpiero Moioli 2022
G. Moioli, *Introduction to Blender 3.0*, https://doi.org/10.1007/978-1-4842-7954-0_6

Eevee is a fast, real-time render engine introduced in Blender 2.8, allowing real-time rendering in the 3D Viewport. It can render PBR materials quickly. In Blender 3.0, Eevee has a new architecture that will serve as the base for future improvements. The Cycles engine takes more time to render but leads to more realistic results. In Blender 3.0, the Cycles X version speeds up render times considerably. Workbench is the third internal renderer, but it is optimized only for better visualization in the 3D Viewport.

I've introduced you to the primary features and the fundamental differences between the two renderers in Chapter 1. This chapter will demonstrate the options to fine-tune the result.

To summarize about renderers, we can say that:

- Eevee, the Extra Easy Virtual Environment Engine, uses rasterization via OpenGL 3.3. As a result, it's a very fast, high-quality renderer.

- The Cycles renderer is a path tracer, and it works with paths of light. Currently, it gets more photorealistic results than Eevee but is slower.

- Workbench allows us to visualize objects in the 3D Viewport easily.

- With Freestyle instead, we can achieve cartoon and nonphotorealistic line-rendering effects.

Eevee will continue to improve in future software versions; the Eevee reactor will probably come soon. And it looks like the Blender Foundation will be betting heavily on Eevee, which is already Blender's default renderer or render engine, as we can see in Figure 6-1.

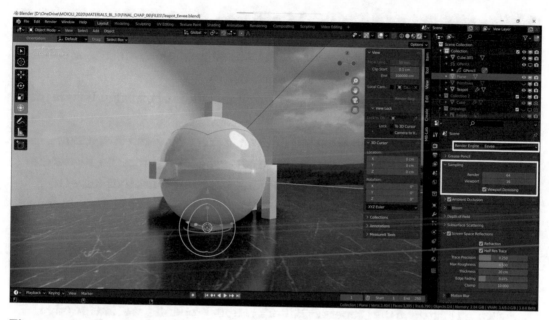

Figure 6-1. *The Blender Viewport in Eevee's Rendered mode*

In the white box highlighted in Figure 6-1 on the right side of the screen in the Properties Editor's Render Properties panel, we find the button to change the renderer. Here we can switch and select either Eevee or Cycles or Workbench.

Let's analyze some standard common features of the first two, which are the ones that give us the final result. Workbench, instead, as we have said, helps us to work efficiently in 3D view. The following are some of the most exciting features:

- Both allow us to work in a real-time viewport preview. However, the Cycles rendering speed is slower than Eevee's.

- The Cycles renderer gives us the possibility to choose CPU or GPU rendering. That is an opportunity to render with the computer's graphics card or processor. Unfortunately, this is not yet possible in Eevee.

- Both support PBR shaders and HDR lighting. We discussed PBR materials in Chapter 4. The first are physically based materials, which mainly consider the interaction between lights and surfaces. The second are high dynamic range images used to illuminate scenes because they allow an increased luminance range.

- Finally, both renderers allow VR rendering.

Now let's see the common standard settings to adjust when running a render.

Cycles and Eevee's Shared Settings

First, in the Render Properties panel, we see the Sampling window, which is important for the quality of the render with both Eevee and Cycles.

The Samples value is the principal option to control the image quality, both in the render and in the viewport.

The higher the Samples value, the less noise in the final rendered image. But, unfortunately, the counterpart is the slowdown of the rendering times: the higher the samples, the longer the rendering time will be. Then there are numerous values to adjust; we will see how to set options separately for Cycles and Eevee in the subsequent sessions.

At the bottom of the same panel, we can activate Freestyle by selecting the Freestyle box. This renderer creates cartoon effects using contour lines in post-production. We will see this tool in the "Introducing the Freestyle Render" section of this chapter.

Switching instead to the Properties Editor's Output Properties, we find the other functions to control our image or video features.

Let's start with the Format panel. We can edit all the options of the rendering format and the resolution on the x- and y-axis (that is, the number of pixels of the rendered image, which allows us to create pictures or videos of any format and resolution). In addition, on the same panel, the Percentage Resolution button enables us to adjust the resolution percentage to create renderings with a different original size without changing the original resolution. The percentage is proper when we want to make test renders, keeping the proportions of the final render and rendering at a smaller size to decrease the rendering time.

Then, in the same panel, we find the frame rate that establishes the ratio between the seconds and the number of frames contained in each second of the movie. Again, this value can vary according to the final file format we want to save our video.

Below, in the Frame Range panel, we have the settings related to the number of the movie's frames, from Frame Start to Frame End, to determine where we want to begin and end the video.

In the Stereoscopy panel, we find all the settings to set up, both in Eevee and in Cycles, stereoscopic rendering in Blender. Then, we set the 3D rendering mode to select the box next to Stereoscopy.

In the Output panel, we must choose the computer's folder to save the rendered image or video after selecting the image or video file format, respectively, such as PNG, JPEG, etc., for pictures, and AVI, FFmpeg, etc., for videos.

Then, we can choose one of the Color options to save our image in black and white or color, or we can choose colors with an Alpha channel for transparency after selecting the Color Depth and Compression options.

Switching to the Cycles render engine box, we get the result we see in Figure 6-2.

Figure 6-2. *The Blender viewport in Cycles' Rendered mode*

Figure 6-2 visualizes a preview in Cycles with similar settings as used in Eevee. If we compare Eevee's Sampling with Cycles, we notice that the samples are the same, but Eevee's result is much sharper. As we can see when comparing Figures 6-1 with 6-2, the render with Cycles is noisier: we can notice white dots of disturbance, especially in the light reflection points. However, we do not see these disturbances so much in Eevee.

Once the render is made, we can subdivide the image into different layers and passes, working on post-production to realize special effects.

This method allows us to use nodes such as Denoise or passes such as Denoising Data to decrease image noise in post-production for both render engines, as we will see in the exercises of this chapter.

In the following two sections, we see more closely the characteristics of the two renderers. Still, before going deeper into the rendering part, we must introduce two elements of great importance for controlling our renderers: render layers and passes.

Render Layers and Passes

To control the render effects and modify them in the Compositor, Blender provides us with layers and passes. These tools help us limit the impact of nodes to certain parts or characteristics of the image.

Render Layers

The layers allow us to divide the rendered image into several levels that we can edit separately and then merge into a final image. We can add a new view layer at the right of the Topbar by clicking the Add View Layer ➤ New button, framed in white in Figure 6-3.

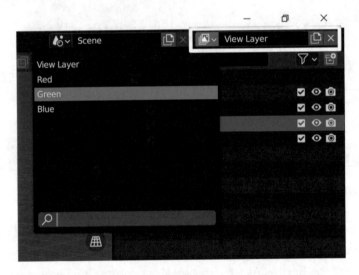

Figure 6-3. *The View Layer box and window*

From the same box, we can remove the created layers. We open the View Layer and Passes panels in the Properties Editor's View Layer Properties section. From here, we work with renders and passes. These panels show the settings of the active layer. Each render layer has an associated set of collections and displays all the objects of the related collections if visible. In the Outliner, we select the collections and enable or disable them from view in the chosen view layer, with the Exclude from View Layer button shown in Figure 6-4.

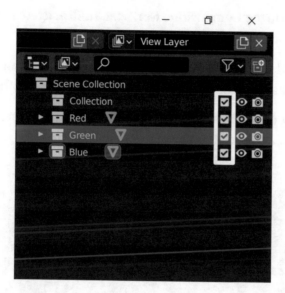

Figure 6-4. *The Exclude from View Layer button*

With the render layers, we can apply compositing effects to objects separately, for example, by using a Blur node to the background and not the foreground of an image. Let's see how they work in practice with a simple exercise.

1. Open Blender and activate the Rendered Viewport shading in the 3D view header; then add two cubes to the default cube. Call them **Red**, **Green**, and **Blue**; create simple materials; and give them colors corresponding to the names.

2. Create a collection for each cube, put every cube into a different collection, and give them the name of the cube they contain.

3. Create three new layers by selecting Add View Layer ➤ New. Call them Red, Green, and Blue.

4. Then select the Red layer, and in the Outliner, click the button Exclude from View Layer of the Green and Blue collections.

    Repeat the same operation for the other two collections and exclude Red and Blue for the Green layer and Red and Green for the Blue layer.

5. Now, move to the Compositing workspace and activate the button Use Nodes in the header of the Compositor editor.

    Render, and you will see the three cubes present in the render. This thing happens because you have rendered the view layer.

6. In the drop-down menu at the bottom of the Render Layers node, select Layer Red and render again. You will see only the red cube, as shown in Figure 6-5.

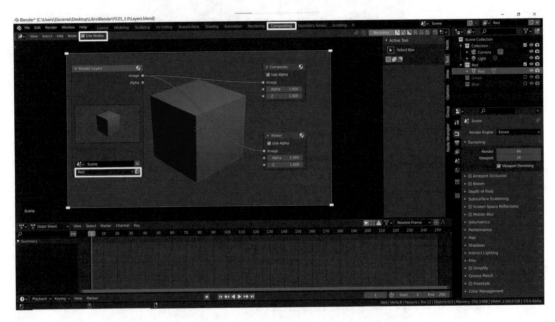

Figure 6-5. *Working with the view layers in the Compositor*

In this way, we have divided into three different layers the three objects that later we can edit individually in the Blender Compositor.

Now we see the render passes that have similar characteristics.

Render Passes

Render passes allow us to select information about particular aspects of the rendering. For example, we can use them to separate the rendered images into different colors and lights or get some data separately, such as the 3D data of the scene, like depth.

Once separated with render passes, we can easily edit these data and then reassemble them into a single image.

In the Blender Compositor, we can modify and combine them in various ways to improve the final render result by changing only the elements that interest us.

Combining render layers and render passes allows us to modify our renders in post-production in a flexible way.

Currently, Cycles still has a higher number of passes than Eevee. There are also some differences between the two renderers. For example, Eevee has the Bloom render pass in the Effects category that Cycles does not have.

We can activate from time to time only the render passes that we need in the Passes window of the View Layer Properties of the Properties Editor, as in Figure 6-6 that shows those of Eevee.

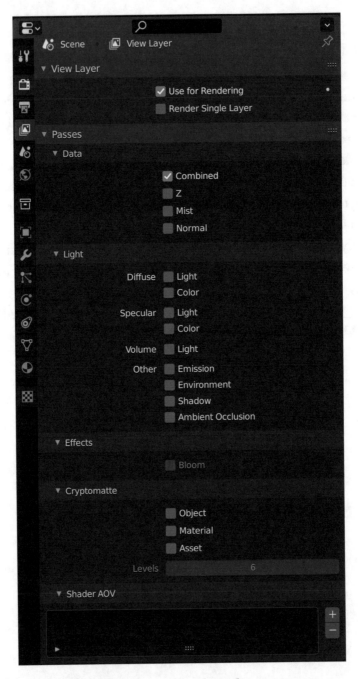

Figure 6-6. *The Eevee View Layer panel and render passes*

There are different categories. Let's quickly see their features.

- The Data category collects 3D information of the scene with nodes like Z, Mist, and Normal.

- Light subdivides the data of the different parts of the lighting.

  For Cycles, we can separate each type of lighting into Direct, Indirect, and Color for Diffuse, Glossy, etc. Instead, for Eevee, we have a more limited number of light passes.

  In addition, there are other types of lighting controls to modify the Emission, Shadow, Ambient Occlusion, etc.

- The Effects category is only for Eevee and contains the passes to edit Bloom's data.

- Criptomatte is powerful and is used to create masks for renderings.

For example, Ambient Occlusion extends our control over shadows; Mist instead allows us to control depth of field, etc.

When we activate render passes from the View Layer panel of the Properties Editor, Blender adds the respective output sockets in the Render Layers node of the Compositor to connect them with the inputs of other nodes.

In this way, we can extrapolate the data from part of the rendered image, modify its characteristics, and add it back to the final image.

Now let's deepen our knowledge of Blender's two main renderers: Eevee and Cycles. Let's take a closer look at them.

Rendering with Eevee

The Blender's default renderer can make a real-time rendering in the 3D Viewport, achieving faster rendering times and creating high-quality images and videos. Eevee supports PBR materials and implements ambient lighting with HDRI effectively.

Cycles and Eevee's materials use nearly the same shader nodes. Eevee, unlike Cycles, does not calculate the path of each ray of light but uses a different process called *rasterization.*

This process currently limits the quality of Eevee's renders with the number of usable lights, shadows, and several other features.

Settings of Eevee

Before starting to work with Eevee, it is advisable to make some changes to the interface to set some essential functions to obtain advanced effects.

1. Open the file Teapot.

2. To get a real-time rendering, press the Z key, choose Rendered in the menu, or click Rendered in the Viewport Shading display on the right of the 3D view header as shown in Figure 6-7.

3. In the 3D view header, disable the buttons Show Gizmo and Show Overlays, highlighted in Figure 6-7. So, you hide all the gizmos and outlines and get the detailed preview of the final render in the viewport.

Figure 6-7. *The Show Gizmo and Show Overlays buttons*

4. Then move to the Properties Editor's Render Properties panel and activate the Ambient Occlusion, Bloom, and Screen Space Reflections buttons. Then enable Refraction in the Screen Space Reflections window.

    Enabling Ambient Occlusion improves the objects' shading and adds realism to local reflection patterns.

    Activating Bloom, you add glow to materials and create brighter pixels. You can control the intensity with the Threshold value in the Bloom window.

    Instead, the Screen Space Reflections option creates reflections and refraction effects on materials. It is essential for glass. In the same window, to improve the quality, you can disable Half Res Trace.

    But to have good reflections on materials, you must also enable Screen Space Refraction in the Material Properties and select Settings.

5. To check the camera's focus, select it and reactivate Show Overlays in
    the 3D Viewport header. Then, in the Properties Editor, from Object
    Data ➤ Viewport Display, select the Limits box. Select the Depth
    of Field box, from the path Properties Editor ➤ Object Data. Then
    modify the Focus Distance value, and see that in 3D view, a yellow
    cross moves on a line that indicates the camera's focus. Finally, by
    pressing 0 in the Numpad, activate the camera view. Notice that
    you can control the focus distance just as you used a real camera, as
    shown in Figure 6-8. With F-Stop we can control the depth of field.
    Decreasing the value decreases the area where objects still appear
    sharp and increases the blurring effect on more distant objects.

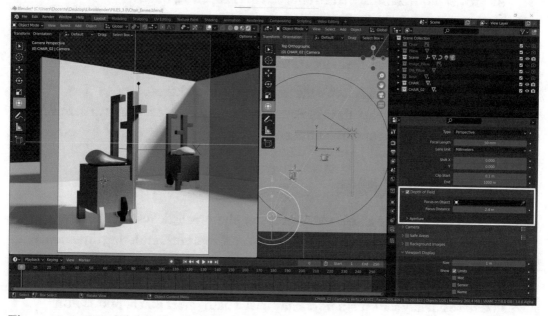

Figure 6-8. *Modifying the depth of field*

6. As far as shadows are concerned, we also need to adjust some
    parameters.

    First, in the Properties Editor, go to Render ➤ Shadows and
    change the Cube Size value from 512 to 1024. Then, to further
    improve the quality of the shadows, we can also check the High
    Bitdepth box.

    We can also increase the incidence of shadows by unchecking the
    box Soft Shadows.

7. To further improve how the shadows render, we can also activate Overscan from the Properties Editor by selecting Render ➤ Film. We can also enable the Alpha channel for the background in the render by clicking the Transparent box to get a transparent background.

8. It is also vital to enable the contact shadows of the lights by selecting each light, selecting the box Contact Shadows in the Properties Editor under Object Data Properties, and increasing the Thickness value to cover the shadows zones in the point closest to the objects.

9. To get more contrast in the render in the Properties Editor's Render Properties ➤ Color Management window, we can modify the light difference by changing the Look value from None to Medium High Contrast, High Contrast, etc.

In this way, we have set a suitable file for our renders in Eevee.

After setting some crucial values in Eevee render engine, we see how to perform the same operations in Cycles for the same scene.

Rendering with Cycles

At the moment, this engine allows us to get better photorealistic results than Eevee, even if with longer rendering times. The arrival of Cycles X shortens rendering times and does not change the features from the original Cycles interface. In Blender 3.0, Cycles X is four to eight times faster than Cycles when rendering the same scene.

As we have already said, it is a physically based path tracer that supports PBR materials, has excellent flexibility, and obtains incredible realism in the results. The renderer set in Blender 3.0 is Eevee, so to use Cycles, we have to choose it in the Properties Editor's Render Properties ➤ Render Engine.

The most important thing to do when using Cycles is to optimize the rendering time.

The Cycles renderer calculates the reflections of light on the surface in a similar way to the real world because, from every source of light, it calculates the rays that bounce in the scene reflecting the light itself. The effect is realistic, and we set up the options faster than Eevee.

Long rendering times are the other side of the coin.

First, to speed up rendering times, if we have a powerful graphics card, we can switch from rendering with the processor to the graphics card. We just need to change two parameters. Let's see how to do it.

1. Select Edit ➤ Preferences in the Topbar and open the Blender Preferences window. Next, select the System panel on the left side of the Blender Preferences window.

    Then in the Cycles Render Devices panel, enable CUDA or OptiX if you use an Nvidia Graphics Card or HIP if you use an AMD graphics card.

    This option allows you to choose the Blender hardware tool to render: the processor or the graphics card.

2. Also, in the Properties Editor's Render Properties ➤ Scene, click the drop-down in Device next to the CPU down arrow. Select GPU Compute. Render Engine, of course, must be set to Cycles because Eevee does not support this option yet.

From now on, Cycles X will use the graphics card to render instead of the computer's processor. This feature can significantly speed up rendering times. But let's see Cycle's main settings.

Setting of Cycles

To compare the results of the two rendering engines, we now render with Cycles the same scene as Eevee. The Cycles renderer is already preset to realistic render, and it is not necessary to change all the settings as we have that we set up in Eevee.

The most important thing for quality rendering in Cycles is the Sample setting in the Sampling window. If we increase the samples, we enhance the quality of the rendered image, but we extend the rendering time.

In the last versions, however, we are provided with the Denoise node that helps to decrease the disturbance created by a low number of samples.

Blender 3.0 also provides three crucial boxes: Noise Threshold, Min Samples, and Max Samples. In Blender 3.0, the Noise Threshold box is active by default. With this box checked, the Noise Threshold option and Min and Max Samples are active, as we can see in Figure 6-9.

Figure 6-9. *Modifying the depth of field*

So in Blender 3.0, it is advisable to set the Noise Threshold value and let Cycles do the work. It will analyze the noise level of the render, and it will automatically set the necessary samples per pixel within the number of samples we have given it in the Min and Max Samples boxes.

It is advisable to keep Noise Threshold values from 0,1 to 0,001.

Lower values mean less noise.

We can also set a maximum time with the option Time Limit for the rendering in the Render panel of the Render Properties. And, always in the Render window, the Denoise box is also active by default.

It is elementary!

Now let's run our Cycles render. But first, let's do a rendering with Eevee to make comparisons.

1. So, reopen the file Teapot, where you set the options for Eevee, and rename it **Cycles**. Then, press the Z key and choose Rendered in the menu or click Rendered in the 3D view header's Viewport Shading.

2. Run a rendering with Eevee to compare it later with Cycles.

   The image obtained is in Slot 1, set by default, as shown in the header of the Blender Render window, in Figure 6-10.

Figure 6-10. *The Blender Render window*

   In the Blender Render window, on the right of the Blender Render header, we click the Select Slot button set to slot 1. Other slots appear.

   In these slots, we can put up to eight different versions of our rendering to compare them and understand the best settings for our final image.

3. Click Slot 1 and select Slot 2. Cycles will place the following renderings on this slot, keeping that one on slot 1.

Warning, though, because Blender will save the images only temporarily, and this operation is not equivalent to saving the rendering but only helps to compare the different versions.

4.   Change the render engine from Eevee to Cycles in the Render Properties panel. Many options in the Properties Editor will change contextually, and the real-time view navigation will become slower if we have enabled Rendered Viewport Shading.

If real-time rendering becomes too slow from the Properties Editor's Render Properties ➤ Performance ➤ Viewport window, change the Pixel Size value from Automatic to a precise value that could be 2x. So, while the rendering quality in the viewport decreases, the browsing time will become faster.

5.   Run the render with Cycles on slot 2.

Then switching from slot 1 to slot 2, you can easily compare the results of the two render engines.

6.   Let's save the file `Chair_Cycles.blend`.

At first glance already, we can see that the results of Cycles, compared to those of Eevee, have softer lighting, more diffused light, less dark shadows, and more defined details.

However, we can also say that the sharp and well-defined image of Eevee is, in some ways, more captivating than that of Cycles.

We can improve our renders by modifying the colors, modifying the contrast, and creating special effects. Still, we will deepen the various rendering systems with Eevee and Cycles in the exercises later in this chapter.

Now let's see Freestyle.

Introducing the Freestyle Render

Before using Blender as a Compositor and Video Editor, we introduce a device to get cartoon effects and line-only special effects in post-production rendering.

With Freestyle, we can create the contour lines of our render geometries. In Blender 3.0, the developers have modified the interface a little.

The Freestyle space reproduces the contours of three-dimensional objects according to various settings in the rendering control panels.

It is a nonphotorealistic (NPR) rendering engine edge/line-based, which allows us to obtain a two-dimensional drawing while rendering three-dimensional objects quickly.

Freestyle allows us to render different line styles to simulate drawings with a technical or artistic stroke, hand-painted drawings, or cartoons. Thus, we can use it for technical drawings, graphics, or cartoon styles.

We can modify the line style and parameters in a predefined way. For example, we can create a sketch with defined contours with different thicknesses or simple volumes, substantial distortions, etc.

Using Freestyle

We activate this tool from the Render Properties window of the Properties Editor by selecting the Freestyle box, as shown in Figure 6-11.

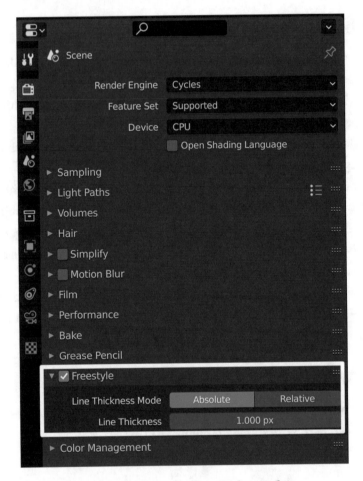

Figure 6-11. *The checkbox to activate the Freestyle renderer*

We can directly control the Line Thickness Mode value and the Line Thickness value from this panel.

Line Thickness Mode has two options:

- We must select Absolute for a constant line thickness.

- Instead, we can use Relative for a variable line thickness, which is one pixel of width every 480 pixels of the height of the rendered image.

From the same panel, we control the Line Thickness value. This box holds the line thickness in pixels when the Absolute line thickness mode is active.

First, we must consider that Freestyle does not render objects without surfaces.

We find the Freestyle settings in the Properties Editor's View Layer Properties.

Here there are a few panels:

- Freestyle, which contains the most general settings

- Freestyle Line Set, which includes the contour line settings

- Freestyle Strokes, which controls the properties of the final lines to render

- Freestyle Color, which defines the stroke's color

- Freestyle Alpha, which modifies the line transparency

- Freestyle Thickness, which establishes Freestyle Stroke thickness

- Freestyle Geometry, which alters the geometry of the line

- Freestyle Texture, which creates a texture

Let's see what we can do with these panels.

The Freestyle Panel

The Freestyle panel contains some general settings and defines the parameters for the contour detection to render, as shown in Figure 6-12.

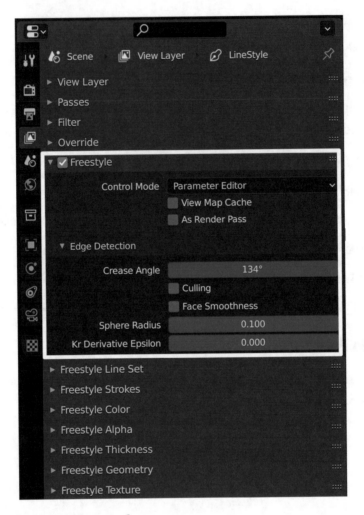

Figure 6-12. *The Freestyle panel*

In the Control Mode box, we can choose between two options.

- The Parameter Editor mode allows us to define the settings with manual control through the Parameter Editor.

- Instead, the Python Scripting mode allows us to create scripting in Python to define the settings and control the rendering more precisely.

Moreover, in the Edge Detection window, we determine the Crease Angle value, the minimum angle between two faces to display the edges in the rendering. Above this angle, the strokes are invisible.

The out-of-view edges are invisible if we enable the Culling box.

If we check the box Face Smoothness, Freestyle will consider the Shade Smooth/ Shade Flat option we can activate and deactivate on the Object context menu.

This panel has two other options: Spere Radius and Kr Derivative Epsilon. These are helpful when rendering more complex human characters or organic objects.

The second panel to control the render is Freestyle Line Set.

The Freestyle Line Set Panel

In this panel, we begin to control the lines' characteristics to render precisely. Here we can select the lines generated according to a predefined line style.

In this panel, as shown in Figure 6-13, we have four different ways to render the contour lines of our object. In addition, we can enable rendering for one or more contour lines simultaneously.

Figure 6-13. *The Freestyle Line Set panel*

The following are the modes:

- Visibility selects the contours to render based on their viewability.

- Edge Type chooses the edges to show based on the different edge types.

- Face Marks selects the silhouettes to render based on the marked faces.

- Collection renders the contours based on the different groups of the Outliner Editor. So we can choose to render with a particular LineSet all the objects of a collection.

In the Visibility section, we can select what Freestyle will display or not in the rendering, by settings things to visible or hidden, or based on quantitative visibility.

In the Edge Type section, we can choose what to render by checking the respective box:

- Silhouette creates the edges at the boundary of the objects.

- Crease shows the edges between two faces whose angle is less than the Crease Angle in Edge Detection value.

- Border renders the border of the open meshes.

- Edge Mark renders edges marked with the Mark Freestyle Edge button that we can find in the path Edit Mode ➤ Edge ➤ Mark Freestyle Edge from the menu of the 3D view header.

- Contour renders the outer shapes of objects.

- External Contour renders the outer contours.

- Material Boundary renders the contours between two different materials.

- Suggestive Contour renders contours randomly;

- Ridge and Valley render contour lines between concave and convex surfaces.

We then have six more panels dedicated to the display control of the rendering line style.

Let's see the first three in the following section.

The Strokes, Color, and Alpha Panels

In the previous versions of Blender, the Freestyle Line Style panel grouped these three windows and the other three of the following section.

In version 3.0, developers have subdivided the tools into six panels, each dedicated to a specific purpose.

The first is Freestyle Stroke, which selects the final lines' properties to render.

We can modify the strokes in different ways. So we can create effects of continuous or dashed lines and so on in an exact way.

Instead, the Freestyle Color panel determines the lines' color. First, we have to select a primary color. Then we can choose different modifiers to modify it such as Along Stroke, Crease Angle, Curvature 3D, Distance from Camera, Distance from Object, Material, Noise, and Tangent, which we will see shortly.

The third window, Freestyle Alpha, modifies the transparency channel. Also, in this panel, we have at our disposal the same modifiers of the Color panel to change the final result of the rendering.

The Thickness, Geometry, and Texture Panels

Three other panels allow us to control the effects of Thickness, Geometry, and Texture.

Freestyle Thickness controls the stroke thickness. Also, in this case, we can apply the following modifiers: Along Stroke, Calligraphy, Crease Angle, Curvature 3D, Distance from Camera, Distance from Object, Material, Noise, and Tangent.

We use the Freestyle Geometry window to modify the geometry of the line.

In this panel, the modifiers are many and obtain the most varied line types.

The last panel, Freestyle Texture, allows us to create a texture assigned directly to the strokes at rendering time. We can set an image texture. Checking the Use Nodes box, we can also operate with the different Blender procedural textures.

Now let's see modifiers more closely.

The Freestyle Modifiers

To conclude this introduction to Freestyle, let's see the Freestyle modifiers to edit Color, Alpha, Thickness, and Geometry.

We use these tools to introduce changes in the various parameters of the rendered line. Let's see the most important ones.

Along Stroke

This modifier applies a linear variation of color, transparency, and thickness to the lines.

Calligraphy

This is only for line thickness; it creates different thicknesses concerning the line orientation and imitates some signs such as fountain and calligraphy pens.

Crease Angle

This modifies the strokes according to the angle between two adjacent faces. If the faces do not form the corner within the values defined in the window, the line is not modified.

Curvature 3D

This modifies the line by referring to the radial curvature of the underlying 3D surface.

Distance from Camera

This creates different types of thickness related to the distance of the object from the camera.

Distance from Object

This modifier edits strokes according to the distance from a specific object.

Material

The material modifier changes the base properties of color, thickness, and transparency, referring to the material of a particular object.

Noise

The noise modifier distributes a disturbance along the lines of the drawing to make its characteristics irregular.

Tangent

This changes its effect concerning the direction of the lines evaluated at the vertices of the drawing.

More on Freestyle

We can use this renderer to make technical drawings or free-hand sketches.

We can combine Freestyle's contour lines and effects with Eevee and Cycles' materials to mix cartoon with photorealistic results.

We introduced here the main elements of this particular renderer.

To deepen this topic, we can refer to `https://docs.blender.org/manual/en/3.0/render/freestyle/parameter_editor/index.html` that leads us to the part of the Blender Manual site dedicated to Freestyle.

Now let's see how to use Blender for post-production.

Compositing

After seeing the features of Blender renderers, we will move on to post-production with compositing. The Blender Compositor allows us to edit and enhance images and videos.

We can improve our renders by modifying the color, contrast, and special effects. We can do all this in the Compositor through the nodal system. We already saw how nodes work with materials in Chapter 4. We will learn about post-processing with the Blender Compositor to improve our renders, images, and videos.

The Compositor Workspace

In the Blender Compositor, we can edit a video, an image, or a sequence of images.

For example, we can merge two movies with Compositing nodes and edit the whole sequence altogether. Moreover, we can import images or videos, edit them, and add many special effects through nodes.

To work with the Compositor, we use the Compositing workspace that we can open from the Topbar by clicking the button Compositing, as in Figure 6-14.

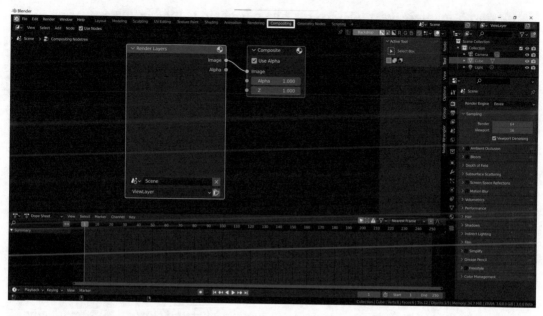

Figure 6-14. *The Compositing workspace*

The default interface presents the Compositor as the main window. Below this window, there are the Dope Sheet and the Timeline. Finally, on the right of the interface, we find the Outliner and the Properties Editor.

Let's start inserting the Render Layers node and the Composite node by checking the box Use Nodes in the Compositor's header, as shown in Figure 6-15.

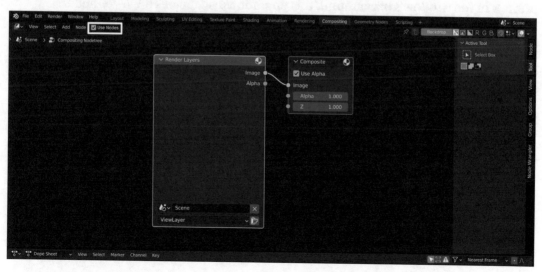

Figure 6-15. *The Compositor with Render Layers and Composite nodes*

We start from these two nodes to create a node chain to modify images:

- The Render Layers node lets us input the scene in the Compositor and connect it to the Composite node. In addition, with the Render Layers node, we modify the render passes that help us control which image data to use to edit the scene image.

- Instead, the Composite node is the final output of the entire blockchain and contains the modified final image.

We don't have any Render Layers node image available at the moment because we haven't launched a render yet.

However, we can do it from the Topbar in the main menu by selecting Render ➤ Render image or directly from the Compositor by clicking the Render Active Scene button at the bottom-right corner of the Render Layers node.

Before executing the render, let's move to the Properties Editor's View Layer Properties ➤ Passes ➤ Data and activate two passes: Mist and Normal. Automatically in the Render Layers node the output sockets of the two nodes will appear. These two functions will help us have better compositional results adding a more specific control over the render display.

Now we play the render again. Again, the rendered image automatically updates in the Render Layers node.

We use the shortcut Ctrl+Shift+LMB in the Render Layers node to see the render preview in the window's background; this operation also creates a Viewer node.

We also preview each output channel of the Render Layers node in the Backdrop by clicking Ctrl+Shift+RMB on the individual output sockets of the various passes. We can change the size and position of the background image in different ways. We use the shortcut V to zoom out and reduce the image, while we use Alt+V to zoom in and close the picture. Also, we can zoom in and out or move our backdrop image, modifying the values of the Zoom and Offset boxes of the View panel in the Sidebar we open and close with N.

Now let's see how the Compositor works in practice.

Setting the Compositor

First, we set the compositor interface to work on the 3D view rendered image.

1. Open the Teapot.blend file previously created and save it as Teapot_Compositor.blend.

2. Choose Eevee or Cycles. Then, from the Properties Editor, select Output, set the Resolution Percentage setting of the Dimensions panel to 50 percent, and render.

3. Click the Compositing workspace, and activate Use Nodes. Then click the Backdrop button on the right side of the Compositor header.

4. Click the Image output in the Render Layer node by pressing Shift+Ctrl+LMB and add a Viewer node to the node chain. The Render Output Image appears as the background of the window.

By selecting the Viewer node and clicking the two crossed diagonals in the center of the background image, we can move the backdrop. Then, clicking one of the white rectangles in the corners of the image, we can resize it. In this way, we can place the image as we wish.

With the shortcut Ctrl+spacebar, we can maximize and minimize the entire window to more easily perform our movements.

We find the same commands in the View panel on the Sidebar to the right of the View window that we can open with N.

Up to now, we have adjusted the interface setup. Now let's learn how to create a newly rendered Image with a few samples.

The Denoise Node

There will be a very accentuated image disturbance in a render with Cycles with few samples.

But even with Eevee, samples improve the rendering quality but lengthen the rendering time. So, we must use as few samples as possible with Cycles and Eevee.

We can reduce the render noise with a simple post-production modification.

In Blender 3.0 for the Cycles renderer, we can use the Denoise boxes for Viewport and Render from the Properties Editor: Render Properties ➤ Sampling path. This operation allows us to control noise in both the viewport and the render.

Instead, in Eevee, we must use the Denoise node. With this tool, we reduce the rendering time by using a low number of samples for the render but maintaining a good quality for the final render result.

Let's go back to the Compositing workspace and add a Denoise node in the Compositor.

It has several inputs; we connect the output image of the Render Layers node with the input Image of the Denoise node.

By creating a straightforward nodal chain like this one, shown in Figure 6-16, we can quickly improve the quality of our render in post-production.

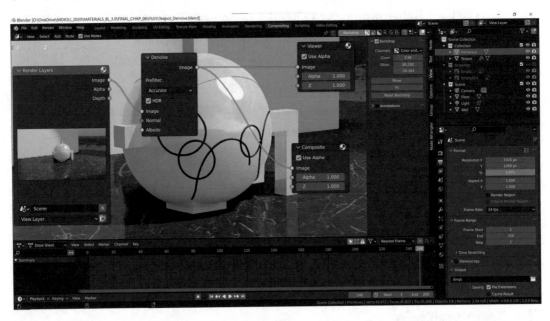

Figure 6-16. *The nodal chain with the addition of the Denoise node*

By adding the Denoise node, we get a noticeable image improvement compared to the original render. We performed the render in Figure 6-16 using Eevee, with the Sampling Value set at 2 for Render and Viewport.

We can set the samples in the Properties Editor by selecting the Render Properties ➤ Sampling window, and in this case, the disturbing effect in the original render is evident. However, as we see in Figure 6-16, the final image improves considerably with the addition of the Denoise node in post-production.

We can use this node also in Cycles.

In Blender 3.0, the Denoise box in the Render window is selected by default.

Moreover, in Cycles, by clicking in the Properties Editor, selecting View Layer Properties ➤ Passes ➤ Data, and checking Denoising Data, we add several other passes to the Render Layers node. We can use them to refine the effect and control it more precisely through the specific passes for editing images or videos. Next, in this chapter, we'll see how to use them in practice in Exercise 14.

Now let's delve into the topic, analyzing the most crucial Compositing nodes individually.

Compositing Nodes

These nodes allow us to work in post-production directly in Blender on external videos and images or directly inside Blender.

These video editing tools allow us to assemble and improve our multimedia content.

This part of the chapter will discuss the different types of nodes for compositing. Blender offers many of them divided into ten different categories. There are many nodes, and we will get an idea of their characteristics and how we can use many of them.

Input Nodes

We use input nodes to enter information in a node chain. They are the first link in the chain, with only an output socket and no input. We can import images, videos, colors, and textures with this node type.

Bokeh Image Node

This node generates blurs in a render. Therefore, we need to connect it to a Bokeh Blur node to make it work.

It simulates camera parameters such as lens distortions and aperture shape to create effects in the blurred parts of the image rendered.

Image Node

We use this node to import images in the Blender Compositor.

There are two output sockets:

- We use the Image output when we want to utilize all image data.

- We use Alpha output when we want to use transparency data only.

We can load the image from the New and Open buttons at the bottom of the interface.

Mask Node

The Mask node allows us to use the mask data-block to control the effects applied to an image. For example, we can use the mask as a factor input and hide some image parts.

We can also select the image part to apply other nodes such as HSV, Hue Saturation, and Value. For example, with this node, we can control the color effects applied to an image.

Movie Clip Node

We can use this node to import video clips of any format supported by Blender. This node provides us with different kinds of outputs:

- Image outputs image data.

- Alpha uses transparency data.

- Offset X outputs the offset value X.

- Offset Y outputs the offset value Y.

- Scale outputs the scale.

- Angle outputs the lens angle.

We can load a sequence of frames or a movie file from the Open button at the bottom of the interface.

Render Layers Node

The Render Layers node is essential. As we learned earlier, this node is the most effective way to introduce a rendered image of one of the Blender scenes into the Compositor's node chain.

RGB Node

We can use this type of node to introduce color into the Compositor. It has no input and only one output, RGBA color value, which allows us to insert colors into images or videos in the Compositor.

Texture Node

This node allows us to insert textures into the Compositor. It has two input sockets to change the image's origin and scale. It also has two outputs to use the grayscale values or the texture's colors.

Time Curve Node

We can modify the Timeline with this node, controlling its changes with a curve graph.

It consists of a curve graph and a time interval to determine the start and the end with the respective boxes.

By changing the curve, we can adjust the Timeline variations; instead, we can modify the duration of the video by changing the Start and End frames.

Track Position Node

We use this node to introduce the information about the position contained in a tracking marker into the Compositor.

Value Node

It is a simple and powerful node that allows us to use numerical values in the Compositor. In addition, we use it to control the values of many other nodes.

Output Nodes

This category of nodes allows us to concretize and visualize the results achieved with the chain of nodes in the Compositor.

Composite Node

As we have already seen, this node receives the final output of the node's chain and connects it with the renderer. Blender updates it after each render.

File Output Node

This node allows us to save the renders in a chosen path automatically. Blender does not perform this operation directly.

It has only one image input box and the button to select the folder to save the files at the bottom of the interface. It can save a single image or a specified frame range.

Split Viewer Node

This node puts two images together vertically on the x-axis or horizontally on the y-axis in the Viewer node. First, we must connect the two images with the two inputs and choose the reflection axis. We can also use the same image modified with different nodes.

Viewer Node

The Viewer node outputs the Compositor's processed image when it is connected. This node is a temporary, in-process viewer. As shown in the previous section, it is automatically added to the Compositor when we select the Use Nodes button in the Compositor editor header.

Color Nodes

Through these nodes, we can control the color of the image. In addition, Blender has many color nodes that allow us to combine, mix, and overlay colors. Thus, they offer us many possibilities to modify both colors and contrast and image overlay.

Alpha Over Node

This node is one of the most frequently used in compositing.

Just like that, we use the Alpha Over node to superimpose two images.

We put one image on top of another using the foreground image's Alpha channel and controlling the foreground image's transparency with the Factor button.

Bright/Contrast Node

We modify the brightness and contrast of an image or rendering with this node.

So we increase or decrease the brightness, the average value of the image's pixels. We can also change the contrast between the lightest and darkest tones.

Color Balance Node

The Color Balance node can control the image's color and value separately for shadows, halftones, and lights.

Color Correction Node

Also, the Color Correction node allows us to modify the color of an image separately for shadows, halftones, and lights. In addition, we can change the saturation, contrast, exponential gamma correction, gain, and lift of the image separately.

Hue Correct Node

This node allows us to edit an image's hue, saturation, and value using a curve. In the beginning, the curve is a straight line placed in a horizontal position. When we modify it, we change the levels of one of the three values that we can select through the three H, S, V buttons in the upper-left corner of the node interface.

Hue Saturation Value Node

The Hue Saturation Value node applies the color transformations in the Compositor using the HSV color space.

Note   We can use this node to modify existing colors in an image. Instead, if we want to color a black-and-white picture, we must use the Mix node to add an RGB node to the image or rendering.

Invert Node

This node reverses the colors or the transparency of the images by inverting the Alpha or the RGB channels. So, we can change white to black or change a color to its complementary color, for example, blue to yellow or red to cyan.

Mix Node

The Mix node joins the image's colors as specified with a factor and a blend mode.

Factor 0 corresponds to the top input socket, as in the other nodes, and Factor 1 corresponds to the bottom. This node has many blending modes. For example, the Mix blend mode combines the two images averaging between them. Instead, the Add mode joins one picture to the other, as in Figure 6-17.

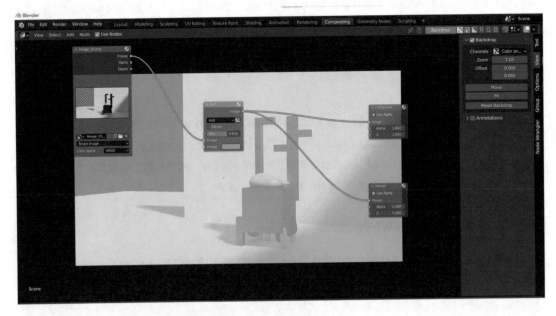

Figure 6-17. *The Mix node in the Compositor*

In Figure 6-17, we added green to the red chair image with the Mix node and the Add blending mode.

The node added the color to the image that acquires a green tone. If we change the blending mode from Add to Subtract, Blender will subtract the green giving us a picture with a preponderance of its complementary color, purple, which is the mix of the two remaining colors: blue and red.

For a deeper understanding of color theory, refer to Chapter 5.

RGB Curves Node

We use this node to modify the saturation and value of an entire image with Curves within the Compositor. For example, we can change the individual color levels or every color channel, Red, Green, or Blue.

Tone Map Node

We can use this node to edit HDR images or High Dynamic Range Images rendered with Blender or imported from a digital camera. These images have high contrast and a vast range of colors. When we use tools that can't reproduce these high-quality features, we can reduce and convert them into standard images or videos with this node.

Z Combine Node

Z Combine node mixes two images based on the pixel's Alpha channel value and is similar to the Alpha Over node but combines images using the Z value that is the distance from the camera.

Converter Nodes

This group of nodes converts different properties of images or videos within the Compositor. With these tools, we can modify colors, transparency, and more. We can also use Converter nodes to alter or add channels to an image, and they also allow us to work on different channels individually. We can edit pictures in various formats and color models with the HSV, RGB, HDMI, etc.

Alpha Convert Node

We use this node to modify the Alpha channel of an image.

Color Ramp Node

Blender uses ramps extensively to specify a range of colors based on color stops. Color stops are points that indicate clear color choices. The intervals between one color stop and another result from their interpolation. So, for example, we can use a ramp to produce a range of colors starting from a single color.

The Color Ramp node in the Compositor allows us to convert and modify the colors of an image using gradients.

For example, through this node, we can change a color image into a black-and-white one by choosing different shades of gray. Or, inversely, we can add color to black-and-white pictures.

Combine and Separate Nodes

These nodes combine or separate individual color channels. For example, the Separate RGBA node allows us to separate the Red, Green, Blue, and Alpha channels to edit them separately.

Later, after editing the individual channels separately, we can combine them into a single image with Combine RGBA.

These nodes do the same things in different color spaces: HSVA, RGBA, YCbCrA, YUVA.

We can divide them into the following:

- Separate splits an image in its different color or transparency channels such as Red, Green, Blue, and Alpha.

- Combine combines the other channels within a single image.

These nodes allow us to work separately for different color spaces on each channel.

Math Node

The Math node allows us to introduce mathematical operations in the Compositor.

RGB to BW Node

The RGB to BW node transforms colors into black-and-white shades.

Set Alpha Node

This node allows us to add an Alpha channel to our image.

Switch View Node

The Switch view node lets us merge two views of the same object to create a single stereo 3D output.

Filter Nodes

This category of nodes allows us to modify the pixels of the images to apply particular effects.

Bilateral Blur Node

We can use this node to apply a kind of a blur to the image while maintaining sharp and defined edges.

Blur Node

The Blur node allows us to blur an image using various algorithms to obtain different types of blur. So we have other blur possibilities that enable us to control the angles and the kind of gradient and, at the same time, allow us to preserve the image's tones.

The Blur algorithms are Flat, Tent, Quadratic, Cubic, Gaussian, Fast Gaussian, Catmull-Rom, and Mitch.

Defocus Node

The Defocus node uses a map or mask to blur parts of the image. For example, we can simulate the depth of field in post-processing.

Denoise Node

This node, which we have already talked about in this section, allows us to correct the Cycles' render noise when we use a low number of samples.

Glare Node

The Glare node helps us simulate the lighting effects, blur, and other imperfections caused by a photographic or cinematographic lens, thus adding realism to our scenes.

Pixelate Node

We can use this node, associated with the Scale node, to obtain pixelated images like in Figure 6-18.

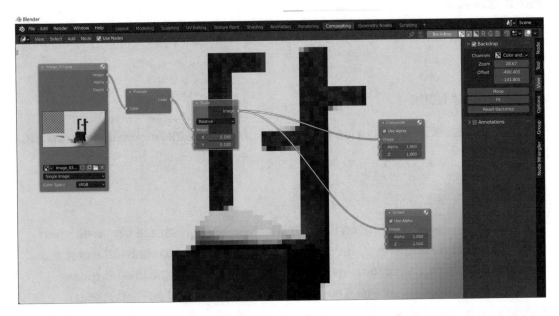

Figure 6-18. *Obtaining a pixelated effect with the Compositor*

In Figure 6-18, we can see the effect of the Scale and Pixelate nodes to get a pixelated result for the render of our chair.

Vector Blur Node

We can use this node to simulate the motion blur effect in post-production to emulate moving objects.

Vector Nodes

We use these nodes to modify vectors. A vector combines magnitude and direction; we display it with intensity, direction, and verso as an arrow.

Blender calculates the vectors of the represented objects.

We use this information in the Compositor to simplify some values through the Vector nodes.

Map Value Node

This node allows us to scale, offset, and clamp values to a specific, more restricted field. So, it transforms a vector or value range set, reducing it to a minor lapse.

Normal Node

The Normal node creates a normal vector that precisely controls the display. We can use it, for example, to edit the orientation or size of a texture.

Normalize Node

This node allows us to transform one set of values into another more accessible and straightforward to understand and use.

Matte Nodes

These nodes are useful for creating effects with overlay images and video. For example, they allow us to create a matte for pictures or videos without an Alpha channel.

Matte nodes allow us to make a pixel transparent, basing the transparency on some aspect of the pixel itself.

Once we have obtained the transparency of some parts of the image, we can use an Alpha Over node to composite the picture over a background.

So, realizing video shooting using blue screen or green screen, we can make some photomontages by inserting matte painting or virtual backgrounds.

Channel Key Node

This node separates foreground objects from background objects, using the differences in the selected channel's levels to create masks.

Chroma Key Node

We effectively use this node to edit images or videos shot in front of a green or blue screen.

The Chroma Key node can determine the difference between foreground and background according to the chroma values of each pixel of the image.

Color Key Node

This node creates a matte for the picture based on the input image colors.

Color Spill Node

We use this node to edit images or videos shot in front of a green or blue screen. When we take a picture or shoot a video in front of a green or blue screen, if the foreground object is reflective, the scene objects will contain shades of the predominant color.

Color Spill allows us to remove the green or blue reflections from the scene objects quickly and easily.

Cryptomatte

Cryptomatte is a post-processing tool. It is a feature of Blender that serves to create masks starting from materials, objects, or groups of things. This node makes mattes for Compositing with the standard Cryptomatte that we can edit in the Compositor.

We can then work on image superimpositions through transparencies using the render layers and render passes of Eevee and Cycles.

Luminance Key Node

This node separates the foreground from the background by relying on a range of brightness values.

Distort Nodes

We use this node to modify images by distorting them. For example, we can uniformly deform images or create special effects using masks or other types of filters.

Crop Node

This node serves to crop or trim the image in the Compositor.

Displace Node

Displace node moves the position of the image pixels based on an input vector that can be, for example, an image, a normal map, or a black-and-white map.

Flip Node

This node flips the image on the x-axis or y-axis, or both simultaneously.

Lens Distortion Node

We can use this node to simulate the distortions that the objectives of a real camera produce.

Rotate Node

We use the Rotate node to pivot an image in the Compositor.

Scale Node

We use this node to change the size of an image in the Compositor.

Translate Node

The Translate node is used to move an image.

Transform Node

This node combines the functions of the three previous nodes; it allows us to translate, rotate, and scale the image in the Compositor.

Node Groups

Like material nodes, we also can group composite nodes to simplify node trees.

Make Group

To create a node group, we must select all the nodes we want to include; we cannot insert either Input or Output nodes.

Then we press Ctrl+G, or from the Compositor Editor header menu, we select Node ➤ Make group; after that we press Tab to display the whole group as a single node.

Pressing Tab a second time, we can open the node group and see every node.

There is a name field in the middle of the node group named NodeGroup.001; we can click this box to rename it.

Edit Group

With a node group selected, we press Tab to open it; then, we can move and modify the nodes inside the group. Finally, by clicking Tab again, we can close it again.

Ungroup

To delete the group, we must use the keyboard shortcut Ctrl+Alt+G. In this way, we will return to the separate nodes in the Compositor Editor.

To disconnect one or more nodes and detach them from the group, we must press Tab, select the node we want to separate, press P, and select Move; we can also copy the node by pressing P and selecting Copy.

This is the same procedure as when working with a mesh in Edit mode and we must divide some subobjects from the current mesh; in that case, we press P and select Selection.

Appending Node Groups

We can also import a node group directly into Blender, as we do with objects, materials, etc., from the Topbar: select File ➤ Link or Append.

Then we can insert them in the scene with the shortcut Shift+A and by selecting Add ➤ Group and then the appended group.

Layout Nodes

These nodes help us control the layout and the connectivity between the various nodes within the Compositor.

Frame Node

This node creates a framework for how to insert nodes to group them visually.

It creates the frame. Then we select the nodes to add and press Ctrl+P or drag the nodes inside the frame.

Reroute Node

This node is helpful to insert a node between the connected nodes.

Switch Node

We use this node to switch from one image to another by selecting the checkbox that its interface makes available to us. We can also animate this node with the keyframes system.

We will practice how some of these nodes work in Exercise 15 later in this chapter.

After studying compositing in Blender and analyzing the Compositing nodes, we can look more closely at video editing.

Editing Videos

In this section, we will learn about video editing. Blender 3.0 provides a powerful and flexible Video Editor to merge multiple images and movies and add complex effects.

This system is called the Video Sequence Editor (VSE) or the Sequencer.

We can load images and video sequences and edit them one after the other, overlapping them and adding fades and transitions to join the different content in the best way. We can add other content, such as sounds, masks, colors, texts, Blender's three-dimensional scenes, etc. Finally, we can add special effects, audio, and texts and synchronize everything easily and naturally.

Let's start working by setting up a video-editing interface.

The Video Editing Workspace

Open Blender, and in the Topbar, click + and then select Video Editing ➤ Video Editing to open the workspace shown in Figure 6-19.

Figure 6-19. *The Video Editing workspace*

This interface comprises a file browser on the left side of the screen to import contents quickly. In the top center, there is the video sequencer in preview mode, in which we can see the movie during editing. On the right, the Properties Editor is opened in the Output Properties panel. Below on the left is a Video Sequencer Editor in Sequencer mode, and on the right, we find this editor's Sidebar.

We can see the various channels to import images and videos and edit them in the Video Sequencer.

If we want to import an image or video, we use the usual shortcut Shift+A ➤ Add in the Sequencer Editor; here, we choose our contents in the window highlighted in Figure 6-20.

Figure 6-20. *The Sequencer Editor*

The three principal objects are Movie, Sound, and Image/Sequence.

In the image, we can see the main menu at the top, as well as the toolbar with the Select and Blade tools on the left.

The menu contains the View, Select, Marker, Add, and Strip drop-down menus. If we press T in the Sequencer, the toolbar provides two instruments on the left.

- Select, which allows us to select one or more strips with the Tweak or Select Box commands

- Blade, or Shift+K, which splits the selected strips in two

The Sequencer has various channels containing different strips.

For what concerns the visualization, the higher channels overlap the lower ones: the top channel sequences cover the ones below.

So, we must put background images in the lower tracks and foreground pictures in the upper.

All the tools and keyboard shortcuts are similar to those of other editors. So, we can use G to move, R to rotate, S to scale, etc.

Now we take a closer look at the features of Blender's Video Editor and the many possibilities it offers us.

Let's start by taking a look at the playhead.

Playhead

The playhead is the blue vertical line we see in the Timeline. It marks the current frame, the moment in time in our animation.

We can move the playhead by clicking and dragging it with the left mouse button or by directly clicking the number of the frame we want to place it.

Below the Sequencer Editor is the Timeline. We can open it by moving the cursor on the line that divides the Sequencer from the Timeline header, and when it turns into a double arrow, we drag the mouse upward, as in Figure 6-21.

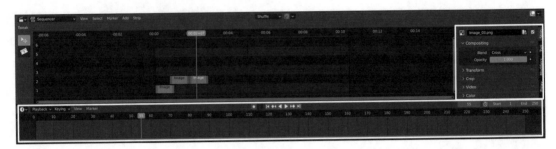

Figure 6-21. *The Sequencer, the Timeline, and the Sidebar*

We can also use the value in the Timeline header that indicates the current frame to the left of the Start and End values to determine our movie's Start and End frame. These two values define the length of the film itself.

We can also move the playhead back and forth with the left and right arrows; by pressing Shift and one of these two arrows, we move to the beginning or end of the Timeline. As we switch the Timeline, we display the frames one by one with the precise moment of the animation depicted in that frame.

For example, when we execute the render from the Topbar by selecting Render ➤ Render image, we render the frame displayed in the playhead.

Now let's see how to add content to the strips.

Adding Strips

We can add content in Blender's Video Editor via strips. A *strip* is a storage container with a length, a Start frame, and an End frame.

Blender represents a strip in the Sequencer as a colored horizontal rectangle of which we can change the duration.

In the Sequencer, we can add four different types of strips: Action, Transition, Sound clip, and Meta.

We can insert strips with the usual methods to add objects in Blender. So, either using the Add key of the Sequencer header menu or pressing the shortcut Shift+A, we import the content we want to add from the Add window, as shown in Figure 6-22.

Figure 6-22. *The Add Strip menu*

Blender offers us several possibilities to develop and edit a video with various content. We can add all this content through the strips.

To create a video, we can add different types of content.

- We can add images, videos, and sounds. These are the main contents that make up our video and are the basis of the story we want to represent.

- We can also directly add text and color. We specify the elements and make them easier to understand with these tools.

- Then we must develop strips for transition effects. These components link the previous content together and make the story seamless.

Finally, we have to render the video to get the final result. This operation leads us to the last step, which is to create the final result and get a finished product.

To practice with some of these tools, we refer to Exercise 16 at the end of this chapter. Now let's see Blender Compositor's effects and transitions.

Adding Effects and Transitions

When we edit our videos with Blender, we can add many effects to our sequences.

To add an Effect strip, we must first introduce at least one Base strip: a movie, an image, etc. Then we must select the Base strip and the effect we want to add from the Add item of the header menu. For example, if we're going to add a transition effect between two strips, we have to choose them by selecting the first one with LMB and then the second one with Shift+LMB.

After, from the Add menu, we select the desired transition.

The effects and transitions inserted will be displayed in the Sequencer Channel above the strips to which they are applied.

Now let's closely see the different types of content that we can add and edit in the Blender Video Editor.

Movie and Image Strips

We introduce the contents with these strips: videos, single images, or sequences that form the basis of all the subsequent work.

We can drag them from the file browser at the top left to the Sequencer at the bottom of the Video Editing workspace.

If we add a single Blender image, Blender inserts it with a standard length of 25 frames; then, we can change the duration by selecting the right end of the strip and dragging it to the desired size.

If we want to insert whole sequences of Images, Blender will import them all together in numerical order: 0001, 0002, etc.

Scene Strips

This strip is exciting because it allows us to directly import the 3D objects created in Blender into the Sequencer. We can insert the render output of another scene of the same Blender file through a Scene strip directly into our sequence.

Sound Strips

We need this type of strip to insert audio tracks in our videos. The audio can be imported with the video or inserted later. The formats available are many and professional, from Waveform Audio format WAV to MP3, etc.

Color Strips

With this strip, we can add solid color frames to the video. As in the case of the picture, Blender inserts a 25-frame-long strip, but we can extend the duration by selecting and moving one of the ends.

From the Strip window of the Sidebar on the right of the interface, we can modify the color and transparency and add transformations. We can also add Strip modifiers from the Modifiers window of the Sidebar.

For example, we can use this tool to adjust the color of an entire strip movie or image or use it to provide a fade-in or fade-out effect or transition, etc.

Text Strips

This content is attractive and allows us to insert text directly into the Sequencer.

Also, in this case, from the text window on the right of the interface, we can modify different parameters such as color and transparency, etc., as shown in Figure 6-23.

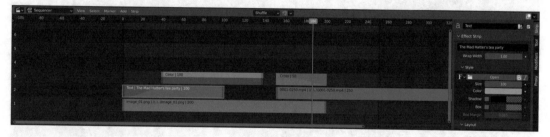

Figure 6-23. *The Text strip in the Sequence Editor*

For example, we can choose to use one of the many fonts available by clicking the Folder icon; or we can load and use an external font of our choice.

With the Blender Compositor, we can also create various special effects.

Let's see how to do it.

Effect Strips

We need Effect strips to add some effects to the Base strips.

To add an Effect strip, we must select the Base strip; then, with Shift, join the upper Strip. Next, with the shortcut Shift+A, we can open a window and choose the Effect strip to add from the menu.

Let's see them one by one:

- Add combines the effects of two strips. So, for example, we can use it to connect a Movie strip with a Color strip, another movie, an image, or a mask.

- Subtract has the opposite effect. It takes away one strip's color from the other, such as subtracting a green strip color from a Video strip, as shown in Figure 6-24.

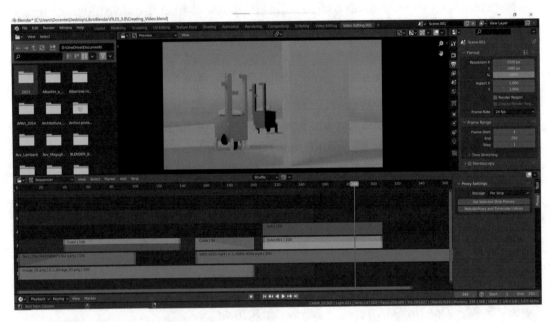

Figure 6-24. *The Subtract effect*

Removing green from the RGB colors of the video leaves red and blue, which creates the violet atmosphere of the picture.

- The Multiply effect multiplies one strip by the other. Basically, like any Multiply Blend mode, it darkens the image or video by increasing the RGB channel numbers of both strips.

- Over Drop, Alpha Over, and Alpha Under use the strip's Alpha channels modification to control the transparency in three different ways.

  - By applying Alpha Over, the two strips are superimposed according to the selection order. The first selected strip is the background; the second remains in the foreground. Opacity controls the transparency of the foreground.

  - Alpha Under has the opposite effect. The first selected strip becomes the foreground and overlaps the second, which acts as a background. In this case, the Opacity modifies the transparency of the ground.

  - Over Drop mixes the two previous effects. As for Alpha Under, the first selected strip is the foreground, but as for Alpha Over, Opacity controls the transparency of the foreground.

- Color Mix combines the two selected strips by mixing their colors and getting an emotional effect, as shown in Figure 6-25.

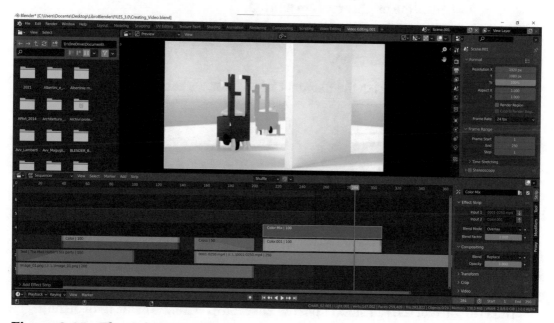

Figure 6-25. *The Color Mix effect*

We see a Color Mix effect superimposed on a video and a green color in the image.

- Multicam Selector allows us to select and edit several cameras simultaneously.

- Transform allows us to modify a basic image or video by moving, rotating, or scaling it inside the video screen.

- Speed Control allows us to speed up or slow down a Base strip.

   The Multiply Speed base value is set to 1 by default. If we raise this value above 1, the strip becomes faster. Instead, we choose a setting lower than 1, and the Base Strip slows down.

   The Speed Control strip can help us produce, for example, a slow-motion effect. In addition, with this strip, we can also play with animation effects by keyframing the speed control.

- Glow adds light to the strip to which we apply it. It modifies the luminance channel of the Base strip, giving it a significant shine effect. Also, the bright areas are blurred.

- Finally, we use Gaussian Blur to fade the Base strip in a predetermined direction.

In addition to the effects in the Blender Compositor, we can also insert transitions between contents.

Transitions

We add a Transition strip to two Basic strips with the Transition button.

We can create different results for both video and sound with this effect. Moreover, they are fast and straightforward to use.

First, we select the strip below and then the one above with Shift+LMB. Then we add the transition with the keyboard shortcut path Shift+A and select Add ➤ Transition and the desired effect. A third strip appears above the first two.

Then we can edit the transition from the Effect Strip window on the right of the Sequencer Editor.

Let's see the most important:

- Sound Crossfade allows us to change the volume of two sound strips by mixing their sounds. This transition does not create a separate strip from the two Base strips because it only animates a value.

- Cross instead fades the passage from one image or video strip to another, creating the so-called Crossfade effect. If the two Base strips overlap, the transition is softer in the case of movies because the movements overlap.

  We can apply it even if the two Base strips do not overlap; in this case, if we overlap movies, we can have defects because the two strips are stretched and the final frames are repeated.

- Gamma Cross behaves like Cross but uses color correction instead of dissolution for the transition. In many cases, it is more effective than the previous one because it allows softer transitions.

- Wipe gradually superimposes one strip on the other using different overlapping methods.

After having also analyzed the essential functions of the Video Editor, in the next session, we put into practice the theoretical notions learned.

Exercises: Rendering and Compositing

Earlier we learned about the differences between the two internal renderers: Eevee and Cycles. Then we delved into compositing and video editing.

After having deepened the theoretical fundamentals, we dedicate this section to some exercises to learn the hands-on techniques of rendering, video editing, and post-production. So, starting from objects and scenes created in the previous chapters, we will do the following steps:

1. We will first render images and videos with Eevee and Cycles.

2. Then we will see the process of video editing and post-production by modifying the images with Blender compositing using some Composition nodes that we studied in the "Compositing Nodes" section.

3. Finally, we will do some video editing using the tools studied earlier in this chapter.

Let's start by rendering a scene with Eevee.

Exercise 13: Rendering with Eevee

Now it is time to learn more about rendering options. We will start with the Eevee render engine and first make an image and then a video.

Let's start to render an image.

Rendering an Image with Eevee

First, we choose the format and resolution of the image to create. These depend on what we want to use the image for.

This time we want to create an image to print. We can refer to the exhibition presentation brochure in the Art Gallery in Milan, *The Mad Hatter's Tea Party*, which we can find at https://issuu.com/giampieromoioli/docs/mad_hatter.

We want to create an A4 size image of 21 x 29.7 centimeters (8.3 x 11.7 inches) for typographic printing with a definition of 300 dots per inch (dpi).

For digital printing, a resolution of 150 dpi may be sufficient. Instead, we can reduce it to 72 dpi if we want to produce images for a screen.

To obtain the size in inches from centimeters, we must divide by 2.54. Then we need to multiply the image size by the resolution we want to obtain.

1. Open the file RedChair.blend with the red chair created in Exercise 5 of Chapter 3.

2. Perform a simple calculation by dividing 21 x 29.7 by 2.54 and then multiplying by 300. In this way, you will get the pixel size of the image you want to render, 2480 x 3508.

3. Move to the Properties Editor's Output Properties section and select Format; set Resolution X to 2480 and Resolution Y to 3508. Then adjust the camera frame for your shot.

4. Adjust the camera and run a first test render by setting the Percentage Scale for Render Resolution value to 20 percent, with the button below Resolution X and Y.

5. From the Topbar, select Render ➤ Render image, or use the
    shortcut F12, and get the result shown in the Blender Render
    window, as shown in Figure 6-26.

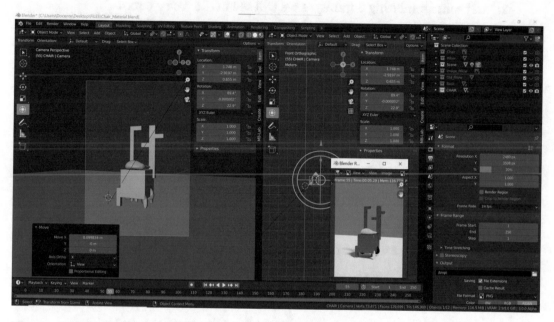

Figure 6-26. *Rendering the red chair with Eevee*

6. Set the lights and the camera's framing, set the Percentage for
    Render Resolution to 100 percent, and repeat the rendering.

7. Once you have obtained the desired result from the Blender
    Render window header, select the image and Save as, choose the
    PNG format and the file path, and click Save as Image.

Now let's see how to render a movie with Eevee.

Preparing a Camera Animation

In the second part of the exercise, we will create a video with Eevee.

Making a Blender video takes a little bit more preparation. For example, we need to
create an animation before we start.

To make videos, we must first prepare the scene by following these steps:

1. Create an animation.

2. Set some rendering options, as we will see in the next exercise.

3. After rendering the scene, we can apply some Compositing nodes in the Compositor to the movie.

We continue with the same file and object from the previous exercise.

We want to make a walk-through video with a pan around the red chair. This kind of animation is valuable and straightforward if we want to show a design object or an architectural environment from all points of view in a video.

Let's start by organizing the camera movement around the object we want to film.

1. Open the file RedChair.blend as in the previous assignment.

2. First, select the CHAIR collection in the Outliner by right-clicking the collection itself and choosing Select Objects in the window.

3. In Object mode, in the header of the 3D Viewport, select Object ➤ Snap ➤ Cursor to Selected.

4. Still in Object mode, add an Empty Object by pressing Shift+A and selecting Add ➤ Empty ➤ Arrows.

5. Select the camera and apply a constraint from the path Properties Editor ➤ Object Constraint Properties ➤ Add Object Constraint ➤ Tracking ➤ Track To. Set the Target to Empty and set the two variables Track Axis to -Z and Up to Y.

6. Then, in 3D view on the right, press 0 on the numeric keypad to go to Camera view. Finally, move the Empty if you need to frame the Chair in Camera view.

7. Add a Bézier curve by pressing Shift+A and selecting Curve ➤ Circle in 3D view. Enlarge it by pressing S ➤ 4; then click Enter to confirm the transformation.

8. In Object mode, select the camera and the circle with Shift+LMB on the curve. Next, click Ctrl+P and choose Follow Path.

   If you prefer, you can also give your camera a Follow Path constraint with the curve as the target in the Object Constraint panel.

Now the camera follows the circle path; to verify, press the spacebar to preview the animation. But in this way, the camera movement only reaches up to 100 frames.

We want to slow down the camera movement and increase the movie frames.

9. Select the curve, transform the left 3D view in a Graph Editor, select the Evaluation Time channel on the left, display the Sidebar panel on the right with N, and from the Modifiers tab, add a Generator modifier.

10. Keeping the curve selected, go to the Properties Editor and select Object Data ➤ Path Animation. Play with frames and evaluation time to change your animation time. You can see the interface in Figure 6-27.

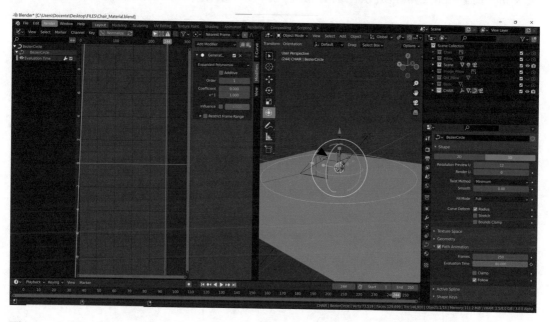

Figure 6-27. *The camera follows a path turning around the chair*

11. If you want to occupy all the animation's frames with the camera movement, you must set the Frames value to 250, the same as the default rendering range.

After creating the camera animation, we render and make the movie.

Rendering a Video with Eevee

So, let's prepare the render settings to create a video clip. Before rendering the scene, we need to set some more options for the rendering.

We keep the length of 250 frames, the default setting, as the duration time of our video. We will choose a file format of 24 frames per second, so our movie will last 10.4 seconds approximately (250:24 = 10.4).

1. First, set the dimensions of the video in the Properties Editor
    ➤ Output Properties ➤ Format.

We choose the format preset and set the Resolution, Percentage, and Frame Rate values in the Format panel.

We can choose to select one of the templates available in the menu that opens by clicking the icon to the right of the Format panel header, as shown in Figure 6-28.

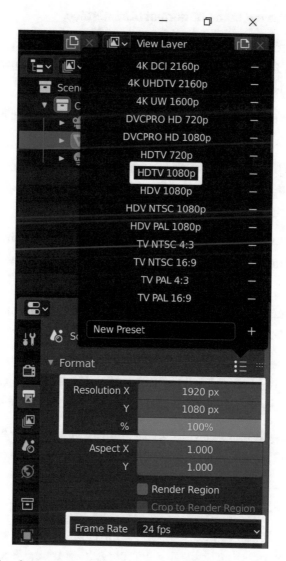

Figure 6-28. *Blender format presets and the Format panel*

Choosing the template will automatically set Resolution X, Resolution Y, and Frame Rate.

2. Choose HDTV 1080p as a template from the Format button. This format is for Full HD Video.

3. Choose the Output folder by selecting from the Output window the folder icon on the right, open the file browser from which you can choose the location for the final file, and give it the name Red_Chair.

Then click Accept at the bottom of the interface.

4. Choose the file format by clicking in the File Format box, where the PNG image file format is the default, and choose the FFmpeg video.

5. Then in the Encoding window from the FFMPEG presets button, choose h264 in MP4.

6. In Output Quality, you can choose the final quality of the video and click High Quality. But, of course, the higher is the rate, the heavier the output file.

7. Finally, choose the Render ➤ Render animation option in the Topbar menu or use the shortcut Ctrl+F12 and start the video rendering.

8. You will find the final file in the destination folder with the name Red_Chair0001-0250 in MP4 format.

We can also render our video as a sequence of images and then import them into the Blender video sequencer and render it as a video file. This approach also allows us to work on individual images. To use this method, we follow this procedure:

1. Render everything in PNG frame by frame by choosing PNG instead of FFmpeg video in the File Format box as step 4 of this exercise.

2. Press Ctrl+F12 to render the image sequence.

3. Move to the Video Editing workspace and import the image sequence by pressing Shift+A, selecting Add ➤ Image/Sequence, choosing all the provided images, and clicking Add Image Strip.

4. Repeat steps from 2 to 8 of this exercise to create the video.

We rendered an image first and then a video with Eevee; in the next exercise, we will change the rendering engine and start using Cycles.

Exercise 14: Rendering in Cycles with Denoise

As we have already said in this chapter, in Cycles, the most crucial thing is to reduce rendering times. By modifying the noise threshold and the number of samples, we can achieve this goal. However, if we lower the samples too much, the quality of the image worsens considerably, showing a disturbance of the rendered image.

In this case, the Denoise node supports us.

Denoising the Render

So let's render the file ChairsCycles.blend with a few samples, the Denoise node, and the Denoising Data corrections.

Let's straightforwardly see how to do this.

1. Open the file ChairCycles.blend and activate Rendered shading mode.

2. Change the renderer to Cycles, click 0, and go to the camera view.

   Enable Denoise in the Render Properties panel for both the viewport and rendering. By default it is enabled only for Render.

Immediately when we navigate 3D view, we see a significant decrease in image noise.

3. Move to the Compositing workspace and enable Use Nodes in the Compositor header. Add a Denoise node with Shift+A and select Add ➤ Filter ➤ Denoise. Connect the image output of the Render Layer node with the image input of the Denoise node and then the image output of Denoise with the image input of the Viewer and Composite nodes.

4. In the Properties Editor's View Layer ➤ Passes ➤ Data, you can enable Denoising Data and perform the first render. By checking the Denoising Data box, Blender automatically displays new outputs in the Render Layers node corresponding to control passes, as shown in Figure 6-29.

Figure 6-29. *The Render Layers node with Denoising Data Activated and the Denoise node*

We can modify the image precisely and monitor the disturbance's decrease with the Denoise node and Denoising Data channels.

Note   We have to render the scene again every time we add some passes to update changes.

Changing Rendering Colors

Now we continue the exercise in the Compositor by applying some more changes to our render. For example, we can change the colors of the rendered image.

1. Press Shift+A to open the Add window, choose the Color category in the menu, and click Hue Saturation Value to add the node.

2. Connect the Image socket output of the Denoise node with the Image socket input of the HSV node and the output Image of the HSV node with the input Image of both the Composite and the Viewer nodes, creating a nodal scheme like the one in Figure 6-30.

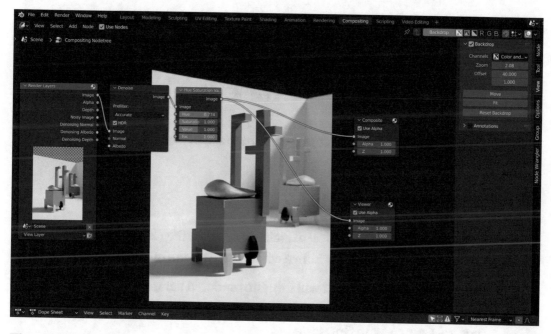

Figure 6-30. *Changing the color of the rendered image with the Hue Saturation Value node*

We made some first renders in Cycles and used denoising data in this exercise. We also started to deepen the practical use of the Compositor and Compositing nodes. In the following two activities, we will continue to deepen the techniques of compositing and video editing, practicing them with Compositing nodes and other effects.

Exercise 15: Deepening Compositing Techniques

The post-production techniques available in Blender via the compositing nodes are very effective. Let's see what we can do with a few simple node schemes. This exercise brings together a set of simple examples to help us to understand how the Compositing Editor works.

Let's start by preparing the work environment.

1. Open the file `ChairCycles`, move to the Compositing workspace, and, in the Compositor header, check the box Use Nodes.

2. In the Render Layers node, click the Render Active Scene button to create a render to work.

3. Click Ctrl+Shift+LMB on the Render Layer node to visualize the backdrop and add a viewer node to the chain.

4. Open with N the Sidebar and in View window adjust the values for Zoom and Offset to position the preview where you like while working.

In this way, we have prepared a convenient interface to work effectively with nodes in the Compositor.

From Colors to Black and White

First, we do a straightforward, practical exercise to see how the Compositor works: we transform the rendering of the chair from a color image to one in shades of gray.

1. Add a Color Ramp node. It will turn the rendered color image into a black-and-white one, and it will give you the possibility to control Contrast and Grayscale.

2. We can see the nodal chain and the effect in Figure 6-31.

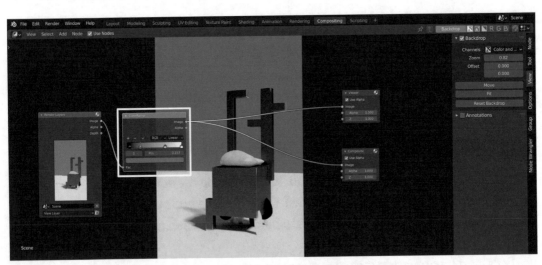

Figure 6-31. *Creating a black-and-white image with the Color Ramp node*

Now we analyze other nodes to modify the images and understand more deeply how they work.

Playing with Colors and Desaturation

We want to achieve the effect of Figure 6-32 by modifying the rendering of the file Chair_Cycles.blend that we have already used in Exercise 14.

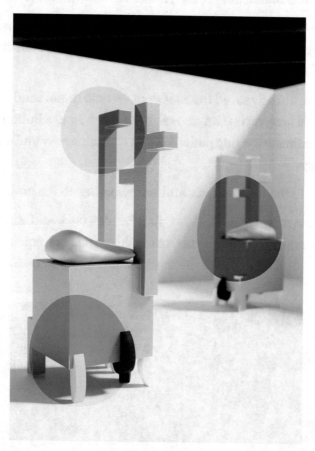

Figure 6-32. *The masked rendering*

In the figure, we masked the image with some circles, and we desaturated the background keeping the colors vivid inside the masked spaces.

To achieve this effect, we follow the steps in the next section.

Creating a Mask

First, let's see how to create the mask in the Image Editor.

1. Open the file ChairsCompositor.blend. Divide the Compositor into two windows and turn the one on the right into an Image Editor.

2. In the Image Editor header, click the View button and change it
    to mask so you can create a mask as in Figure 6-33 on the left.
    Blender will add several tools and properties to the editor panels,
    and it will automatically create a mask. Rename it **Chair**.

3. Add the rendered image to the Image Editor from the Browse
    Image button in the Image Editor header as in Figure 6-33 in the
    center of the Image Editor interface.

    If you have already saved the render or want to import and edit
    an external image, you can also click the Open Image button and
    follow the image loading path. You can also click New and add a
    new image.

4. Continue in the Image Editor and start working on the mask.

    In the main menu of the Image Editor header, click Add. A window
    opens from which you can choose to add a circle or a square. Add
    a circle and edit it to create the mask shapes in Figure 6-33.

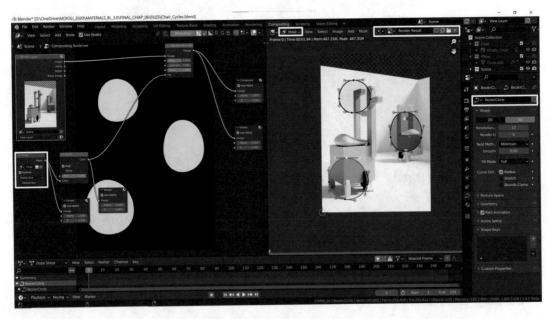

*Figure 6-33. The mask created in the Image Editor and the effect on the
masked parts*

The figure shows the tools we have talked about in the previous part, highlighted in white from left to right. We can also see the mask on the left, in the backdrop of the Compositor. We added Bézier curves with the control points and the handles.

We can use all the usual Blender commands and shortcuts to edit them. For example, we can move, rotate, and scale the shapes of our mask with G, R, and S. We can also add new control points to our forms by holding Ctrl and left-clicking the curve.

Moreover, we can change the curves' handle type by selecting it, right-clicking it, and choosing the option that interests us among those available. We can change, for example, an orthogonal angle into a rounded one. Finally, we can also add more shapes to mask everything we want.

Once we have created the mask to modify the image, we prepare the nodal chain.

Preparing the Nodal Chain

In this case, to obtain some circular colored parts of the image on a black-and-white background, we continue as follows by creating the nodal chain:

1. Add a Hue Saturation and Value node by pressing Shift+A and selecting Color ➤ Hue Saturation and Value. Place it between the Render Layers node, and the Viewer, and Composite nodes in the blockchains' position shown in Figure 6-34.

2. Try varying the Hue Saturation and Value values to understand how they work and how they change the preview.

3. Add a Mask node and choose the mask Chair from the "Browse Mask to be linked" button. Then add an Invert node. Duplicate the viewer. You will get the nodal chain represented in Figure 6-34.

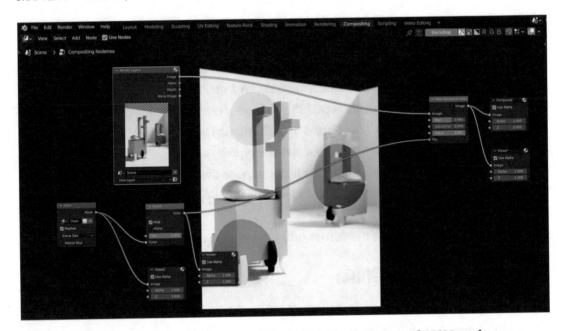

Figure 6-34. *The final nodal chain with the Mask, Invert, and HSV nodes*

After experimenting with what we can do with Blender's internal Compositor, we continue with the Video Editor.

Finally, we will edit images and videos to create a sequence for the *Mad Hatter Tea Party* presentation.

Exercise 16: Creating a Video for *The Mad Hatter's Tea Party*

In the previous exercise, we experimented with the possibilities of Blender's video editing. Now we create a short promotional film for *The Mad Hatter's Tea Party* exhibition, a short film presenting the event. We edit it in the Sequencer using different types of strips that we learned about earlier.

1. Open Blender. In the Properties Editor's Output Properties ➤ Format, click the icon Format Presets on the right of Format to choose the HDTV 1080p format preset. Then select an output directory by clicking the folder icon in the Output window.

2. Choose the FFmpeg Video file format in File Format box, and the H264 in MP4 preset in the Encoding window on the FFmpeg presets. In Output Quality, choose High Quality as the final quality of the video.

    Then save the file as `Creating_Video`.

We have set up the Blender interface for video editing, and we are ready to import content and edit it in various ways.

Importing Content

We have chosen the Full HD format with the dimensions of 1920 x 1080 pixels, so now it's essential to import the contents uniform to this format if we don't want deformed images and videos.

1. In the Topbar, click the + icon, then choose Video Editing ➤ Video Editing so you open the same workspace.

2. In the Sequencer, import an image by pressing Shift+A and selecting Image/Sequence, choose `Image_01.Png` from the directory, and then click Add Image Strip.

    We can also import content easily by dragging and dropping files directly from the File Browser editor at the top left of the interface into the Video Sequencer channels below.

    We can move the image in the Timeline by left-clicking the strip center and dragging the mouse. Instead, by clicking either end, we change the frame number, which is the length of the display.

3. Left-click the right end of the strip and drag while holding the mouse to increase the image duration to 200 frames.

    The frame rate of our format is 24 frames per second, so currently the length of our video corresponds to about eight seconds.

    By pressing Ctrl+T in the Timeline and Sequencer, we can go from the unit of measure in frames to using seconds and vice versa.

4. Import a movie by pressing Shift+A and selecting Movie, choose `Red_Chair0001-0250.mp4`, and move it to frame 150 to the channel above the image. This way, you superimpose it to the image of 50 frames or about two seconds.

Now that we have imported the contents, we can edit the video and add some transitions and effects.

Adding Transitions and Effects

As we have seen in the theoretical part, there are many effects we can add to the Video Sequencer. Let's start with a Cross Transition effect.

1. Select the picture first and then Shift+LMB on the movie.

2. Then click with the right button and, in the window that opens, select Add Transition ➤ Cross.

    In this way, we have inserted a Cross Transition effect between the image and the video, as shown in Figure 6-35.

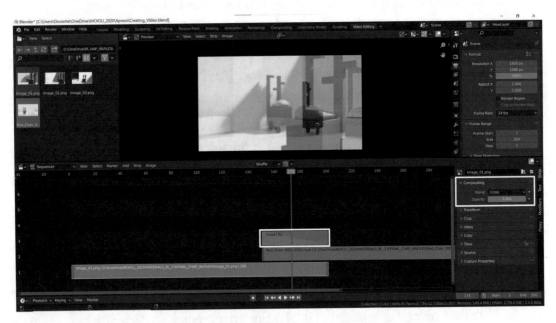

Figure 6-35. *A Cross Transition effect between image and video*

3. Now continue adding the other effects offered by Blender for video editing. Two exciting and straightforward tools are Color and Text.

    First, place the playhead in Frame 1 and add a Text effect with Shift+A and Add ➤ Text.

4. Increase the Size value to 100 in the Sidebar on the right of the Sequencer interface in the Strip ➤ Effect Strip ➤ Style window. Then change the color in the Color and Layout panel and, finally, edit the location of the text by placing it where you prefer.

5. Write the title *The Mad Hatter's Tea Party* in the Effect Strip panel box and increase the Text duration to 100 frames by clicking and dragging the right side of the strip.

We can see the result in Figure 6-36.

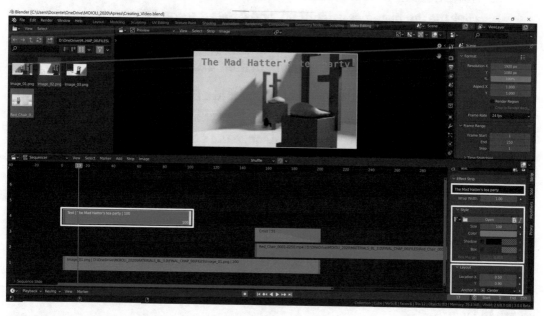

Figure 6-36. *The Video Editing workspace*

This Text Effect is Blender's Basic Text, which is straightforward and intuitive to use and is quite malleable.

We can choose among many fonts by clicking the Fonts button. We can also create many other effects. For example, by animating the Location X and Location Y boxes with the keyframes, we can have the text scroll over the images or videos. We can materialize or dematerialize it slowly using the Opacity button, etc.

Let's apply an animation to the text now. So, we make it appear at the beginning of the movie by gradually increasing its opacity.

1. Make sure you place the playhead at Frame 0.

2. Select the text and, in the Sidebar of the Sequencer interface, in the Strip panel, change the Opacity value to 0. Then click the black dot on the right of the Opacity box to insert a keyframe. The dot becomes a diamond.

3. Move the playhead to Frame 50, change the Opacity value to 1.00, click the dot becomes a diamond, and create a second keyframe. With this effect, the title gradually appears in the video.

Another simple effect we can easily insert in the video is Color.

1. So place the playhead at Frame 100 and add a Color strip with Shift+A and select Add ➤ Color. In the Effect Strip window of the Sidebar, turn the color to red, change the opacity to 0.3, and increase the effect duration to 100 frames.

2. Move the playhead to Frame 140, and insert an Opacity key by clicking the black dot on the right of Opacity.

3. Then move the playhead to Frame 199, change Opacity to 0, and insert a second key for the opacity by clicking the diamond again.

In this way, we have inserted a red color effect that fades after about four seconds, as shown in Figure 6-37.

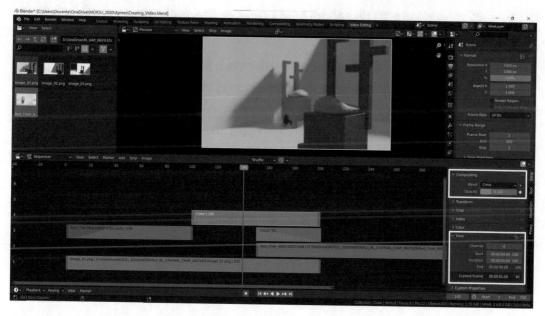

Figure 6-37. *Adding a Color strip*

We end the chapter with an exciting addition: a 3D scene modeled in Blender.

Introducing a 3D Blender Scene in the Video

As the last effect, we will model inside Blender a three-dimensional Text object to add to the video instead of the text effect that we added to our video. But we could model any object in Blender, animate it and add it to the video.

1. Delete the last two effects: select Text and Color, and click X; then in the 3D View, delete the default cube.

2. Add a new scene by clicking the New Scene ➤ Full Copy button on the right of the Topbar. Rename it **Text**.

3. Press 0 on the Numpad and go to Camera view. Next, add a Text object with the shortcut Shift+A, select Add ➤ Text, open the Add Text window on the left side of 3D view, and choose Align ➤ View. The text will align with Camera view.

We will now create a 3D title of the *Mad Hatter Tea Party* and an animation that has text enter from the left of the screen.

1. Make sure you have the text selected, switch from Object to Edit mode with the Tab button, delete the word *Text*, and write **Mad Hatter tea party**. Then, back to Object mode, select Properties Editor ➤ Object Data ➤ Geometry ➤ Extrude, and type **0.25** to give thickness to the text.

2. Make sure the playhead is set to Frame 1 and move the text out of Camera view on the left. To more easily move the text, you can switch from Global to Local transform orientation from the header and then use the red arrow of the Move gizmo.

3. Select the text, press I, open the Insert Keyframe menu, and click the location. You have inserted a Text Keyframe position.

4. Move the playhead to Frame 250, move the text out of the Camera view on the right, and insert a new set of keyframes for the location. Make sure that the Z value is unchanged.

5. With the spacebar, check the text animation that enters the video from the left and exits on the right. Save the file.

6. Now return to the previous scene by selecting it in the Scenes box on the Topbar.

7. Select the Video Editing workspace, move the playhead to Frame 1, and add the scene text to the Sequencer by pressing Shift+A and selecting Scenes ➤ Text.

8. To make the background of the text transparent, go back to the Text scene, and activate the Transparent checkbox from the path Properties Editor ➤ Render Properties ➤ Film.

9. In the Sequencer's Sidebar, back to Scene, and edit Blend from Cross to Alpha Over in the Compositing window.

To change the characteristics of the text, we can change it on the Text scene. For example, we can add a color to the text, scale or rotate it, change the animation, etc.

Note   Sometimes, some properties don't appear directly in the preview of the Video Sequencer. So now and then, to check, make a rendering of some frames.

If we want to add color directly from the Video Sequencer, we can add a modifier. Besides, we can add many other effects directly from the Video Sequencer. Let's see some of them.

1. Now, color the text green by selecting it and adding the Color Balance modifier from the Modifier panel of the Video Sequence's Sidebar. So, click the Add Strip Modifier button and choose Color Balance.

2. Finally, in the Strip panel, flip the text by pressing the X key in the Transform window. Then invert the text entry from left to right by selecting Reverse Frames in the Video window in the Strip panel, as shown in Figure 6-38.

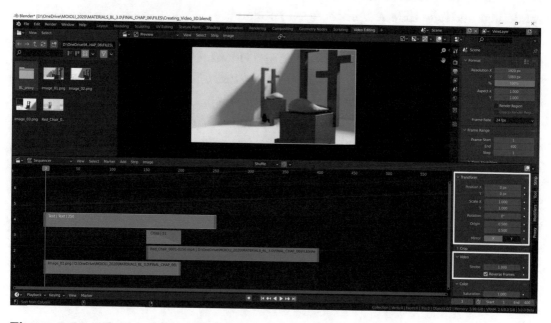

Figure 6-38. *The Mad Hatter's Tea Party final video*

3. To launch the final render, lengthen the duration to 400 frames;
   then with the settings you used in Exercise 13, render the scene
   with Eevee.

There is an example in the CreatingVideo.blend file that accompanies the book.

We could add many more things to our video, either by editing it directly in the Video Sequencer, modifying the existing objects, or modeling others in 3D view. We could also add more scenes and more material. But we have reached the end of this chapter dedicated to render and video editing, so we leave you to experiment with the other features of the software.

Summary

This chapter analyzed how to render with Blender's two internal renderers: Cycles and Eevee. They have similar aspects, support the same materials, and have more or less the same settings and nodes. But we have seen they produce very different final results of the renderings and have different procedures to obtain it.

Next, we looked at compositing and video editing; we saw how Blender is comparable to other software to edit images and videos.

Blender offers us the versatility of the nodal system and the opportunity to insert internally modeled three-dimensional scenes in a video.

The software combines different design possibilities, from creating 3D objects to producing materials to animation and physical simulation and virtual reality. But that's another story! The possibilities offered by this software are too wide to be contained in one book only.

This single interface contains many tools.

Index

Printed in the United States
by Baker & Taylor Publisher Services